ALSO BY ALAN EHRENHALT

The United States of Ambition

The Lost City

Democracy in the Mirror

THE GREAT INVERSION AND THE FUTURE OF THE AMERICAN CITY

THE
GREAT INVERSION
AND THE FUTURE OF
THE AMERICAN CITY

Alan Ehrenhalt

ALFRED A. KNOPF · NEW YORK · 2012

THIS IS A BORZOI BOOK
PUBLISHED BY ALFRED A. KNOPF

Copyright © 2012 by Alan Ehrenhalt
All rights reserved. Published in the United States by Alfred A. Knopf,
a division of Random House, Inc., New York, and in Canada
by Random House of Canada Limited, Toronto.
www.aaknopf.com

Knopf, Borzoi Books, and the colophon are
registered trademarks of Random House, Inc.

Portions of this work were previously published in
Governing magazine and *The New Republic*.

Library of Congress Cataloging-in-Publication Data
Ehrenhalt, Alan, 1947–
The great inversion and the future of the American city / Alan Ehrenhalt.—1st ed.
          p.   cm.
ISBN 978-0-307-27274-4 (hardback)
1. Cities and towns—United States—Case studies.
2. Gentrification—United States—Case studies.
3. Sociology, Urban—United States—Case studies.
I. Title.
HT123.E37   2012
307.760973—dc23   2011035139

Jacket satellite imagery courtesy of TerraServer.com
Jacket design by Chip Kidd
Maps by David Merrill

Manufactured in the United States of America
First Edition

To Suzanne,
with love

CONTENTS

THE **GREAT INVERSION** AND THE **FUTURE** OF THE **AMERICAN CITY**

TRADING PLACES

A LITTLE MORE THAN thirty years ago, the mayor of Chicago was unseated by a snowstorm. A blizzard in January 1979 dumped more than twenty inches of snow on the ground, leading, among other problems, to a curtailment of transit service. The few available trains coming downtown from the Northwest Side filled up with middle-class white riders near the far end of the line, leaving no room for poorer people trying to board on inner-city platforms. Blacks and Hispanics blamed this on Mayor Michael Bilandic, and he lost the Democratic primary to Jane Byrne a few weeks later.

Politically, this is ancient history. Demographically, it leads us to a picture of what has happened in Chicago over the past three decades. No such event could take place now. This is not because of climate change, or because the Chicago Transit Authority runs flawlessly. It is because the trains would fill up with minorities and immigrants on the outskirts of the city, and the passengers left stranded at the inner-city stations would be members of the affluent professional class.

In the years since 1979, Chicago has undergone changes that are routinely described as gentrification, but are in fact more complicated and more profound than that. A better term is "demographic inversion." Gentrification refers to the changes that happen in an individual neighborhood, usually the replacement of poorer minority residents by more affluent white ones. Demographic inversion is something much broader. It is the rearrangement of living patterns across an entire metropolitan area, all taking place at roughly the same time.

Chicago is gradually coming to resemble a traditional European city—Vienna or Paris in the nineteenth century, or, for that matter,

Paris today. The poor and the newcomers are living on the outskirts. The people who live near the center are those, some of them black or Hispanic but most of them white, who can afford to do so.

Events like this rarely occur in one city at a time, and indeed the present demographic inversion is taking place, albeit more slowly, in metropolitan areas throughout the country. For much of the past decade, the national media paid relatively little attention to it. While they were focused on Baghdad and Kabul, our own cities changed right in front of us, changed from year to year, faster than even the most attentive students of urban life could easily keep up with.

In some places, the phenomenon of demographic inversion is centered on racial rearrangement. Atlanta, for example, has long been overwhelmingly black, but between 2000 and 2010, according to census figures, the percentage of African Americans within the city fell from 61 percent to 54 percent; in 2009, the city came within a few hundred votes of electing a white Republican mayor. Within a few years, demographers agree, blacks will be a minority there. This is happening in part because the white middle class is moving inside the city borders, but it has more to do with blacks moving out. In the past two decades alone, two of Atlanta's huge suburban counties, Clayton and DeKalb, acquired substantial black majorities, and immigrants arriving from foreign countries began settling in overwhelming proportions in suburban counties, not within the city itself. The numbers for Washington, D.C., are strikingly similar to those of Atlanta. Washington, once roughly 70 percent African American, is now barely 50 percent African American.

Race is not always the critical issue in, or even especially relevant to, the process of demographic change. At the time of the September 11 attacks in 2001, the number of people living in lower Manhattan south of the World Trade Center was estimated at fifteen thousand. Seven years later it was approaching fifty thousand. Close to a quarter of these people were couples (nearly always wealthy couples) with children. The average household size had become larger in lower Manhattan than in the city as a whole. It is not mere fantasy to imagine that in, say, 2020, the southern tip of Manhattan will be a residential neighborhood with a modest residual presence of financial corporations and financial service jobs. What happened in lower Manhattan isn't exactly an inversion in the Chicago sense: Expensive condos replaced offices, not poor people. But it was a dramatic demographic change nevertheless.

If you want to see this sort of thing writ very large, you can venture just across the Canadian border, to Vancouver, British Columbia. Vancouver is a city of about six hundred thousand, roughly the size of Washington, D.C. What makes it unusual—indeed, unique in all of North America at this point—is that roughly 20 percent of its residents live within a couple of square miles of one another in the city's center. Downtown Vancouver is a forest of slender green condo skyscrapers, many of them with three-story townhouse units forming a kind of podium at the base. Each morning, there are nearly as many people commuting out of the center to jobs in the suburbs as there are commuting in. New public elementary schools have opened in downtown Vancouver in the past few years.

For several decades now, cities in the United States have wished for a 24/7 downtown, a place where people live as well as work, and keep the streets busy, interesting, and safe at every time of day. This is what Jane Jacobs preached in the 1960s, and it has long since become the accepted goal of urban planners. The irony in Vancouver's case is that it has not merely done well at attracting downtown residents, it has done too well. The condominiums are crowding out office space. Relatively few commercial building projects have been launched in the past decade, and there is little vacant land to build them on anyway. This is Vancouver's problem today; it may be Wall Street's problem in the not-too-distant future.

Some of Vancouver's center-city residential boom is the plain result of its dramatic physical setting: blue water and snowcapped mountains visible from downtown in nearly every direction. Much of it stems from deliberate public policy: In 1991, the city adopted a program called Living First, which raised the ceiling on downtown density in exchange for developer-provided amenities, such as parks, waterfront walkways, and community centers. But part of it is simply demographics. A large proportion of the city's six hundred thousand residents, especially those with money, want to live downtown. The dramatic changes over the past decade have reflected this demand.

No American city looks like Vancouver at the moment. But quite a few are starting to move in this direction. Demographic inversion of one sort or another is occurring in urban pockets scattered all across America, many of them in seemingly unlikely places. Charlotte, a city roughly Vancouver's size that was hit exceptionally hard by the meltdown in the financial industry, is nevertheless still experiencing the effects of a decade-long downtown building boom dominated by new mixed-use high-rise buildings, with office space on the bottom and condos or rental units above.

We are not witnessing the abandonment of the suburbs, or a movement of millions of people back to the city all at once. The 2010 census certainly did not turn up evidence of a middle-class stampede to the nation's cities. The news was mixed: Some of the larger cities on the East Coast tended to gain population, albeit in small increments. Those in the Midwest, including Chicago, tended to lose substantial numbers. The cities that showed gains in overall population during the entire decade tended to be in the South and Southwest. But when it comes to measuring demographic inversion, raw census numbers are an ineffective blunt instrument. A closer look at the results shows that the most powerful demographic events of the past decade were the movement of African Americans out of central cities (180,000 of them in Chicago alone) and the settlement of immigrant groups in suburbs, often ones many miles distant from downtown. Central-city areas that gained affluent residents in the first part of the decade maintained that population in the recession years from 2007 to 2009. They also, according to a 2011 study by Brookings, suffered considerably less from increased unemployment than the suburbs did. Not many young professionals moved to new downtown condos in the recession years because few such residences were being built. But there is no reason to believe that the demographic trends prevailing prior to the construction bust will not resume once that bust is over. It is important to remember that demographic inversion is not a proxy for population growth; it can occur in cities that are growing, those whose numbers are flat, and even in those undergoing a modest decline in size.

America's major cities face enormous fiscal problems, many of them the result of public pension obligations they incurred in the more prosperous years of the past two decades. Some, Chicago prominent among them, simply are not producing enough revenue to support the level of public services to which most of their citizens have grown to feel entitled. How the cities are going to solve this problem, I do not know. What I do know is that if fiscal crisis were going to drive affluent professionals out of central cities, it would have done so by now. There is no evidence that it has.

The truth is that we are living at a moment in which the massive outward migration of the affluent that characterized the second half of the twentieth century is coming to an end. And we need to adjust our perceptions of cities, suburbs, and urban mobility as a result.

Much of our perspective on the process of metropolitan settlement dates, whether we realize it or not, from a paper written in 1925 by the University of Chicago sociologist Ernest W. Burgess. It was Burgess who defined four urban/suburban zones of settlement: a central business district; an area of manufacturing just beyond it; then a residential area inhabited by the industrial and immigrant working class; and finally an outer enclave of single-family dwellings.

Burgess was right about the urban America of 1925; he was right about the urban America of 1974. Virtually every city in the country had a downtown, where the commercial life of the metropolis was conducted; it had a factory district just beyond; it had districts of working-class residences just beyond that; and it had residential suburbs for the wealthy and the upper middle class at the far end of the continuum. As a family moved up the economic ladder, it also moved outward from crowded working-class districts to more spacious apartments and, eventually, to a suburban home. The suburbs of Burgess's time bore little resemblance to those at the end of the twentieth century, but the theory still essentially worked. People moved ahead in life by moving farther out.

But in the past decade, in quite a few places, this model has ceased to describe reality. There are still downtown commercial districts, but there are no factory districts lying next to them. There are scarcely any factories at all. These close-in parts of the city, whose few residents Burgess described as dwelling in "submerged regions of poverty, degradation and disease," are increasingly the preserve of the affluent who work in the commercial core. And just as crucially, as we will see over the course of this book, newcomers to America are not settling on the inside and accumulating the resources to move out; they are living in the suburbs from day one.

So FAR, I haven't used the words that make the most dramatic case for the reality and importance of demographic inversion. But I will use them now: the price of gasoline. It's impossible at this point to say with any certainty just what energy costs will do to American living patterns over the next decade. Urbanists predicted a return to the city during previous spikes in the cost of gasoline, notably during the two episodes of shortage in the 1970s. They were wrong. Gas prices came down, and the suburbs expanded as never before. But I have seen no convincing evidence that the recent period of volatility in the cost of gasoline has anything to do with the previous ones. Today's prices at the pump are not the result of political pressures by angry sheikhs in the Persian Gulf. They are the result of increased worldwide demand that is only going to increase, not recede, when the worldwide economy emerges, even if fitfully, from its current doldrums.

I don't know how many families living in outer suburbia will make a decision in the coming years to stop paying $100 every few days for a tank of gasoline that will allow them to commute forty or fifty miles a day, round-trip. Some will simply stay where they are and accept the cost. But some will make the opposite decision. The problem for major cities in the coming decade will not be finding people who want to live in the center. It will be finding places to accommodate them. At moments of real estate price deflation, such as the current one, there is a predictable shift in demand and in construction from condominiums to rental apartments. But that does not detract from the reality that the demand for central living space will be a lasting one.

A significant cadre of urban advocates, including mayors of some of the nation's largest cities, continue to insist that the middle class will not return to the central city in meaningful numbers until the public school problem is "fixed." I would be just as happy as anyone else to see schools improve, but I think these people have it backward. The schools improve after the middle class arrives. Schools are not the first piece of the urban revival puzzle that falls into place. They are among the final pieces. The important questions are whether young adults are attracted to the idea of living downtown, whether they will still want to live there once they have children, and whether they will stay when the children reach school age. I think the answer to the first two questions is clearly yes. The strollers have reached Wall Street, and they are not leaving. Take a walk down there some Saturday morning and you will see for yourself. The answer to the third question is one upon which reasonable people may differ. I think that in the coming decade, we will see that question answered in the affirmative as well.

WHY HAS demographic inversion begun to happen? One might start by recounting the factors that seem obvious, or at least ought to be. The deindustrialization of the central city, for all the tragic human dislocations, has eliminated many of the things that made affluent people want to move away from it during much of the twentieth century. Since nothing much is manufactured downtown anymore (or anywhere near it), the noise and grime that prevailed through most of the twentieth century have gone away. Manhattan may seem like a gritty and noisy place now, but it is nothing like the city of tenement manufacturing, rumbling elevated trains, and horses and coal dust in the streets that confronted the inhabitants of a century ago. Third-floor factory lofts, whether in SoHo or in St. Louis, can be marketed as attractive and stylish places to live. The urban historian Robert Bruegmann goes so far as to claim that deindustrialization has on the whole been good for downtowns because it has permitted so many opportunities for creative reuse of the buildings. I wouldn't go quite that far; I doubt most of the residents of Detroit would, either. But it is true that the environmental factors that made middle-class people leave the central city for streetcar suburbs in the 1920s, and for station-wagon suburbs in the 1950s and gated enclaves in the 1970s, do not apply anymore.

Nor, in general, does the scourge of urban life in the 1970s and 1980s: random street violence. The dramatic decline in all violent crime that took place over the past two decades does seem to have leveled off in the last few years. Cities such as Chicago, Philadelphia, and Cleveland have watched murder rates climb in some recent years from the reduced levels of 1995 or 2000. But this increase has been propelled almost entirely by gang- and drug-related violence. Middle-class people of all colors began to feel safe on the streets of urban America in the 1990s, and they still feel that way.

The paralyzing fear that anyone of middle age can still recall vividly from the 1970s—that the shadowy figure passing by on a dark city street at night stands a good chance of being a mugger—does not occur much these days, and it hardly occurs at all to young people. Walk around the neighborhood of Fourteenth and U streets in Washington, D.C., on a Saturday night, and you will find it perhaps the liveliest part of the city, at least for those under twenty-five. This is a neighborhood where the riots of 1968 left physical scars that still have not disappeared, and where outsiders were afraid to venture for more than thirty years.

Millions of words have been written in an attempt to understand why crime declined so dramatically in the 1990s, but with no convincing answer to the question. Some scholars attribute reduced crime to the policing reforms that featured more careful collection of statistics and focused on prevention rather than response; others to the simple fact that so many would-be offenders were in prison and unable to cause trouble. There have been arguments that the number of muggings fell because people started carrying less cash in their pockets; there has, much more controversially, been the economist Steven Levitt's contention that the decline in crime was related to abortion. In Levitt's view, legalized abortion in the 1970s led in the 1990s to a much smaller cohort of young underclass males most likely to perpetrate crimes. But no one can honestly claim to know for sure.

Whatever the reasons for the change, the young newcomers who have rejuvenated Fourteenth and U streets in Washington are nearly all convinced that this recovering slum is the sort of place where they want to spend time, and, increasingly, where they want to live. This is the generation that grew up watching *Seinfeld, Friends,* and *Sex and the City,* mostly from the comfort of suburban sofas. I do not claim that a handful of TV shows has somehow produced a new urbanist generation; obviously it is more complicated than that. But it is striking how pervasive the pro-city sensibility is within this cohort, particularly among its elite.

In recent years, teaching undergraduate and graduate students at two universities on the East Coast, the majority of them from affluent suburban backgrounds, I made a point of asking where they would prefer to live in fifteen years: in a suburb or in a neighborhood close to the center of a city. Very few ever voted for suburban life. I make no claims to the statistical validity of this inquiry, or to the randomness of the sample, but I can't help finding it interesting and revealing.

They had not necessarily devoted a great deal of thought to the question: When I asked them whether they would want to live in an urban neighborhood without a car, many seemed puzzled and said no. I think we are a long way from producing a generation for whom urban life and ownership of an automobile are mutually exclusive. In downtown Charlotte, a luxury condominium has been designed that will allow residents to drive their cars into a garage elevator, ride up to the floor they live on, and park right next to their front door. I have a hard time figuring out whether that is a triumph for urbanism or a defeat. But my guess is that except in Manhattan, the carless life has yet to achieve any significant traction in the affluent new enclaves of urban America.

Not that cars and demographic inversion aren't closely related; they are. This was true before the price of gasoline shot up in 2008. In Atlanta, where the middle-class return to the city is occurring with more suddenness than perhaps anywhere in America, the most frequently cited reason is traffic. People who did not object to a twenty-mile commute in from the suburbs a decade ago are objecting to it now. Of course, that is partly because the same commute takes quite a bit longer than it did in the 1990s. Atlanta is traffic-obsessed to a degree that, among major American cities, perhaps only Los Angeles can match.

And it is the place where traffic and demographic inversion seem, at this point, to be most closely tied together.

Ultimately, though, I don't think an inversion of the sort now occurring is mostly a result of middle-aged commuters changing their minds, any more than a political realignment is normally a matter of middle-aged people changing their partisan loyalties. It has far more to do with the emergence of new adult cohorts with different values, habits, and living preferences.

Consider these statistics, compiled from census data by the demographer Arthur C. Nelson. In the peak baby boom period after World War II, roughly half of American households were engaged in the process of raising children. In 2020, extrapolating from census figures, the number will be closer to 25 percent. The increase in the number of single-person households, Nelson reports, will be more than twice the increase in the number of households with children. The percentage of Americans over age sixty-five was 13 percent in 2010; in 2030 it will be 19 percent, an increase of roughly half. This latter number is not a matter of opinion; it is as close to being a statistical fact as anything in demographic projection can possibly be.

When one thinks of the larger demographic changes that have taken place in America over the past generation—the increased number of people who remain single, the rise of cohabitation, the later age of first marriage, the smaller size of families, and at the other end, the rapidly growing number of healthy and active adults in their later years—it is hard to escape the notion that we have managed to combine virtually all of the significant elements that make a demographic inversion not only possible but likely. We are moving toward a society in which millions of people with substantial earning power or ample savings will have the option of living wherever they want, and many—we can only guess how many—will decide in favor of central cities and against distant suburbs. As they do this, others will find themselves forced to live in places less desirable—places farther from the center of the metropolis. Statistics from the U.S. Census Bureau in October 2011 revealed that in the first decade of the new century, poverty increased by 53 percent in the nation's suburbs, compared to only 26 percent in the cities.

This has been true for the bulk of Western urban history; since the

Middle Ages, the center of life in urban Europe has normally been the area closest to the core, where commerce, culture, and affluence all congregated together. There is more evidence that the pattern is reasserting itself than that it has come to an end. And as this happens, suburbs that never dreamed of being entry points for immigrants are having to cope with new realities. It should come as no surprise that the most intense arguments about hiring and educating the undocumented have occurred in the relatively distant reaches of American suburbia, such as Prince William County, Virginia, and the exurban territory of Chicago. They are not occurring, for the most part, in the cities. That is not where the immigrants are landing.

There are plenty of responsible critics who look at what appears to be happening and say that a lot is being made out of relatively little. One may object, and plausibly so, that much of what occurred from 2000 to 2008 could be categorized as pre-recession change, a result of the housing bubble that generated a large supply of luxury condos in dozens of American cities, and led to an increase in speculative investment as well. Once conditions return to "normal," it might be predicted, the supply of high-priced in-town residences will exceed the demand. Indeed, there are estimated two-year to five-year backlogs of empty condos in the downtown areas of cities from Miami to New York, and Chicago to Phoenix. It is possible to envision the supply of urban residences outstripping the demands of prosperous people willing to live in them for years to come.

Recession or no recession, it is true that the return to the urban center has up to now been modest in absolute numbers. In most metropolitan areas, in the first decade of the twenty-first century, more people still moved to the suburbs than moved downtown. A city of half a million that can report a downtown residential population of twenty-five thousand—5 percent of the total—can claim that it is doing relatively well in this respect. Charlotte, for all the local excitement it generated about upscale in-town living, still has no more than twelve thousand residents downtown. Moreover, these twelve thousand are not a representative sample of the area's overall populace. Unlike in Vancouver, there are few families with school-age children. Downtown Charlotte has mostly attracted the familiar gentrification cohort: singles, gay and straight couples, older people whose children have left home. The bulk of the married-with-children middle class has not only been living in the suburbs, it has been moving to the suburbs. Joel Kotkin, perhaps the most prominent of the downtown debunkers, declares flatly that until families begin turning up in significant numbers on downtown streets throughout America, we are talking about a blip rather than a major cultural phenomenon.

There is no question that Americans like to have living space, and the latter half of the twentieth century is a testament to that. There is a reason the average size of a new house built in the United States grew from about one thousand square feet in the years immediately after World War II to more than two thousand today. But the combination of rapid decline in household size and frequently expressed living preferences of the emerging adult generation for walkable compactness suggests that the demand for cul-de-sacs, oversize garages, five-thousand-square-foot suburban residences, and long commutes, even among the most affluent of the millennial generation, will be receding in the years ahead. It seems likely, as suggested above, that more of the social life of the next adult cohort, compared to that of the previous one, will be lived in a public realm, not a closed-off private one, in a more active and vibrant streetscape and in parks and other public spaces. They will have to do with less private living space and more shared urban territory. But this is a choice that a good percentage of them seem prepared to make.

Even if the critics are right when it comes to the overall numbers—even if the vast majority of cities never sees a downtown affluent residential boom of massive proportions—the significance of demographic inversion for the future of American urban life seems difficult to dispute. The crucial issue is not the number of people living in and near downtown, although that matters. The crucial issue is who they are, and the ways in which whole metropolitan areas are changing as a result.

WHAT WOULD an American city in the full grip of demographic inversion actually look like? In one plausible scenario, it would look like many of the European capitals of the 1890s: an affluent and stylish urban core surrounded by poorer people and an immigrant working class on the periphery.

Vienna might be the most interesting example to consider. In the mid-nineteenth century, the medieval wall that had surrounded the city's central core for hundreds of years was torn down. In its place there appeared the Ringstrasse, the circle of fashionable boulevards where opera was sung and plays performed, where rich merchants and minor noblemen lived in spacious apartments, where gentlemen and ladies promenaded in the evening under the gaslights, where Freud, Mahler, and their friends held long conversations about death over coffee and pastry in sidewalk cafés.

If you were part of the servant class, the odds were you lived either in the dirty and ill-lit alleys just outside the Ringstrasse circle of prosperity, or else far beyond the center, in a neighborhood called Ottakring, a concentration of more than thirty thousand cramped one- and two-bedroom apartments, whose residents endured a long horsecar ride to get to work in the heart of the city.

Paris was a different story. It had always had a substantial inner-city working class, the breeding ground for political unrest and violence over and over again in French history. But the narrow streets that housed the Parisian poor were largely obliterated in the urban redesign dictated by Baron Georges-Eugene Haussmann in the 1860s. The Paris that Haussmann created was the city of fashionable inner-ring boulevards that remains largely intact a century and a half later. The poor and the newly arrived were essentially banished to the suburbs—where they remain today, though they are now mostly Muslims from North Africa rather than peasants from the south of France.

Nobody in his right mind would hold up the present-day physical arrangement of metropolitan Paris, with thousands of unemployed immigrants seething in shoddily built suburban high-rise housing projects, as a model for what twenty-first-century urbanism ought to look like. At the same time, I think it is difficult to fashion a convincing argument that a city is morally better off simply by virtue of the poor being on the inside and the rich on the outside, or vice versa. The moral obligation is to treat people humanely, whatever their circumstances. Citizens of metropolitan regions deserve decent places to live, and convenient transportation to their jobs. Which part of the region they inhabit is an economic and planning question, sometimes an aesthetic question, but, in my opinion, not a moral one. I find it hard to see demographic inversion as either a menace or a godsend. But it is a phenomenon that deserves our attention.

I PAY ATTENTION to it every time I return to Chicago, the city in which I was born and grew up. My grandfather arrived there in 1889, found his way to the Near West Side, and opened a tailor shop that remained in business for fifty years. The building was torn down in the 1960s when the University of Illinois built its Chicago campus in the neighborhood. The street corner where the store stood now houses a science center.

The UIC campus is, to my eyes, one of the ugliest in America. But I have made my peace with that. What interests me is what is going on all around that West Side neighborhood, now called University Village. Before the 1960s, this part of the West Side was a compact and somewhat culturally isolated enclave of Jewish and Italian families. (It was also the location of Hull House and the early home of the Chicago Cubs.) For a while after the university was built, the areas around it constituted a sort of residential no-man's-land, dangerous at night and unattractive to the young academics who taught there. Assistant professors at UIC generally don't live there now, either, but that is for a different reason: They can't afford it. Demand for the townhouses and condominiums on the Near West Side has priced junior faculty out of the market. One can walk a couple of blocks down the street from the spot of my grandfather's shop and order a steak for $24. My grandfather wouldn't have understood paying that much for a steak, but he would have understood people paying a premium to live near their work.

You might respond that there is nothing especially noteworthy in all this. A college setting, liberal academics, houses close to the city's cultural attractions: That's garden-variety gentrification. What else would you expect?

If you feel that way, you might want to ride an elevated train going northwest, to a lesser-known place called Logan Square, a few miles beyond the Loop. Whatever Logan Square might be, it is not downtown chic. It is a moderately close-in nineteenth-century neighborhood with a history fairly typical for a city that A. J. Liebling once called "an endless succession of factory-town main streets." Logan Square was developed mostly by Scandinavian manufacturers, who lived on the tree-lined boulevards while their workers, most of them Polish, rented the bungalows on the side streets. By the 1960s, nearly all the Poles had grown more prosperous and decamped for suburbia, and they were replaced by an influx of Puerto Ricans. The area became a haven for gangs and gang violence, and most of the retail shopping that held the community together disappeared.

Logan Square is still not the safest neighborhood in Chicago. There are armed robberies and occasional killings on its western fringe, and, even on the quiet residential streets, mothers tell their children to make it home before dark. But that hasn't prevented Logan Square from changing dramatically again—not over the past generation, or the past decade, but in a period of five years. The big stone houses built by the factory owners on Logan Boulevard have sold for close to a million dollars, even in a housing recession. The restaurant that sits on the square itself sells goat cheese quesadillas and fettuccine with octopus, and attracts long lines of customers who drive in from the suburbs on weekend evenings.

To describe what has happened virtually overnight in Logan Square as gentrification is to miss the point. Chicago, like much of America, is rearranging itself, and the result is an entire metropolitan area that looks considerably different from what it looked like when the last decade started. Of course, demographic inversion cannot ever be a one-way street. If some people are coming inside, some people have to be going out. This is occurring in Chicago as in much of the rest of the country.

DURING THE PAST ten years, with relatively little fanfare and surprisingly little media attention, the great high-rise public housing projects that defined squalor in urban America for half a century have essentially disappeared. In Chicago, the infamous Robert Taylor Homes are gone, and the equally infamous Cabrini-Green is all but gone. This has meant the removal of tens of thousands of people—a huge number, although it was always hard to say precisely just how many public housing residents Chicago had. Most of them have moved beyond the city limits. The 2010 census showed a decline in the city's black population of 180,000; the demolition of the big housing projects was one of the reasons for this, and helps to explain why the city as a whole suffered a population loss of 6.9 percent. At the same time, suburbs stretching out as far as forty miles from Chicago are housing many more African American residents than they did a decade ago. The city government in Chicago promised to construct new mixed-use housing for large numbers of those displaced by the removal of the projects, but reporting by the *Chicago Tribune* at the end of the decade documented that only a small proportion of the mixed-use units had been built. Even if they had, it seems indisputable that there would have been a mass exodus of blacks from the city in the first decade of the new century; this is what was taking place in cities all over the country, including those that did not tear down large numbers of high-rise housing projects.

At the same time, tens of thousands of immigrants are coming to Chicago every year, mostly from various parts of Latin America. Where are they settling? Not in University Village. Some in Logan Square, but fewer all the time. They are living in suburban or exurban territory that, until a decade ago, was almost exclusively Anglo, middle-class, and white. Chicago is not nineteenth-century Vienna—it never will be—but this is one more sign that its demographic inversion is well under way.

Now is the time to begin talking about the consequences of demographic inversion, and the possible futures it might set in motion. On the extreme dystopian end, one can conjure up gated enclaves of the wealthy clinging to the center, with the poor out of sight and largely forgotten, Paris-style, in some new kind of high-rise. I think this is the least likely scenario. We do not have to worry about a return of the idea of warehousing the poor in vertical Corbusian ghettos. That is one beast we have managed to slay. Large American cities are not integrated today the way idealists hoped they would be by this time; poor people and minorities still live in clusters; but those clusters now exist in many different sections of cities and metropolitan regions. Segregation may not be gone, but it is not what it was in 1960.

The people who are moving downtown are doing so in part to escape the real or virtual "gatedness" of suburban life. The condos that house them in the coming years may feature elaborate security systems, but the inhabitants will not be walled off from the street. They will want to be in contact with the street.

This will mean different things to different people. Some will want the funky qualities of Jane Jacobs's 1950s version of Hudson Street in New York's Greenwich Village, with locally owned and slightly messy bookstores, coffeehouses, and bars, and a concentration of art galleries and studios. Others will be willing to accept the less adventurous urban world invaded by chain stores, with street-level rows occupied by the Gap, Cheesecake Factory, and Barnes & Noble, and with apartments perched above them on upper residential floors, either rental or condominium. Some of these will be, already are, in the middle of downtowns. Others will be in neighborhoods on the fringe of downtown, in close-in suburbs on the city border, or even in more distant suburbs trying to create an urban ambience of some sort. But the crucial component will be the desire for an atmosphere of urbanism, with the opportunity to walk between living space and commercial and recreational opportunities.

Christopher Leinberger, the real estate developer and urban planning scholar, believes that a dramatic increase in middle-class central-city population will in fact take place throughout America, and today's tract homes in the far suburbs will deteriorate into the slums of 2030. I don't think this will happen, at least not in such extreme form; there simply are not enough lofts and townhouses to double or triple the number of people living in the center of most large American cities. The central-city population will continue to grow, but massive growth would require concentrations of skyscrapers that very few cities have shown much inclination to accept. Nor does it seem likely that exurbia will turn into a wasteland. The prices of the houses will continue to go down and render them more attractive for newcomers trying to rise in the American economy and society. Urbanists have complained for years that immigrants and poor people in the inner city have a hard time commuting to the service jobs that are available to them in the suburbs. If they live in the suburbs, they will be closer to the jobs. Transportation will remain a problem, but not one that can't be solved.

Demographic inversion will also mean different futures for different cities. It goes without saying that the phenomenon will not apply in the same way or at the same pace in every big city in America. It will not come to Detroit or Buffalo in the way it is coming to Chicago, New York, and Washington, D.C. Some cities will lack the central job base to generate a large-scale affluent urban revival, and will lag behind their more fortunate counterparts by a long period of years, if they ever get there at all. This is the argument of scholars such as Edward Glaeser and Richard Florida, who see an increasing bifurcation between cities economically equipped to regenerate themselves in the twenty-first century and those whose obsolete industrial economies will leave them mired in the downtown blight and exurban outward pressures of an earlier era. They have a point. There is no evidence that Detroit will produce a large cohort of downtown dwellers anytime soon. But despite the unevenness, demographic inversion will apply in more cities than many critics have imagined thus far. The living habits and preferences of the emerging adult generation are simply too strong to prevent it from occurring to some degree in every healthy urban area.

Somewhere in the midst of all these differing prophecies lies the vision of Jane Jacobs. Much of what Jacobs loved and wrote about will never return: The era of the mom-and-pop grocer, the shoemaker, and the candy store has ended for good. We live, for the most part, in a big-box, big-chain century. But I think the youthful urban elites of the present are looking in some sense for the things Jane Jacobs valued, whether they have heard of her or not. They are drawn to the densely packed urban life that they find vastly more interesting than the cul-de-sac world that they grew up inhabiting. And to a great extent, I believe central cities will give it to them. At the same time, much of suburbia, in an effort to stay afloat, will seek to reinvent itself in a newly urbanized mode. That is already taking place: All over America, the car-created suburbs of the 1970s and 1980s have built "town centers" in the past five years, with sidewalks and as much of a street grid as they can manage to impose on a faded strip-mall landscape. None of these retrofit efforts looks much like an old-fashioned city. But they are a clue, I think, to the direction in which we are heading.

In the 1990s, a flurry of academics and journalists (me among them) wrote books lamenting the decline of community and predicting that it would reappear in some fashion in the new century. I think that is beginning to happen now in the downtowns of America, and I believe that, for all its imperfections and inequalities, demographic inversion ultimately will do more good than harm. We will never return—nor would most of us want to return—to the close-knit but frequently constricting form of community life that prevailed fifty years ago. But, as we rearrange ourselves in and around many of our big cities, we are groping toward the new communities of the twenty-first century.

CHAPTER ONE

A BACKWARD GLANCE

IN THE LAST QUARTER of the twentieth century, as poverty, violence, and abandonment settled over most of the big cities in America, the great urban historian Donald Olsen made an intriguing remark. "If we are to achieve an urban renaissance," Olsen wrote, "it is the nineteenth-century city that will be reborn."

It was a cryptic comment, and Olsen is no longer around to be asked precisely what he meant, but he was not the only urbanist of taste and judgment who voiced similar sentiments. Jean-Christophe Bailly, the French architect and critic, looked at cities all across North America around the same time and declared that "the nineteenth century invented modernity, and it must now be reinvented to make up for the damage done by the systematic negligence of twentieth-century urban planners."

Two decades later, at least a part of this vision seems to be coming true. Not all of it involves changes that most of us would desire. It does not take much effort to enumerate a long list of the features of pre–World War I urban life that none of us would wish to emulate, features that were ubiquitous in the old-fashioned cities we actually tend to admire the most.

No one would wish to cope with the East End of London as H. G. Wells described it in 1910: six-story walk-up tenements, bedrooms little more than ten feet square, and all through the stairwells the smell of unwashed bedding and stale food. There were nine hundred thousand people living in the East End in 1910, and one-third of them, according to the London Poor Law Commission, were living in extreme poverty.

Nor is there any reason to be nostalgic for the conditions of working-class Vienna, in which hundreds of thousands of immigrant factory workers lived in the shadow of the textile mills and chemical plants where they worked, many of them seven days a week, at jobs whose nonexistent health and safety standards all but guaranteed them frequent illnesses and short life spans. Similarly, the most passionate advocate of urban density would be wary of the physical environment of even middle-class Paris flats, where, as historian Sharon Marcus wrote, paraphrasing the cultural criticism of Honoré de Balzac, "Apartment houses destroy private life by making each apartment simultaneously function as an observatory, theater, and mirror in which the residents of one apartment spy on those of another, provide unwitting spectacles for each other, and see their own lives reflected or inverted in their neighbors'."

So let us stipulate one point right away: To admire London, Paris, or Vienna in 1900 is not to admire squalid tenements, lethal working conditions, or the absence of privacy. It is instead to admire other qualities that those cities possessed.

Street life, for one. The late twentieth century considered the street so preeminently an instrument of movement that we forget what it was in the great European cities of a century before: a center of activity, much more than of motion, a center of commerce and sociability, of nonstop human drama, of endless surprises and stimulation. One might call it, as many did at the time, a theater for living. To talk about a crowded city thoroughfare of the nineteenth century as "mixed use" urbanism in the modern sense is to miss the point altogether. This was essentially "all use" urbanism.

Of course, people were out in the streets of London, Paris, and Vienna in part because they did not want to be inside. In 1860, in a piece of social analysis aimed at describing and understanding Parisian social life, the critic Alfred Delvau wrote that "as soon as it awakes, Paris leaves its abode and steps out, and doesn't return home until as late as possible in the evening—when it bothers to return home." He went on to write that "Paris deserts its houses. Its houses are dirty on the inside, while its streets are swept every morning. . . . All the luxury is outside—all its pleasures walk the streets." Delvau did not specify particular streets, but he did not need to. In mid-nineteenth-century

Paris, anything wider than a narrow lane, any street twenty-five or thirty feet across, was bursting with activity day and night. Left and Right Bank, east or west of the city center, all hosted essentially the same form of raucous street life. They differed considerably in the wealth and status of their residents, but the scene at ground level was essentially the same throughout.

These were streets in which traffic was often gridlocked and nothing moved very fast, so there was plenty of time for the resident or visitor to take in the human drama at leisure. At first glance, there was little charm to them. They were not the quaint European streets down which foreign tourists like to stroll today. To a great extent, they resembled the streets of New York's Lower East Side that nearly all of us have seen in pictures: unrefined, menacing to some, and occasionally violent, but full of the raw energy of day-to-day human existence.

Everything and everyone was visible on these streets: prostitutes; horse-drawn carriages filled with well-dressed ladies and gentlemen who traveled at speeds of no more than a few miles an hour, or walked if they wanted to arrive at their destination more quickly; vendors who crowded the sidewalk; peddlers with no fixed place of business carrying their goods in handcarts or wheelbarrows, or on their backs; children inventing games and playing them all day in the midst of the confusion.

In a work published in 1862, Delvau had argued that "we find it tiresome to live and die at home . . . we require public display, big events, the street, the cabaret, to witness us for better or worse . . . we like to pose, to put on a show, to have an audience, a gallery, witnesses to our life." Some Parisians even warned that the street was becoming too enticing, almost irresistible. The Goncourt brothers, perhaps the city's most important publishers, lamented that "the interior is going to die. Life threatens to become public." As a later historian put it, Paris was an extroverted city.

AFTER THE MID-NINETEENTH CENTURY, Paris became a different sort of urban example: a city of boulevards, created with autocratic efficiency and painstaking attention to detail by Baron Georges-Eugene

Haussmann under the direction of the Emperor Napoléon III in the 1850s and 1860s.

The Paris of the boulevards is the place that foreigners romanticize and tourists love to visit. In many ways, it represents a break with the street-dominated city life that preceded it; in other ways, it is remarkably similar. When people make the claim that Paris is the most beautiful city in the world, as they often do, it is normally the boulevards that they have in mind. Sometimes it is difficult to see why. The boulevards Haussmann created are, for one thing, monotonous; he made sure of that. They are long corridors of stylistically similar, often nearly uniform stone apartment buildings, invariably gray, because Haussmann disliked color as a form of surface building ornamentation. Virtually every building had an identical number of window openings, all the same size. Each one had cast-iron balconies. The mansard roofs were almost all the same. Only the doors presented much opportunity for individualization. One critic commented that the long rows of apartment buildings looked like books neatly arranged in a bookcase. It is easy to understand how any one of these buildings can be admired for craftsmanship, sense of proportion, and overall aura of elegance. Understanding why endless boulevards full of them seem beautiful is a more complex question, but visitors have been lavishing praise upon the boulevards for the past century and a half.

One reason is very simple: the quality of light. It's not entirely clear that Haussmann knew in advance what sort of reflection his long rows of gray buildings would create, but one must give him the benefit of the doubt. He did, after all, like to proclaim that "light before all else" was his guiding principle. And the unrelenting gray of Haussmann's boulevards somehow gave off a visual impression that struck those who saw it as not only mysterious but somehow magical.

"Gray does not have a good name," the modern architectural historian Jean-Christophe Bailly wrote, "but in the very special light of Paris, it becomes a sort of receptacle for every nuance, creating a pearly refinement that excludes all shrillness." More than a century before him, the Italian novelist Edmondo de Amicis, coming upon Parisian boulevards for the first time, put it even more lyrically: "It is not an illumination but a fire. The boulevards are blazing. Half closing the eyes it seems as if one saw on the right and left two rows of flaming furnaces. The shops cast floods of brilliant light halfway across the street, and encircle the crowd in a golden dust."

But for the most part, it was neither the light radiating from the buildings nor the buildings themselves that made the Parisian boulevards of 1900 into an icon of Western civilization. It was the scene at ground level.

In part, this was a function of decoration. Haussmann was an artist of street furniture. The most trivial-seeming objects were designed with ingenuity and great care: Litter bins, sun and rain shelters, drinking fountains, public bathrooms, awnings, kiosks, pillars, and especially lampposts were decorated with silver or even small amounts of gold. The Métro stations, most of them appearing first in the 1890s, were decorated with the art nouveau signage and trim that makes them striking even today. There were iron benches on every boulevard, and long rows of trees. Haussmann preferred chestnut trees when he could get them; otherwise plane trees sufficed.

Above all, the Parisian boulevard was another version of human theater, merely two or three times larger than the midcentury street. Edmondo de Amicis saw it with a foreigner's clarity: "Everything is neat and fresh and wears a youthful air. . . . Between the two rows of trees is a constant passing and repassing of carriages, great carts and wagons drawn by engines and high omnibuses, laden with people, bounding up and down on the unequal pavement, with a deafening noise. Yet the whole air is different from that of London—the green open place, the faces, the voices, and the colors give to that confusion more the air of pleasure than of work."

The boulevards were crowded even at a width of eighty feet; the sidewalks were the most crowded part. Besides the iron benches, there were signs anywhere a spot could be found for them, and kiosks advertising and selling everything from luxuries for elite apartment dwellers to utensils for the day-to-day needs of their servants. All of this left little room for strolling on the sidewalks, often as little as four or five feet of room, but strollers were omnipresent nevertheless. "The sidewalks provided an outdoor living area for the city," the modern historian Norma Evenson explains, "an all-day circus and fair accessible to

The Boulevard des Italiens, one of the four "grand boulevards" of Paris in the late nineteenth and early twentieth centuries, was thronged with pedestrians, vehicles, and vitality almost twenty-four hours a day.

everyone." Those lucky enough to live in flats above these sidewalks could watch the circus from second- or fifth-floor balconies—and they could be watched themselves by pedestrians looking up from below.

The apartment buildings that lined the boulevards were highly desirable living spaces. Paris had more or less invented upscale apartment living as early as the eighteenth century, but Haussmann's Paris refined it and created an apartment-dwelling population many times larger. These buildings, nearly all five or six stories high, preserved the hierarchy of class separation that had existed earlier. The more affluent tenants lived on the lower floors, with the most affluent of all generally on the second floor, in a large flat with a wrought-iron balcony, and one moved downscale as one climbed the stairs, so that the top floor was often the province of the servants who waited upon those below. Children had their own territory in the form of a large nursery, from which they emerged in late afternoon for inspection or tea before returning for the evening.

This arrangement for living had its share of critics: The architect Viollet-le-Duc wrote that "nothing can more thoroughly demoralize a population than those large apartment houses which efface individual personalities and where love of family life is barely admissible." But for most Parisians in the late nineteenth century, and for most critics ever since, urban boulevard life represented a genuine achievement in the progress of Western civilization.

It was an ordered city, but it was one that proved remarkably hospitable to artists, bohemians, and misfits of various kinds. From the 1880s onward, the hill neighborhood of Montmartre, at the far north end of the city on the Right Bank, became the clubhouse of the creative class. As Nigel Gosling put it, "Montmartre was to become the dynamo charging the revolution which overturned the whole European art world." Peter Hall wrote: "The young artists, thrown together by poverty and isolation, formed close and intense networks; in the cafés, in the cabarets, on the river, in the salons of the dealers and the critics. They lived and worked in each other's pockets." Haussmann had never touched the Montmartre hillside, so housing was far cheaper than on the boulevards down below. Cabarets, bars, and restaurants were ubiquitous. Picasso practically lived at Vernin Bistro, eating his meals on credit when he was broke. A member of his circle recalled that "the smells from the kitchen and the rough wine mingled pretty disagreeably. Nobody minded that, though. You could eat well and there was always a lot going on."

Just beyond Montmartre, the Paris suburbs began. They had nothing in common with the modern American image of a suburb. For one thing, they were more densely populated than the city itself, and possessed little in the way of sanitation, because they were outside the geographical boundaries of Parisian sanitary requirements. In a sense, they were Haussmann's creation. He had no interest in these suburbs, but they provided a place to live for the thousands of immigrants who flocked to Paris to realize his plans: construction workers, ironworkers, stonemasons, all able to make the journey from rural France because of the train lines that reached out to the hinterlands to pick them up. Eventually they became home base for the children and grandchildren of the Haussmann brigade, most of them still working at jobs of hard physical labor, though in plastics and rubber factories rather than building boulevards. Grimy suburbs like Belleville and Ménilmontant became the ancestors of the squalid suburban housing projects north of Paris that house the North African immigrant underclass today—even though, somewhat ironically, these suburbs right on the urban border are growing more gentrified every year.

Even with eyesore suburbs on its northern fringe, Paris was a city that seemed to enchant practically every visitor who showed up. It is still enchanting them. Just a few years ago, the urbanist James Howard Kunstler exulted of Haussmann's Paris that "the great ordering system of the street walls, the balconies, the mansard roofs, the ubiquitous white limestone facades of the buildings . . . all induce a tremendous sense of satisfaction that you are finally in a human habitat that completely makes sense." A couple of decades earlier, François Loyer put it more concisely: "Second Empire Paris became one of the most coherent cities imaginable."

ONE OF THE MOST. Some might award the prize for urban coherence to turn-of-the century Vienna, the capital dominated by one big circular boulevard, around which the social and cultural life of the vast Austro-Hungarian empire seemed to revolve.

Vienna's Ringstrasse was a boulevard of Haussmannesque grandeur, but it was not created by anything resembling Haussmann's methods. In the 1850s, the medieval wall that had enclosed the Hapsburg palace and the cathedral was declared obsolete and torn down, leaving an empty circle more than four miles in circumference and 160 feet wide. Emperor Franz Josef seized on the opportunity to create a unique urban street, and he fixed its dimensions and height limits, but he didn't make rules for every window and cornice the way Haussmann did. The actual character of the Ringstrasse was determined by thousands of individual decisions, the product of the wealthy bourgeois families and minor nobility who developed it, owned it, and lived on it.

The apartment buildings that lined the street were magnificent to look at—they still are—but the boulevard itself was the magnet. It was a promenade at all hours, a place where Vienna's industrial and commercial elite spent much of its time seeing and being seen. One impoverished young painter living in Vienna in 1910 found himself utterly transfixed by the entire scene. "For hours I could stand in front of the Opera," he wrote, "for hours I could gaze at the Parliament; the whole Ring Boulevard seemed to me like an enchantment out of 'The Thousand-and-One-Nights.'" Such was the spell that Vienna's show-place boulevard cast over Adolf Hitler.

When the Ringstrasse opened in 1865, the imperial government and the city offered thirty-year property tax abatements to encourage the elite to live there. Probably they were unnecessary: In the Vienna of those days and in the generation to come, it simply made sense for the city's elite to live on the Ringstrasse, or on the smaller avenues that ran alongside it. It was said that a third of the residents were aristocrats, and that the other two-thirds were the commercial rich: industrialists, bankers, rentiers of various sorts. To a certain extent, they grouped themselves by occupation: There was a "textile quarter" right off the Ringstrasse where the Jewish clothing magnates who had

The wide Ringstrasse that made a circle through the Vienna of a century ago was an outdoor playground and showcase for the wealthy bourgeoisie and members of the nobility.

made late-nineteenth-century fortunes installed their modestly scaled businesses on the ground floor and their apartments above, mostly in buildings four to six stories tall, sixteen apartments to a building. Vienna was about 10 percent Jewish in 1900, but Jews made up most of the commercial elite and a majority of the city's doctors, lawyers, and journalists. Nearly all of them lived on or near the Ringstrasse and took part in its cultural temptations.

Apartment life on the Ringstrasse was, by today's standards, an unusual form of urban life. Most of the private living areas were relatively small, even in the most expensive buildings. It was the more public spaces that were large, the front rooms overlooking the street where dinners and parties could be held. And even more money was lavished on the common areas, the entrance halls with grand marble staircases and the front entrances with columns, sculptures, pediments, and friezes. Unlike in Haussmann's Paris, the buildings had their own individuality, or perhaps quirkiness is a better word. There were Gothic apartment buildings with classical ornaments; there were Renaissance-style palazzos with Gothic ornamentation. More than a dozen families would use the same front door and stairway, and take a common pride in the decoration that surrounded them.

The residents shared one crucial value: their belief in culture and entertainment as the core of life in their community. Children grew up with an intimate knowledge of museums, theaters, and concert halls. The novelist Stefan Zweig was to write in his memoirs many years later that "the Minister-President or the richest magnate could walk the streets without anyone's turning around, but a court actor or an opera singer was recognized by every salesgirl and every cabdriver."

As Zweig recalled, "The first glance of the average Viennese into his morning paper was not at the events in parliament, or world affairs, but at the repertoire of the theater, which assumed so important a role in public life as hardly was possible in any other city." Taking the whole family to a play early in the evening and then out for a late supper on the Ringstrasse was not a special treat; it was a routine part of urban living.

The Ringstrasse had a wide selection of formal restaurants for after-theater dining, but for casual dining and sociability at all hours there was the café, an institution that turn-of-the-century Vienna developed to a level of sophistication unmatched anywhere, before or since.

The café was a place to drink strong coffee and choose from an enormous variety of pastries—*apfeltorte,* Sacher torte, cinnamon streusel, *cremeschnitte;* the Viennese had as many names for pastry as the Eskimos did for snow—but for many, it was also a place to spend much of one's day, conversing on subjects that ranged from the upcoming weather to the state of Western civilization. Every café had its regulars, who spent three or four hours a day there, but also a steady supply of smart and talkative strangers. "It is a sort of democratic club," Zweig wrote, "to which admission costs the small price of a cup of coffee. Upon payment of this mite every guest can sit for hours on end, discuss, write, play cards, receive his mail, and above all go through an unlimited number of newspapers and magazines."

Not everyone in Vienna frequented the cafés, of course, or strolled down the Ringstrasse on sunny afternoons, or enjoyed the city's embarrassment of cultural riches. As diverse as the mixture of people was at Vienna's center, a huge proletariat resided far beyond it, across the Danube, in hastily built suburbs where the heavy industry was concentrated—the chemical factories, most especially—and immigrants, from Bohemia, Hungary, and a profusion of other places far to the east. This suburban working class was a quarter of the population of metropolitan Vienna by 1900; its members no longer worked seventy-hour weeks, as they had until the 1880s, but they worked longer and harder and in less sanitary conditions than anyone in a developed country could imagine today. In the suburb of Ottakring alone, there were thirty thousand apartments, most of them two rooms, with as many as ten adults and children sleeping inside every night. Ottakring, Frederic Morton wrote, was a "dismal tenement landscape . . . barracks hidden under laundry lines and the crumbling of pseudo-classic stucco." To the inhabitants of Ottakring, the Ringstrasse must have seemed thousands of miles away.

·   ·   ·

WHEN WE SHIFT our focus to London, the third of the great European cities of the early twentieth century, we are looking at an altogether different sort of place from Paris or Vienna. There were no great boulevards for the affluent to use as promenades; there was no Haussmann or Emperor Franz Josef to impose any plan for urban greatness. "If the British empire was the most powerful the world had ever known," the historian Jonathan Schneer wrote, "it yet lacked an emperor whose every vision of London could become an architect's command."

London, like Vienna and Paris, was an enormous magnet. It brought millions of people together for reasons of economics, government, and culture. But it didn't have a center in the way Paris or Vienna did. Until the very end of the nineteenth century it had few large apartment buildings, and no grand streets to place them on. Instead of a center, it had centers; instead of concentrating, it sprawled—as much as fifteen miles in some directions, a sea of small-scale tenements, townhouses for the wealthy, and small suburban cottages for the emerging middle class.

The closest thing to a center was an entirely commercial place, the "City of London," barely one square mile, a short walk up from the Thames River docks, a chaotic place in which the fundamental business decisions of a global empire were made. The City was, one might say, a downtown to end all downtowns. The daytime population was close to half a million. They were mostly subway commuters: Every morning, tens of thousands of men emerged from the Bank Street Underground station, men in white shirts, white collars, and top hats. They were importers and exporters, bankers and brokers, lawyers and insurance agents. They traded Caribbean sugar, South African gold, East Asian rubber, tea from China and India. They created a pedestrian traffic jam on the narrow City lanes three times a day: at the morning and evening rush hours, and at lunchtime, when the City restaurants were so crowded that customers queued up in long lines behind those seated at the counters, waiting patiently for their turn to eat.

If the City of London lacked the iconic architectural masterpieces of Paris or Vienna, it did have its landmarks: the Stock Exchange; Lloyd's of London; the "Mansion House," where the lord mayor lived and presided benignly over the commercial transactions of the globe; and, a little incongruously for a money-obsessed downtown, St. Paul's Cathedral, built by Sir Christopher Wren in the decades following the Great Fire of 1666.

The City of London was not a place for people to live in—the residential population in 1900 was tiny—but it was a place that Londoners of every class felt proud of. The Underground itself, noisy, dirty, and plastered with advertisements on every inch of available space, was a source of civic pride. The novelist Ford Madox Ford wrote of "a true Londoner, wishing on his death-bed once more to see and savour the smoke of the Underground."

But it was the Strand, the commercial street just a short distance from the Thames, that best reflected what this part of London was all about. "The Strand of those days," the architect H. B. Creswell wrote many years later, "was the throbbing heart of the people's essential London. Hedged by a maze of continuous alleys and courts, the Strand was fronted by numbers of little restaurants whose windows vaunted exquisite feeding; taverns, dives, oyster and wine bars, ham and beef shops and small shops marketing a lively variety of . . . things all standing in rank, shoulder to shoulder, to fill the spaces between its many theaters." Only three unpleasant qualities marred Creswell's enjoyment of the Strand, but they were three fairly important ones: "The mud! And the noise! And the smell!"

The social geography of London in 1900 can be reported pretty accurately in one sentence: The rich lived in the west, the immigrants and the poor in the east, the growing middle class in the suburbs.

The affluent, ensconced in the West End townhouses of Mayfair and Belgravia, lived a much more private life than their counterparts in Paris or Vienna. There was no equivalent to the Ringstrasse cafés in which the bourgeoisie drank coffee and ate pastry among people they didn't know. The City bankers and traders who lived in the West End had their own gathering places in the clubs near St. James's Park and other fashionable parts of the city, but these were private places, closed not just to strangers and the less affluent, but to women of every social class. Even in the theaters of Covent Garden, where the classes actually did mix, there were separate entrances for the elite and the ordinary, unlike in Paris. As Donald Olsen wrote, "The leisure class in London spent more of its leisure out of public view."

The West End encompassed diversity of a unique kind; an estimated 16 percent of its workforce consisted of servants, and they lived either in the basements of the grand townhouses or on side streets nearby. But the genuinely poor had a province of the city all to themselves, and it was a place their more fortunate fellow Londoners rarely even saw. It was the East End. In the words of the historian Tristram Hunt, "The East End became a terra incognita as unknown and as dangerous to the clubs of the West End as the Great Lakes of central Africa."

There were nearly a million people living in London's East End at the start of the twentieth century. It was a vast expanse of six-story tenements with as many as half a dozen people sleeping in rooms no larger than ten by twelve feet. One writer described it as a place "where filthy men and women live on penn'orths of gin, where collars and clean shirts are decencies unknown, where every citizen wears a black eye, and none ever combs his hair." The journalist Will Crooks is said to have remarked that the sun that never sets on the British Empire never rises on the dark alleys of east London.

This was no welfare population; to all intents and purposes, there was no welfare. Most of these people worked. The main employers were sweatshop clothing makers, but many East End residents worked on the London docks, loading and unloading ships at the world's greatest port, twenty-six square miles of territory along the Thames, lined with huge warehouses, some of them six stories tall and an acre across. Most of the dockworkers were casual laborers, showing up at hiring halls early each morning in hopes of finding temporary work.

When their work stints were finished, or when they weren't fortunate enough to get any work, they returned to the East End streets, as crowded as the midcentury streets of Paris, but far more dispiriting. H. G. Wells walked the neighborhood often and described it as "a great mysterious movement of unaccountable beings." D. H. Lawrence found it more ominous still: "some hoary massive underworld, a hoary ponderous inferno, where traffic flows through the rigid grey streets like the rivers of hell through their banks of dry rocky ash."

Turn-of-the-century London was not unique in placing its affluent on one side of the divide and reserving another for immigrants and the working poor. What was unique about London was the rapid expansion of suburbs for the lower middle class, generated almost entirely by rail transportation.

The Cheap Trains Act of 1883 required the railroads to build "workmen's trains." Although it took a while, they built enormous numbers of them: More than six thousand of these trains were running by 1904. That was the year the *Times* of London wrote that "the habit of living at a distance from the scene of work has spread from the merchant and the clerk to the artisan. The suburb is now mainly the residence for the family of small means."

In fact, the term "workmen's train" was something of a misnomer. Dockworkers didn't commute to the suburbs on them; neither did the enormous servant population that waited upon the West End elite. But the bank clerks and bookkeepers of the City found homes in the suburbs, semidetached stucco cottages with small gardens in the rear, each of them looking almost identical and the whole agglomeration stretching for miles into the countryside of Surrey, Essex, and Hertfordshire. They were commonly advertised as "villas," even though they didn't qualify for that status by any definition familiar before or since.

The upper class almost universally derided these developments as sterile, if not hideous. Even those who believed in social reform saw nothing worthwhile there. H. G. Wells, who found the poverty of the East End fascinating, if sometimes grotesque, didn't find the suburbs interesting in any way at all. He described "the little clump of shops about the post-office, and under the railway arch . . . and, like a bright fungoid growth in the ditch . . . a sort of fourth-estate of little red-and-white rough-cast villas, with meretricious gables and very brassy window blinds."

Some of the critics found suburbia not only a dull place but an ominous portent of the metropolitan future. "The center of population is shifting," Sidney Low wrote in the 1890s, "from the heart to the limbs. The life blood is pouring into the long arms of brick and mortar and cheap stucco that are feeling their way out to the Surrey moors."

In many ways, these critics sound like their American counterparts in the 1950s, appalled by the monotony of the suburbs and oblivious to the fact that ordinary families were moving there because they considered a suburban cottage a symbol of comfort, and a step up in the world.

The middle-class suburbs of London were not models for the American suburbs that sprouted up after World War II. Londoners who moved there were not fleeing racial change or failing schools, and they were not fleeing crime. But they were seeking more space; in that respect, the two institutions share a common connection.

IT WOULD BE ABSURD to make the claim that the great European cities of the late nineteenth century will reappear in this country in anything like their original form. No American city will create a Ringstrasse; none could reproduce the City of London even if it wanted to; it is impossible to imagine a Haussmann (or even a Robert Moses) emerging anywhere. But it would also be a mistake to deny the relevance of these older cities to the evolving urban experience, or not to notice that Donald Olsen, hyperbole notwithstanding, was onto something.

American cities all but lost their street life in the last decades of the twentieth century; anybody walking around downtown Philadelphia or Boston or Chicago after five in the afternoon found the streets deserted and dangerous. Today, in various forms, street life is returning. One can walk down Michigan Avenue in Chicago or Walnut Street in Philadelphia long after dark and find the place throbbing with activity and nearly always safe.

Much of this activity, as in the Paris or Vienna of another time, is clustered around entertainment. In the twenty-first century, this is less likely to mean performances at an immense concert hall, although a few cities have built them, and more likely to mean plays at storefront black box theaters and live music coming out of the bars that line the street. Most of all, however, street life in the emerging city means restaurant life. Walk along Tryon Street in downtown Charlotte, that highly untraditional American city, and you will see diners at sidewalk tables on every block. There is little retail shopping in downtown Charlotte, but there are restaurants almost everywhere.

And there are cafés. One can make fun of the ubiquitous presence and the uniformity of Starbucks, but the fact remains that just twenty years ago, the idea of coffeehouses in urban centers seemed a quaint vision of the vanished past. Now one can walk into a Starbucks in the center of any large American city at ten in the morning or eight in the evening and find clusters of coffee drinkers deep in conversation, many of them lingering as much to talk as to consume. It is not going too far to say that Starbucks resurrected the coffeehouse experience in present-day America: Small independent cafés have returned to the street along with it. We have not re-created the Ringstrasse café—but we have taken a step in that direction.

We have also taken a step toward the urban diversity and tolerance that prevailed in Paris a hundred years ago. People with widely different backgrounds and modes of living come together on the sidewalks of Boston, Chicago, San Francisco, and a growing number of other cities in ways that would have been unthinkable in 1980. American cities are also returning to diversity of use: The idea of zoning for segregation of uses is slowly dying in America; virtually every city planning official is now looking for ways to promote mixed-use zoning, perhaps not the chaotic jumble of the old Paris, but a mixture of uses nevertheless.

At the level of the metropolitan region, modern American urban patterns are coming to resemble older ones in a more dramatic fashion. The late twentieth century was the age of poor inner cities and wealthy suburbs; the twenty-first century is emerging as an age of affluent inner neighborhoods and immigrants settling on the outside. The movement of singles, couples, and empty-nest baby boomers back to the center gathered momentum in the first decade of the new century, stalled in the recession at the end of the decade, and will eventually resume.

When it resumes, American cities will come to resemble not only the European capitals of a century ago, but cities all over the globe today. Current European cities have their problems with suburban sprawl, but almost without exception they follow the historic pattern: affluent people in the center, migrants and the poor on the outskirts.

The cities of the developing world follow it as well, perhaps more dramatically. Mumbai, Cairo, and Rio de Janeiro all consist of central districts where tourists and rich locals congregate, surrounded by shantytowns populated by newly arrived urbanites who have left zones of rural poverty to try to make a fresh start amid the chaos of a mushrooming metropolitan population. So do other fast-growing cities on every continent. There are no shantytowns surrounding American cities, and there will not be any. But even the briefest consideration of the rest of the world makes it clear that the inversion taking place in the United States is no global aberration, but a distinctly American version of a phenomenon that exists in large cities everywhere.

In the chapters that follow, we will visit a cross section of cities and suburbs in diverse parts of America, take a detailed look at the way they are changing, and hazard some guesses about what they might look like a generation from now.

N LINCOLN AVE
N SHEFFIELD AVE
N HALSTED ST

Lake Michigan

41

W FULLERTON AVE

Logan Square

DePaul University

Sheffield

Bucktown

W ARMITAGE AVE

Armitage El station

Lincoln Park

W NORTH AVE

Humboldt Park

Wicker Park

90

Chicago River

N LAKE SHORE DRIVE

0   1 Mile

Downtown
Chicago

Loop

290

Grant Park

Chicago O'Hare Int'l Airport

90

Lake Michigan

294

Detail area

Chicago Harbor

41

0   5 Miles

Chicago

S LAKE SHORE DRIVE

55

55

CHAPTER TWO

A NEIGHBORHOOD IN CHICAGO

IT IS SIX THIRTY IN THE MORNING in Sheffield, a quiet neighborhood three miles north of downtown Chicago. I'm sitting by the window at a bagel-and-coffee shop just off the corner of Sheffield and Armitage, across the street from the Armitage elevated train station. Every few minutes a Brown Line train rumbles by directly overhead, its noise so consistent and regular that it feels like an icon of neighborhood life, not an annoyance of any sort.

Armitage Avenue is no Parisian boulevard; there are no boulevards in Sheffield, only business streets and residential streets. But the buildings are about the same age as those in central Paris; nearly all of them were built between 1880 and 1910. The Argo tea shop on the other side of the street reveals the date 1885 in large letters on the second-story wall. By city ordinance, none of the buildings can be more than thirty-four feet tall.

A parade of early risers marches down the street in front of me: joggers, men in suits on their way to the train, art students from nearby DePaul University carrying their supplies to the studio. It is not a picture of diversity as we have come to define it—there are very few blacks or Hispanics on the street—but it is the sort of diversity Jane Jacobs saw in Greenwich Village in the 1950s, a diversity of occupations, ages, and daily schedules. There are people on their way to nine-to-five jobs, others returning from night shifts, young singles who jog this route every morning, older people who cover the same route at a slower pace.

The businesses that line this block of Armitage are, for the most part, neither chic nor shabby. There is a Rugby Ralph Lauren bou-

*Armitage Avenue, in Chicago's Sheffield neighborhood, has managed to
retain its workaday appearance while serving as a commercial center for
one of the city's most affluent communities.*

tique, but that is about the only hint of cosmopolitan sophistication.
The others are nearly all local. There's a sports bar that has huge Cubs
and White Sox banners displayed with seeming impartiality in the
window, also a chiropractor and a dry cleaner. Around the corner on
Sheffield is a Caribbean restaurant. If you look down the next block of
Armitage, you can see empty storefronts.

But the day-and-night street life is undeniably interesting. "There's
so much activity at Armitage and Sheffield," one resident says, "it
almost feels like a movie." Another boasts that "in Sheffield, you wonder what you're going to see next, maybe a famous pro athlete next to
a Filipino immigrant." A third is more grandiose: "This is like the Left
Bank of Paris seventy years ago."

THE ONE THING you won't notice about Sheffield through the windows of the Chicago Bagel Authority may be the most important

thing about the place. It is rich. Actually, very rich. As of 2009, in tract 711, where comparatively modest old houses fill most of the residential blocks north of Armitage, the median family income was $201,125. When mid-decade projections were released in 2007 by Esri, an independent demographic research company, the median home price had surpassed a million dollars. "Gentrification" is not a word that accurately describes Sheffield. It is a neighborhood of stable and substantial affluence where scarcely any of the people we normally consider gentrifiers can afford to live.

It is easier to demonstrate that Sheffield is rich than to explain why. "At first glance," the *Chicago Tribune* wrote in 2006, "it's hard to see why some of Chicago's most wealthy people have chosen this formerly nondescript area as their new enclave. It doesn't have a lake view. It isn't even that close to the lake." And the land is flat as a pancake.

In fact, Lake Michigan is a little more than a mile from the center of Sheffield, and one can walk there in half an hour at a leisurely pace. But few of the residents do that very often. There are other factors that clearly have something to do with what has happened—the fourteen-minute train ride to downtown, the presence of a university, the tree-lined streets and pleasingly eclectic stock of houses—but none of these quite suffice as explanations. It is more instructive simply to say that Sheffield is a small piece of a much larger demographic phenomenon that has enveloped much of Chicago over the past couple of decades. "The city is changing," then-mayor Richard M. Daley proclaimed shortly after taking office in 1989. "You're not going to see the factories back."

But just what Chicago was to see in the ensuing years was not predicted by Daley or anyone else. When the mayor spoke those words, the city had suffered through nearly a generation of economic and demographic decline and social disorder, to which no clear end was in sight.

In fact, however, by 1989 many of Chicago's problems were already beginning to ease up. The loss of factory jobs was indeed horrendous: four hundred thousand of them between 1969 and 1983 alone, or 32 percent of the city's total manufacturing employment base. This was roughly comparable to what was happening in other Midwestern industrial cities, except in one respect: Virtually all the other cities—Detroit, Cleveland, St. Louis—were unable to come up with new kinds of jobs to replace them. Chicago did. In Chicago, the downtown Loop and lakefront corridor running north from it gradually became a magnet for service and professional work: banking, brokerage, insurance, architecture, and various forms of temporary office employment. In 1950, Chicago had three times as many jobs in manufacturing as in services; by 2001, services led by more than two to one. "Manufacturing was still more important in Chicago than in most other big urban areas," journalist David Moberg wrote a few years later, "but smoky mills, clanging presses, and fast assembly—or disassembly—no longer defined the regional economy." Between 1990 and 2006, if you exclude factory jobs—admittedly a large exclusion—Chicago was a net job gainer. It ceased to be one in the recession years that followed, but demographic inversion was well under way, and it has not receded in the years since.

The question of why Chicago escaped the fate of other industrial cities is a subject that has been much debated, but in the end the most satisfying answer may be the simple reality of size. One can argue plausibly that there was room for only one Midwestern city to compete in the new service- and technology-based global economy that was emerging, and Chicago, by far the largest among these cities, was the obvious candidate, even with its serious problems of poverty, weak schools, and scattered violent crime.

Chicago's civic leaders were startled and discouraged to learn in early 2011 that the previous year's census had reported a citywide population decline of 6.9 percent, leaving a population of 2,695,598, fewer people than have lived in Chicago at any time since the 1920s. These are difficult numbers to present optimistically; the media tend to equate raw population growth with urban success, and Chicago had boasted when the 2000 census showed it with a small population gain, in contrast to the losses of other Midwestern cities. But a closer look at Chicago's population changes in the past decade reveals more precisely what happened: In part because of the demolition of the high-rise housing projects, the black population declined by 177,401, accounting for more than three-quarters of the total decline. Many went to suburbs surrounding the city on all sides, including suburbs many miles distant from the city limits. There was a small overall decline in the white population as white working-class families living just inside the city's borders decamped to the suburbs, while Hispanics moved in to replace them, their numbers growing by three percentage points, and constituting the only major population group whose numbers increased in the city in the past decade. The more affluent population of the central areas remained stable. The census did not tell Chicago what it wanted to hear, but when one examines the numbers in detail, one conclusion is inescapable: Between 2000 and 2010, Chicago became a whiter city with a larger affluent population.

LIKE NEW YORK, but unlike most large American cities, Chicago has long had a reasonably large affluent population within a short distance of its commercial center. For most of the twentieth century, though, this population was limited to a narrow strip along the shores of Lake Michigan, stretching north from the Loop. These urbanites lived in tall and elegant apartment buildings constructed during the boom years of the 1920s, when completion of Lake Shore Drive made downtown offices easy to reach by car.

Except for this lakefront strip, however, Chicago roughly resembled other industrial cities: Hardly anyone resided in the center, and the neighborhoods immediately beyond it, most of them abutting factories and warehouses, were not considered fashionable or attractive places to live. During World War II, only 1 percent of what is now called the "central area" was in residential use.

This did not change for a long time. It finally changed mostly because of a widely held civic illusion: that Chicago's population was about to grow substantially. The city's official projection in 1959 was that by 1980, the city would increase from 3.7 million to 4.2 million. The housing director declared that "all large centers of population must plan for accommodating an ever increasing number of people." In fact, he and the other experts were massively mistaken. By 1980, the city's population hadn't increased at all.

But Mayor Richard J. Daley (Richard M.'s father), a fervent believer in population growth, had spent the two decades of his mayoralty (1955–1976) doing everything he could to house the added residents he expected to see. A 1957 zoning code made it much easier for residential developers to build luxury high-rise housing virtually anywhere they chose. Within a decade after that, the developers responded, and in the 1950s and 1960s, 350 new high-rise towers went up. At first, they were still mostly a lakefront phenomenon, pushing just a little farther west of Lake Michigan, onto such streets as Marine Drive and Sheridan Road. But they attracted thousands of upper-class renters and owners who decided they wanted to live the lakefront life. The city was responding to a projected population growth that never took place, but in the process it made possible moves by thousands of affluent residents to close-in apartments they found appealing.

In the 1960s, the elder Daley and the developers discovered downtown itself. The turning point was the construction of Marina City, on the Chicago River just north of the Loop, one of America's oddest residential complexes, but also one of the most influential. A pair of sixty-five-story cylindrical towers that vaguely resembled corncobs, nine hundred apartments perched on the banks of the Chicago River with boat docks for the residents, Marina City was, at the time of its opening in 1964, the tallest apartment building in the world. It was derided by critics but proved to be a huge financial success. In the words of the urban historian Joseph Schwieterman, Marina City was "a watershed in Chicago planning history. . . . [I]t showcased the cosmopolitan lifestyle available to those living in the greater Loop." Never before had Chicago seen residential development on this scale so close to the heart of the city.

Marina City was followed in 1968 by Lake Point Tower, a seventy-one-story curved glass International Style building on the Lake Michigan shore that replaced Marina City as the world's tallest all-residential structure. Lake Point Tower was infinitely more pleasing to look at than Marina City, although it was equally controversial—it obstructed the view of Lake Michigan for passersby and some area residents. It turned out to be equally successful. It drove home the idea that even a city with a declining population, as long as it is large enough, can attract the upper middle class to downtown living.

By 1970, an increasing number of new residential towers were going up in the old commercial sector surrounding the Loop. They brought in enough year-round urban dwellers to support a raft of new businesses that catered to them: restaurants, nightclubs, boutiques, and more than one multistory shopping mall. The more people came to central Chicago to live, the more successful the businesses became; and the more diverse and interesting the businesses became, the more people wanted to live nearby. It was, for the city government and the developers, a truly virtuous circle.

And it was a circle that kept expanding its dimensions—north, south, and especially west, where older blue-collar neighborhoods were filled with compact nineteenth-century houses close to the downtown action and waiting patiently to be reclaimed. That is, in part, the story of how Sheffield became rich.

NOBODY LIVING IN SHEFFIELD in 1970 would have guessed that anything like a demographic inversion was about to take place. The neighborhood was indeed undergoing a transition, but it was a transition from modest working-class enclave to semislum.

The Latin Kings had their official headquarters on the second floor of the 1885-vintage Mueller Building, at the corner of Armitage and Sheffield, and sold drugs next to the tracks of the Armitage El station. The Kings' rival, the beret-wearing Young Lords, were all over the neighborhood, not only selling drugs but demanding protection payments from local businesses. Anyone who chose to refurbish a house—there were just a few at the time—would likely be asked to pay the Lords $2 a month to guarantee that the windows would not be broken. In 1969, the Young Lords and their leader, Cha-Cha Jimenez, seized a building on the nearby DePaul University campus and demanded that the university donate money to the group's "antipoverty" program. Teenagers from the huge Cabrini-Green public housing project, less than a mile away, used to make quick trips into the neighborhood to steal bicycles and ride off. In the early 1970s, the minister of the Armitage Avenue Methodist Church was murdered on the sidewalk in front of the church's entrance.

On the residential streets east and west of Sheffield Avenue, larger buildings had been cut up into small apartments and housed as many as eighty people each. In the words of Erich Teske, who was growing up in Sheffield at the time, "Virtually every garage was covered with graffiti. The garbage was strewn over the alleys." Residents who wanted to preserve a semblance of neatness used shovels to dump the trash into garbage cans. There were signs scattered throughout the neighborhood that read, in big black letters, RID YOUR BLOCK OF RATS. RATS EAT GARBAGE. CLEAN UP THE GARBAGE.

This was by no means a uniformly poor neighborhood. The median family income in census tract 710, on the blocks west of Sheffield, was $9,375 in 1970, only slightly below the national family median of $9,870. Thirteen percent of the people in tract 710 lived beneath the poverty line, a number that matched almost precisely the average for the nation as a whole. Tract 711, the neighborhood's eastern half, was doing a little better. Its median family income was $11,392.

Many of the white ethnic families who had occupied Sheffield for generations continued to live there in 1970, but it was not the place they fondly remembered. Sheffield in 1970 was a dangerous place to be.

THE SITUATION did not change overnight, or even in a couple of years. No single event or series of events made Sheffield into something new. The most accurate thing to say is that something important was happening around the center of America's third-largest city, and Sheffield gradually became part of it.

Certainly one can make a list of factors that contributed. Perhaps first among them, odd as it may seem, is Lake Michigan, a body of water that one can live indefinitely in Sheffield without even noticing.

It is sometimes difficult to explain to non-Chicagoans the mystical significance that the lake possesses. Civic leaders have traditionally talked about it as a civic achievement, almost as if they had built it. "You ride the length of Chicago," the influential newspaper columnist Jack Mabley wrote in 1957, "and think that other cities, corruption or no, should have been able to produce something as beautiful."

In a sense, the city actually did create Lake Michigan. For more than half a century of its existence, the lake absorbed massive amounts of industrial waste that flowed into it from the Chicago River. Year by year, the garbage dumped into the river turned the lake into more and more of an eyesore. Finally, at the beginning of the twentieth century, city engineers found a method of using canal locks to reverse the river's flow, depositing the industrial garbage west into a new Chicago Sanitary and Ship Canal, returning the lake to the more or less pristine condition it had been in when Potawatomi Indians lived along its banks in the eighteenth century.

The engineers who performed this feat mainly felt that they were dealing with a public health nuisance, but they were doing much more than that. They were creating miles of clean blue lakefront suitable for boating, swimming, and other pleasures of urban life. The boosters are correct when they say that no other major lakefront city did this. Nearly all the others concentrated industry along their major waterfronts and left them unusable for much else, essentially creating a wall between the water and the city. More than a century later, most of them are still struggling with this problem. One is not drawn to the splendors of Lake Erie in Cleveland or Buffalo, or Lake Huron in Detroit.

But Chicago, whether it fully intended to or not, made a lakefront that was an attraction rather than an eyesore. When Richard J. Daley decided in the late 1950s that the city needed a whole new collection of high-rise apartment buildings, he had the shores of Lake Michigan to place them on. Of the high-rise apartment buildings constructed in Chicago in the 1960s, 90 percent were within one mile of the lake.

By the end of that decade, most of the opportunities closest to Lake Michigan had been seized, and the process of urban revival began moving into the blocks a little farther west that were known as Lincoln Park. Despite its location, the Lincoln Park neighborhood was more than a little seedy in the 1960s, with many of its 1920s-era apartment buildings turned into multitenant rooming houses. But Lincoln Park was the next closest thing to Lake Shore Drive, and by the early 1970s, its renewal was on the verge of completion. The invasion of the professional class now stretched all the way to Halsted Street, ten blocks from the lakefront park. There it stopped. Lakefront and Lincoln Park parents warned their children not to wander any farther west than Halsted Street. Halsted was the eastern boundary of the ominous residential enclave known as Sheffield.

If riding a bicycle west of Halsted Street was a scary enterprise, then renovating a house in Sheffield was a much riskier one. Nevertheless, people with the means to do that began doing it in the early 1970s. Sheffield was different from Lincoln Park in an important way: Rather than apartment buildings, its residential stock consisted largely of single-family homes—"workmen's cottages," in the local parlance. The neighborhood traditionally had housed German and Irish families whose breadwinners earned modest but stable livings serving as police officers or firefighters, or working for the local gas company, or holding down jobs at the nearby steel factory or the Deering Harvester plant in the industrial corridor just west of the neighborhood boundary.

Although no precise numbers exist, it's estimated that workmen's cottages comprised nearly two-thirds of all the housing in Sheffield at the start of the 1970s. They were modest in size, but they were solidly built and attractive—a quirkily eclectic mixture of Italianate, Romanesque, and Queen Anne architectural styles, nearly all dating from the period between 1880 and 1910. Hundreds of them were available, because their previous working-class owners had begun moving to the suburbs. They were also affordable; in tract 711, the more expensive of the two main Sheffield census tracts, the median home value in 1970 was $23,800. "Living west of Halsted was considered very risky," says Diane Levin, a longtime resident. "But it was a beautiful, undeveloped neighborhood."

It was also a neighborhood that was easy to get to. Trains on the Brown Line, then known simply as the Ravenswood El, rumbled by every few minutes. The Armitage Station, which opened in 1907, was rickety and underused in the early 1970s: It looked like a relic of a very different time. There were no wooden trains anymore—the Chicago Transit Authority had stopped using those in the 1950s—but the tracks and platforms and railings still conjured up the feeling of an old wooden city, and the tiny stations and creaking trains made the

Ravenswood El feel a bit like the Toonerville Trolley of urban mass transit.

The Ravenswood line was in financial trouble throughout the 1970s, and the CTA threatened seriously to close it down in the early 1980s, but suddenly its ridership began to grow again, its mere presence an attraction to the arriving professionals more than it had been to the locally rooted blue-collar workers in the neighborhoods it traversed. Between 1987 and 1998, as overall CTA rail traffic continued to plummet, traffic on the newly renamed Brown Line increased by nearly 30 percent. In 2000, weekend service was reinstated along the line, forty-eight years after it had been discontinued for lack of patronage. By that time, roughly half of Sheffield's workforce was taking the Brown Line to jobs somewhere in the city, and the main problem was overcrowding. All its stations had to be retrofitted to accommodate the longer trains that were necessary to handle the traffic. In the first decade of the new century, the Brown Line corridor was the hot property of Chicago's transportation network, and Sheffield sat right in the middle of it.

The stations along the line are spaced every few blocks, and Sheffield has two of them: one at the south border on Armitage and one at the northern end at Fullerton, in the middle of the DePaul University campus.

Founded in 1898 by the Vincentian Catholic order, DePaul has always been a presence in the neighborhood—many of the priests who taught there grew up in working-class families on the Sheffield streets. But for most of the school's history, it was a modest presence: "the little school under the El," as people liked to call it, overshadowed in local Catholic education by the more imposing Loyola University on the Far North Side. DePaul in 1970 was still almost entirely a commuter school, just as it had been in the 1920s and 1930s, when Richard J. Daley rode the train there four nights a week to get a law degree.

DePaul almost decided to abandon the Sheffield campus in 1967 for more enticing suburban pastures, but it made the opposite decision instead: It stayed and converted its grimy buildings dating from the 1920s into a modern and nationally known school whose twenty-four thousand students made it the largest Catholic college in the United

States. It's a stretch to call twenty-first-century Sheffield a college neighborhood, but the continued presence and growing reputation of the university was one more magnet enticing newcomers to buy the old workmen's cottages that surrounded it on every side.

One other feature of Sheffield attracted newcomers in the 1970s and 1980s: its music scene. Music and theater had come to Lincoln Park in the 1950s, with the arrival of the Second City comedy club and a thriving folk and blues cluster in Old Town, a mile or so south of Sheffield along North Avenue and Wells Street. The glory days of Chicago folk music were over by the 1970s, but the blues began creeping northward, into storefronts on Halsted near Sheffield's eastern border, close to DePaul. Some of them are still there: One of the clubs, B.L.U.E.S., is a reminder of the neighborhood's funkier days, with a tiny stage, wobbly bar stools, and vinyl seats held together by duct tape. Across the street from B.L.U.E.S. is Kingston Mines, which dates all the way back to the late 1960s, a cavernous open space with stages built to look like back porches. These days, you can buy a genuine Kingston Mines jacket for $250. And there is one last conspicuous reminder of the folk scene: the Old Town School of Folk Music, located not in Old Town but along the Armitage shopping corridor between Halsted and Sheffield. It has been mainly a school and music store for several decades, holding on at the same address since 1968.

No one would confuse this with Montmartre in the 1890s, but it was an important part of Sheffield's revival, an amenity that helped to persuade young and relatively affluent home buyers that the neighborhood was worth the indignities that still lingered from the days of overstuffed rooming houses and gangs and drugs on the street. It was a deal that the newcomers were willing to accept; the squalid days are now no more than a distant memory for those Sheffield residents who remember them at all.

THESE DAYS, Sheffield is much more concerned about preservation than it is about attracting development. The commercial corridors of Armitage Avenue and part of Halsted Street have been designated by the city as a historic district, and are unlikely to change very much.

The blocks of storefronts that give the neighborhood the aura of the late nineteenth century seem poised to maintain it well into the twenty-first. On Webster Avenue, in the middle of Sheffield, you can find a jewelry store that calls itself the Left Bank and has done just about everything it can to create the aura of old-fashioned Parisian shopping. But with a few minor exceptions, the residential streets do not have historic protection. Plans to establish it have been debated for years, but have met a wall of resistance from home owners who don't want to lose the right to alter their property as they see fit. Walking down the residential blocks of Sheffield, you find a smattering of lawn signs that read SAY NO TO LANDMARK DISTRICTS.

And so it is legal to do almost anything to a house on a residential block in Sheffield—add on to it, change its architectural style—or, most ominously, tear it down. There are some residents who insist that the neighborhood hasn't changed much in the past few years, but others feel that it has been losing its identity to the teardowns of the last decade. "They're turning what was a vibrant urban neighborhood into

Sheffield combines "workmen's cottages" from the nineteenth century and expensive new homes on narrow lots, built to replace older homes that have been torn down.

a collection of bloated, physically isolated, suburban-style manses," *Tribune* architecture critic Blair Kamin wrote a few years ago, referring specifically to the streets south of Armitage. "Most cities would kill to have billionaires and multi-millionaires putting down this kind of change instead of fleeing to the 'burbs. . . . It's just that they're killing off the architectural style and urban substance that once made this area so attractive."

To an outsider, it doesn't look that way. The vertical McMansions built in the last few years stand mostly as conspicuous exceptions to the long rows of Victorian cottages. They are conspicuous mainly because there are still relatively few of them. But there is no denying that the biggest story in Sheffield, at least until the real estate bust of 2008, was the arrival of the superrich.

Some of them are famous. Kerry Wood, the onetime star pitcher for the Cubs, became a resident of the neighborhood. So did Penny Pritzker, the Hyatt heiress identified by *Forbes* magazine in 2009 as the 647th-richest person in America, who built a home of more than eight thousand square feet on Orchard Street, just south of Armitage, a street that some locals have taken to calling "Gazillionaire's Row."

The McMansions in and around Sheffield don't look anything like their suburban counterparts. The limits on height and lot size guarantee that. A majority of them are simply tall, narrow glass boxes. Some manage to blend in rather well with the surrounding buildings. But their extravagance is undeniable, even if not all of it is visible to the passerby. Many of them have elaborate green-designed rooftop decks on the fourth floor, reachable by elevator. Some of these decks block the view from the surrounding older houses. Some of the new houses have huge wine cellars that run the entire width of the property. There are heating coils under the sidewalks in front. And there are massive curb cuts that critics say ruin the pedestrian flavor of the streets on which they are placed.

The owners of the smaller houses that still dominate the neighborhood can't really be said to have suffered economically. They bought for next to nothing, in many cases have paid off the mortgages, and could sell them for a fortune. The one depressing fact of life for the owner of a Sheffield cottage is taxes. Some home owners whose buildings fall far short of McMansion status find themselves looking at property tax bills that can run as high as $11,000 a year.

The most common complaint that long-term Sheffield residents make about the newcomers, however, is that they don't have much interest in broader community life. There's been "a tremendous diminution in participation in civic affairs," says Martin Oberman, who used to represent Sheffield on the Chicago City Council. "There's a lot more isolation. As people build three- or four-million-dollar houses, they tend not to be community activists."

One hears that all the time in Sheffield. "The young people here don't have kids for my littlest boy to play with," one resident told a writer for *Midwest Magazine.* "They lead their own lives and don't make friends." But it's not a new complaint. That comment was made in 1972. In Sheffield, as in countless neighborhoods around the country, the glory days of civic activism always seem to have occurred a generation before.

If there is a true test of resident commitment to the community, it would seem to be in the schools. The elementary school that serves Sheffield is Oscar Mayer, at the northern end of the neighborhood, next to the DePaul campus. It goes from kindergarten to eighth grade. For most of the past quarter century, the student body at Mayer was overwhelmingly black and Hispanic, with most of the pupils bused in from other parts of the city. There weren't enough children from Sheffield families to keep it operating at capacity. In 2002, Mayer had a white student population of 12.5 percent.

In the past decade, that began to change. By 2007, the school was 27 percent white. It was in the process of conversion to magnet status, as a Montessori school in the lower grades and an International Baccalaureate program in the higher grades, with neighborhood residents guaranteed a place. This move generated criticism that the Chicago school system was mainly trying to make Mayer more attractive to affluent white families living around it, luring them away from private schools. That has been borne out only in a selective way. There are white majorities in kindergarten and first grade, and sizable numbers of white pupils through the early primary school years. But as the children grow older, the percentages change. In eighth grade, Mayer remains a minority-dominated school.

The consensus nevertheless exists among some Sheffield residents that even though it is available to students of any race living anywhere in the city, Mayer in ten years will be a majority-white school primarily serving Sheffield and the neighborhoods around it. And whether we wish to believe it or not, school performance tracks demographics more than it tracks pedagogical approach. The more middle-class students populate a school, whatever their ethnic background happens to be, the higher the test scores rise. An increase in middle-class students is a magnet that draws more middle-class families to the neighborhood, changing the performance of the school further, in what amounts to a virtuous cycle.

IT'S EARLY EVENING now in Sheffield, the busiest time of day on Armitage Avenue. Sipping a glass of wine at the Twisted Lizard side-walk café, around the corner from the train, you can track the changes in the street scene as the evening rush hour wears on. At five o'clock, the sidewalks transport a parade of babies in strollers, many of them just retrieved from the St. Vincent de Paul day-care center on Halsted Street, one of the largest such centers in the state, with nearly five hundred children in attendance. Judging from the profusion of strollers in the late afternoon, and the seemingly ubiquitous presence of children's clothing stores on Armitage and Halsted, you begin to suspect that census data on household size in Sheffield—a median of roughly two people per household in the two main census tracts—is somehow in error.

By five thirty most of the strollers and children are gone, and the scene has begun to change significantly. There are middle-aged men with white shirts and briefcases now, younger men carrying messenger bags, women lugging big round papasan wicker chairs from a neighboring furniture store, and quite a few people carrying clothes on hangers from the dry cleaner that sits next to the station.

The Starbucks on the corner of Armitage and Sheffield is busy at this time of day, as it was early in the morning, but the scene is much more social. Few conversations took place in the store early in the morning; much of the inside crowd was composed of young women working silently on their laptops. At six in the evening, however, little knots of people congregate in front of the store to talk, almost as if each group had an assigned time: One group leaves the corner and another turns up to replace it.

One also gets more sense of Sheffield as a left-leaning urban enclave in the evening than in the morning. There are Greenpeace activists on two of the four corners; adults drift by on skateboards and Roller-blades. I begin to wonder whether this is more a neighborhood of aging hippies than I thought it was. Then I see a red Corvette convertible glide by, and I am reminded of a basic truth: It is still a place where it can cost more than a million dollars to buy a house.

ONE THING most of Chicago's planners felt sure of in the 1980s was that once the westward spread of central-city affluence reached the end of Sheffield, it would face an insuperable physical barrier. The western boundary of Sheffield, Clybourn Avenue, was a wide, ugly thoroughfare lined with strip malls. Just beyond it was an industrial zone called Goose Island, with factories where many of Sheffield's old blue-collar workers used to be employed. After Goose Island came the Chicago River, and a few blocks beyond that, the eight-lane Kennedy Expressway. Any two of those obstacles seemed sufficient to halt the residential boom. It looked like a safe bet that the upper-class march that had moved west from Lincoln Park in the 1970s could not be repeated beyond the river and the freeway.

But anyone who made that bet was wrong. In the two decades after Sheffield became rich, an equally dramatic—although different—transformation took place on the other side of the barrier, in Wicker Park and Bucktown. In retrospect, it isn't that hard to understand. This was a boom generated to a large extent by public transportation. And on the CTA's Blue Line, both Wicker Park and Bucktown were only a few minutes farther from the Loop than Sheffield was. When you are sitting on a train, a factory district, a dirty river, and an eight-lane

freeway don't loom so large as obstacles. Martin Oberman puts it suc-
cinctly: "In Chicago," he says, "gentrification follows the El."

"Gentrification" is a word that fits Wicker Park and Bucktown, even
if it's the wrong term for Sheffield. Both had reputations as havens for
artists and bohemians well before World War II, in the years when
the Chicago poet Nelson Algren entertained the French philosopher
Simone de Beauvoir in a third-story apartment above a Wicker Park
storefront.

The bohemian tradition never really died in these neighborhoods.
Nevertheless, by 1970 they had deteriorated even further than Sheffield. Crime and poverty rates were higher; an even larger proportion
of the white middle-class residents had moved away. North Avenue,
the heart of the area, was shabby and unappealing. "I remember when
that stretch of North Avenue was hubcap shops and liquor stores,"
state representative John Fritchey said a few years ago. "No one wanted
to claim it then, and now everyone wants to claim it."

That's true. Some locals, like Fritchey, believe that North Avenue
is the dividing line between Wicker Park on the south and Bucktown
on the north. Others ferociously claim that the border lies two blocks
farther north, at Bloomingdale Avenue. But it doesn't really matter.
The two neighborhoods just seem to blend into each other.

And they have a frenetic quality that quiet Sheffield has never possessed. Armitage Avenue in Sheffield is a busy and attractive street; on
a summer evening, Damen Avenue as it runs through Wicker Park and
Bucktown is more of an open-air festival, the sidewalks jammed with
so many young people that it feels a bit like SoHo or Greenwich Village in New York. Damen Avenue is lined with bookstores, boutiques,
sidewalk cafés, and art galleries; there seem to be more art galleries
in Wicker Park than there are business offices. If one wishes to make
comparisons to the Left Bank of Paris seventy years ago, and to the
twenty-four-hour public display that its streets presented, then Wicker
Park and Bucktown are a closer fit than Sheffield.

Since the 1990s, though, these neighborhoods have faced some of
the issues that Sheffield did earlier. A single-family house in Wicker
Park can cost a million dollars now; some of the artists who settled
there twenty years ago have been priced out and have moved to places

even farther west, such as Logan Square and Humboldt Park. It is not hard to find someone in the crowd on Damen Avenue who will lament that the glory days of bohemian life are over. But most of those who have lived here over the past couple of decades and remain today seem to accept the change.

SHEFFIELD, WICKER PARK, and Bucktown tell the story of Chicago's demographic inversion, and they tell it colorfully, but they are not the neighborhoods that produce the largest numbers. Sheffield had an estimated population of about eleven thousand in 2007; Bucktown was only a little larger, and even Wicker Park, the largest of the three, had twenty-three thousand. None of these is expected to grow much between now and 2020.

Sheffield is all but built out, and large-scale development in either Wicker Park or Bucktown would face significant community resistance. The big numbers lie elsewhere, along the very borders of Chicago's Loop, and in the Loop itself. This is where the high-rise growth of the central city took place on a massive scale prior to the 2008 recession. The Chicago Planning and Zoning Department estimated in 2009 that what it calls the Central Area—five miles running north and south with the Loop in the center, and a mile west from the lake in most places—-had acquired a residential population of 165,000 by 2007. It had grown 48 percent in the years since the 2000 census was taken. The planning department predicted that the number will be up to 230,000 by 2020.

That may be wishful thinking on the city's part. But even the current estimate of 165,000 is difficult to grasp until you walk around the Central Area and gaze up at the multitude of residential buildings, some of them fifty and sixty stories tall, that did not exist in 2000 and are now filled with home owners or tenants. In the district surrounding the Loop, sociologist John Koval wrote in 2006, "High-rise villages and communities—interspersed with warehouse conversions—are literally popping up like so many mushrooms on a summer morning."

These new high-rise villages have some unexpected touches: trees and flowers in the middle of the wider streets, with wrought-iron fenc-

ing around them; old-fashioned streetlights reminiscent of the ones
Haussmann placed on the boulevards of Paris. Such amenities are no
accident—they came by direct order of Mayor Richard M. Daley, who
had, it seems legitimate to say, a bit of a Paris obsession. On his return
from a visit to Europe in 1996, he decided that downtown Chicago's
larger office buildings should be lit at night in a manner reminiscent
of those on some of the boulevards of Paris. Later, he insisted that
the new condo neighborhoods have at least one shade tree for every
twenty-five feet of street frontage, a somewhat autocratic decree but
one that Haussmann would have approved of. Nearly a thousand
hanging baskets went up on downtown streets in a single year, many
of them three feet tall and marked with the inscription, *urbs in horto*—
"city in a garden," which happens to have been Chicago's city motto
since 1837.

In 2008, the condo mushrooms basically stopped sprouting. Huge
new residential projects—including architect Santiago Calatrava's 150-
story tower on Lake Shore Drive—were put on hold until the real
estate market picked up. By mid-2009, there were more than ten
thousand unsold condominiums in the Central Area. Most of the townhouses and midrise condominiums were maintaining their attractiveness rather well; it was the developers who overdid it, who chose to
build fifty or sixty or seventy stories simply because they could get the
money. Some real estate analysts speculated that by the spring of 2009
there was already a backlog of Central Area condos that could take
as much as five years to clear. But even the pessimists did not dispute
that in the year 2020, no matter how many condos are built or sold,
downtown Chicago is likely to be a nest of center-city urban affluence unequaled in size—or even approached—by anyplace in America
outside Manhattan. Sheffield is unique in its own way, but in other
respects, it is a harbinger of things to come.

One lesson we should not attempt to draw from all this is that
massive numbers of suburban families will return to the city, reversing
the demographic changes of the past half century. Even if the city's
projections are accurate and Chicago's Central Area is home to as
many as 230,000 people in the year 2020, that will still be less than
one-tenth of the population of the city as a whole. The rules of urban

population change that prevailed in the past century are not going to be erased that easily.

The city is likely to grow modestly in the coming decade, and the Central Area somewhat more than modestly. The Census Bureau reported early in 2009 that the percentage of residential permits issued within the city was 7 percent of the metro area total in the early 1990s, 23 percent in the early 2000s, and 40 percent in 2007. That process of change has paused; it has not concluded.

The suburbs of Chicago are not emptying out by any means, but they are no longer growing very fast, and some of them, the most distant, less appealing, and less convenient ones, are not currently growing at all. Some of this is undoubtedly due to a recession that has made it difficult for urban dwellers to sell their houses and move, but much of it is due to the enhanced appeal of the city's close-in neighborhoods.

There are those urban critics who insist that this is a temporary phenomenon, that once national prosperity has fully returned, prosperous families will again be vacating the central city in large numbers to find exurbs where they can spread out. It is not possible to refute such predictions; what can safely be said is that virtually no one who has spent the past decade watching Chicago closely believes that it is going to happen. The consensus is that the abandonment of the central city and the rapid suburban growth that marked the second half of the twentieth century are slowly coming to an end. And so the urban areas of the next generation, not only Chicago and New York but others that have been much less fortunate so far, will be much different places than they were in 1990. In many ways, they will resemble the cities in which our grandparents felt comfortable, rather than the ones in which we ourselves grew up.

The real essence of demographic inversion is based not on numbers but on choice: Increasingly over the past decade, both before and during the recession, people with the resources to live wherever they wished began choosing to live near the urban center—just as Viennese, Parisians, and Londoners at the turn of the previous century elected to do. This will have significant social consequences, especially when it comes to daily communication and casual social life. Central-city dwellers who have the option of communicating with friends almost entirely by electronic device will also have the option of socializing on the street or in neighborhood cafés in ways that suburbanites do not get the opportunity to do. Many of them will be drawn to the urban center by precisely that opportunity.

A hundred years ago, the legendary architect Charles McKim talked about the civilizing effect of wealth. One has to be careful tossing around phrases like that today. But if by civilizing effect McKim meant a richer cultural scene, a more comfortable mingling of races and ethnic groups, a more vibrant outdoor life, and a more diverse array of people using the streets at all hours of the day, it seems fair to predict that the next urban America will be a more civilized place than the current one.

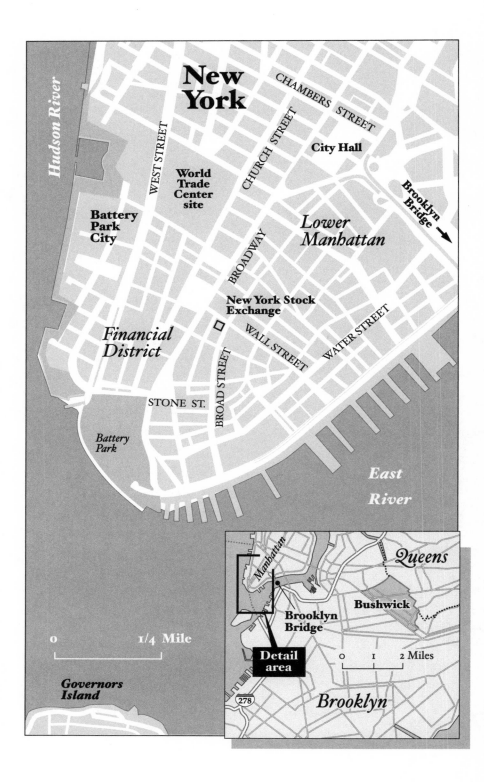

New York

Hudson River

CHAMBERS STREET

WEST STREET

CHURCH STREET

City Hall

World
Trade
Center
site

Battery
Park
City

Brooklyn Bridge →

BROADWAY

*Lower
Manhattan*

New York Stock
Exchange

WALL STREET

WATER STREET

*Financial
District*

BROAD STREET

STONE ST.

*Battery
Park*

East

River

0   1/4 Mile

*Governors
Island*

Manhattan

Queens

Brooklyn
Bridge

Bushwick

Detail
area

0   1   2 Miles

278

Brooklyn

CHAPTER THREE

RE-CREATION IN NEW YORK

THE HISTORY OF COMMUNITY LIFE in New York City over the past three decades, in boom times and hard times alike, has been the reclamation of its oldest neighborhoods, and the invention of new communities where none stood before. From the first conversions of factories into loft apartments in SoHo, in lower Manhattan, in the 1970s; through the discovery of Tribeca, just to the south, in the 1980s; on through the revitalization and soaring condo prices on the Lower East Side and in Chelsea in the 1990s; and the transformation of Brooklyn's Williamsburg, in the first decade of the new century, New York has seen a relentless colonization by middle- and upper-class residents of neighborhoods once thought to have no residential future at all.

By 2007, the process had reached to some of the least likely places one could imagine: the canyons of Wall Street and the surrounding Financial District; and the grimy industrial territory of Bushwick, the forgotten enclave at Brooklyn's far eastern end, on the border with Queens.

IT'S NOT ABSOLUTELY CLEAR why people wouldn't find Wall Street a decent place to live, but for nearly two hundred years, virtually no one did. There were more residents at the lower end of Manhattan—roughly, the area south of the World Trade Center and Chambers Street—at the beginning of the nineteenth century than there were in the last decades of the twentieth. In fact, there were a lot more. The 1800 census shows that the four lower Manhattan wards housed 22,871

people, which was more than a third of New York's total population.
The 1970 census managed to find 833 residents in the same territory,
many of them living in poverty in single-room occupancy hotels.

The first change in this state of affairs was the construction of Battery Park City, the planned community built on filled-in land along
the Hudson River. Opened in 1985, this complex of mostly low-rise
mixed-use buildings, with a riverside park at the edge, was an instant
success and eventually came to house more than ten thousand residents in more than thirty buildings. Battery Park City is cut off from
the center of the Financial District by West Street, which is impossible
for a pedestrian to cross at most places, but its popularity was a hint to
the real estate industry that people of means were willing to live at the
lower tip of Manhattan. It was unclear then whether they would want
to live amid the noise and congestion of Wall Street itself, but soon it
became clear that quite a few of them would.

By the turn of the twenty-first century, the lower Manhattan population had recovered its 1800 numbers. Then, to the surprise of much
of the city's real estate industry, it began to explode. A decade later, the
skyscraper canyons, condo developments, and narrow, twisting streets
at the southern tip of Manhattan were home to something close to
fifty thousand people, by conservative estimates. Some placed the population nearer to sixty thousand.

This would be impressive growth under any circumstances, but it
was remarkable growth given the fact that during that same decade,
lower Manhattan had experienced two catastrophic events: the terror-
ist attacks of 2001 and the financial collapse of 2008.

Following September 11, 2001, many predicted that Manhattan
would experience a hemorrhage of financial industry jobs, and that
residential growth at the bottom of the island would come to a halt.
They were right about the jobs: High-paying work in the financial
industry began to leave lower Manhattan within weeks after 9/11,
some for Midtown, some for what was perceived as the safer precincts of northern New Jersey. Most of the jobs did not return. After
9/11, lower Manhattan lost a great deal of its office space, which was
either destroyed or simply abandoned. But the residential picture was
entirely different. There was a short-term decline of about forty-five

hundred residents in late 2001 and early 2002, but it had been erased by 2004, and the curve of residential occupancy tilted sharply upward in the years after that. In 2007 alone, twenty-one residential buildings opened south of Chambers Street, making 295 in all. Despite what seemed to be an exponential growth in new condo skyscrapers, more than 60 percent of the Financial District's population continued to be renters.

Who were the Wall Street newcomers of this last decade? To an overwhelming extent, they were wealthy people. A study in 2007 showed that new households in the Financial District had an annual median income of $256,000. They were primarily singles and child-less couples (74 percent), but there were more families living in the district than one might expect. In 2009, the median family size of 2.2 was larger than the comparable figure for Manhattan as a whole, and considerably larger than the 2.02 recorded for the same territory several years earlier. Anyone who walked down Wall Street on a Saturday

The stately Beaux-Art Cipriani Building at 55 Wall Street in lower Manhattan, once home of the National City Bank, is now, like most of the buildings nearby, a collection of residences for those who can afford the high price it takes to live in the Financial District.

morning in 2007 or 2008 would run into a cadre of young parents and baby strollers.

Most of these families lived in prewar office skyscrapers that had been retrofitted for residential use. It is hard to take an office building built in the 1920s and modernize it to handle the business technology of the present day. But it is relatively easy—and much cheaper—to turn the same building into condominiums or rental apartments. The departure of financial industry jobs after 2001 left an ample supply of such buildings ripe for conversion.

The owners had an enormous incentive: section 421-G of the state housing code, enacted in 1996. By this time, the number of older and underused Financial District office buildings had already grown substantially. Seeing the residential possibilities—although most of these lay well in the future—the authors of 421-G offered a substantial tax abatement for landlords converting from office to apartment use. The law enabled landlords to keep rents more or less within reason, at least by Manhattan standards. This included luxury dwellings. It soon became significantly cheaper to rent or buy a place to live in the Financial District than in Midtown or on the Upper East Side. In 2005, the median gross rent for a one-bedroom apartment in lower Manhattan was $1,775—higher than for the borough as a whole but much lower than in its most exclusive neighborhoods.

By then, newcomers were being enticed by another plum almost as juicy as the one offered to landlords in the previous decade. New residents of the Financial District were eligible for generous federally funded rent subsidies, depending on how close their dwellings were to the World Trade Center site and how long they committed to stay. In addition, the city issued $1.6 billion in tax-free bonds for new residential construction. With conversions and the rental boom in full swing, the development of new condos also took off, and the neighborhood acquired a set of tall glass condominium buildings, put up seemingly anywhere a developer could obtain land. By 2007, every building on the south side of Wall Street, with the sole exception of the New York Stock Exchange, had become a residence.

At that time, developers were touting the Financial District as the fastest-growing neighborhood in North America. This is hard to verify, but in percentage terms, it may have been true. At one point, there were sixty residential buildings simultaneously being either built or converted from commercial status. This included the seventy-five-story 8 Spruce Street, formerly Beekman Tower, a short distance from the World Trade Center site, a glass-and-titanium building designed by Frank Gehry that laid claim to being the tallest residential structure in the western hemisphere. It includes, in addition to the residences, a public elementary school with one hundred thousand square feet of space.

Then something else happened, the economic wounds from which will take longer to heal than those of 2001. The meltdown that began in earnest with the bankruptcy of Lehman Brothers in the fall of 2008, and continued with a parade of financial industry insolvencies and the erosion of credit for new construction or rehabilitation, brought the condo boom of lower Manhattan to a virtually complete halt.

Developers of condominium buildings completed before September 2008 found it all but impossible to sell their units; work on projects that were in construction that fall largely ceased. The inability of developers to obtain credit was matched by the laying off of thousands of workers in the financial industry. Had money been found to complete the unfinished condos, it's not clear whether there would have been an adequate supply of buyers with enough confidence in the near-term economic climate to purchase them. By the summer of 2009, official city estimates reported 10,445 unsold Manhattan condo units, a large proportion of them in the Financial District, and perhaps another 7,000 "shadow" units in the borough not officially for sale but essentially unmarketable. When an existing condo did sell, the average time between listing and closing was more than six months. Some developers were making unsold units available for short-term stays, essentially turning them into hotels, which is generally against the law.

Yet it's important to consider not only what happened to the lower Manhattan residential market in the deepest recession months, but also what did not happen. While condos languished unsold and few new residents moved to the area, the vast majority of the people who had lived there in 2007 were still there as the decade drew to a close. The population remained virtually unchanged. In midsummer 2009, the rental market vacancy rate was 1.98 percent, a full 11 percent lower than at the beginning of the year. Renters were enticed by generous new concessions from landlords, often including free rent for a period of several months, plus subsidies for brokers' fees and moving costs.

Part of this was the direct result of changes in the Financial District's employment base. As recently as the 1980s, more than 70 percent of the area's jobs were in the so-called FIRE industries: finance, insurance, and real estate. In 1999 the number was down to half; now estimates are that it is closer to one-third. Bankers and brokers have been replaced by people who work in design, advertising, software, and the nonprofit sector of the economy. The estimated sixty-five thousand jobs that Manhattan will lose as a result of the financial crisis will take a serious long-term toll on the entire city and have an impact on the residential future of the Financial District. But because so many of these jobs had moved out of the neighborhood in the preceding decade, the impact on Wall Street and its environs will be lessened.

Couples who had moved to lower Manhattan in the boom years not only stayed, they started families amid the chaos of recession. One building on John Street with 147 condo units reported twenty-two new babies born in 2008 alone. For families that had not suffered serious financial losses in the preceding months, the issue of greatest concern seemed to be finding places for their children to go to school. P.S. 234, a K–5 school in the area that consistently records some of the highest test scores of any public school in Manhattan, was operating at 139 percent of capacity in the fall of 2008, and it was difficult even for Wall Street neighborhood kids to find places there. A makeshift overflow kindergarten was established in the old New York County Courthouse at the north end of the district, near City Hall. In addition to the school in the Frank Gehry skyscraper on Spruce Street and one in Battery Park City, a new public high school for girls was being created at 26 Broadway, in the old Standard Oil Building.

It remains true that the residential families of the Financial District are wealthy ones, even in hard economic times. But it is a myth that they all send their children to private schools, or wish to. They are about as eager as other parents in the five New York boroughs to use the public schools, as long as they can find decent ones. In this respect, parents in lower Manhattan differ little from parents in any neighborhood or community across the country.

WALKING THE STREETS of the Financial District today, one can't help but think that it is, indeed, a throwback to an earlier version of the city's life. But not to the Wall Street of a century ago: That was an economically segregated one-use neighborhood, with offices and virtually nothing else, no residents, hardly a place to shop, only a handful of restaurants to cater to the financial workforce.

But look back farther than that, and you begin to see a resemblance. In some ways, lower Manhattan in the early twenty-first century has come to resemble lower Manhattan in the late eighteenth and early nineteenth: brokers, investors, and insurance agents who live in the neighborhood and walk to work; a social life that does not disappear at quitting time, the way it did twenty years ago; a modest but growing number of families with young children. Ron Chernow offers a picture of this early lower Manhattan in his biography of Alexander Hamilton, who lived there both as a college student and as a young lawyer. "Shaded by poplars and elms," Chernow writes, "Broadway was the main thoroughfare, flanked by mazes of narrow, winding streets. There were sights galore to enthrall the young [Hamilton]. Fetching ladies promenaded along Broadway, handsome coaches cruised the streets, and graceful church spires etched an incipient skyline. Rich merchants had colonized Wall Street and Hanover Square, and their weekend pleasure gardens extended north along the Hudson shore."

It would be foolish to extend the analogy too far, but it's perfectly true to say that conviviality has returned to the Financial District. To notice this, one need do no more than take an evening stroll down Stone Street, one of the shortest and narrowest stretches of pavement in the district, more an alley than a street.

Stone Street is said to have been the first street paved in all of New York, by the Dutch in 1658. It was a gathering spot for British soldiers in the years before the American Revolution, a place for merchants to trade and sell goods of the British West India Company, a place where colonial dissidents argued the pros and cons of independence. Its low-rise redbrick buildings remained a hub of commercial activity through the close of the nineteenth century. To say that it deteriorated in the twentieth would be something of an understatement. It essentially disappeared. One of its two blocks was closed in 1980 and removed from the city map altogether.

But as you turn the corner onto Stone Street now on a summer night, weekday or weekend, you find large numbers of Wall Street workers and neighborhood residents thronging the bars and restaurants that comprise virtually all of its present commercial function. Outside in the middle of the alley are large picnic tables meant for outdoor eating and drinking. They are family-style tables, built to accommodate six or eight people. It is hard to find seating for one anywhere along the pavement. Stone Street exists for socializing, much in the way that it did two hundred years ago. It is a place where young people who work, live, and look for entertainment in the Financial District come and enjoy the atmosphere and the crowd. Taking in this scene on an atypically comfortable August evening in 2009, one had to remind oneself that a serious recession, much of it launched only a few blocks away, was taking place.

Whatever happens to the residential condo market in the coming years, whatever the financial industry's job losses may be, Stone Street will continue to serve the social purpose it serves now. The surrounding neighborhood, having reached what would seem to be critical mass with nearly sixty thousand residents, will retain much of the sense of vibrancy it acquired over the past decade. Now that the baby strollers have reached Wall Street, it is unlikely that they will disappear.

This is a neighborhood, then, but is it a community the way Sheffield is, the way communities existed in the great European cities of a century ago? Is it genuine—or is there something artificial about it? That is a question on which reasonable people may disagree. One can argue that the astronomically high average income of the people who bought residences in the Financial District mandates an inequality that will prevent it from becoming a true neighborhood in the sense in which most of us understand that term. The public school population in lower Manhattan does not mirror the public school population in other parts of the city. Or one can look at the growing vibrancy of the streets and decide that the rudiments of genuine neighborhood life are present, regardless of the economic imbalance of those living in the buildings. Street life is perhaps the most crucial aspect of the urban revival of the twenty-first century, and street life is not dependent on demographic equality, much as we might desire it to be.

Jane Jacobs believed the Financial District could never qualify as a community in the sense in which she used the word. She believed this, in fact, long before the efforts to establish one achieved any sort of traction at all.

In *The Death and Life of Great American Cities,* published in 1961, Jacobs devotes several pages to her argument that Wall Street and its environs could never attract enough residents to acquire a diversity of jobs that would keep workers in the neighborhood beyond the end of the conventional workday, or possess the amenities that could bring in a significant core of visitors from outside. She goes out of her way to ridicule a report by the Downtown-Lower Manhattan Association that insisted "a residential population would stimulate the development of shopping facilities, restaurants, places of entertainment," and similar staples of neighborhood life. She warned that the number of residents was unlikely ever to exceed 1 percent of the daytime workforce. One percent at that time would have been just four thousand people.

Jacobs, for all her prescience about so many things, got much of this wrong. The idea of sixty thousand people living south of Chambers Street would have seemed preposterous to her. In other ways, however, her warnings remain relevant. The neighborhoods that Jacobs admired, including the Greenwich Village in which she lived, were suffused with diversity of use: people coming and going at all hours of the day, working at a myriad of different kinds of jobs, seeing and greeting one another regularly, and maintaining the network of casual but reliable relationships that created a genuine sense of community well-being. The Financial District does not have this, and it would seem a stretch to predict that it ever will. People live there, socialize in the Stone Street taverns, and entertain neighbors in their homes, but it would be a considerable exaggeration to say that they create the kind of street life Jacobs was talking about. The twenty-first-century residents of the Financial District do not walk down Wall or Broad or William streets and run into the local storekeeper with whom they can converse casually and comfortably every day. They walk down crowded streets full of strangers, even though the ratio of residents to daytime workers has changed dramatically in half a century, from the one in one hundred that Jacobs imagined to something much closer to one out of five. And, of course, there are no children playing in the streets in the afternoons.

Even if the residents of the Financial District wanted to make a special effort to cultivate local merchants and stop to talk to them, they couldn't do it, because the merchants themselves are not there. The area has its share of retail facilities, but they are to a large extent boutique retail aimed at affluent tourists. Wall Street has a Tiffany & Co., but it does not have a local jeweler who can fix a watch; it has a Thomas Pink clothing store selling shirts and ties at high prices, but no independent clothing store owner sitting on a folding chair in front of his store, greeting familiar passersby. It has Duane Reade drugstores scattered throughout the area, but these are staffed by employees who come and go every few months, do not live in the neighborhood, and know scarcely anyone who does.

Four new high-end retailers opened stores south of Chambers Street in the spring of 2009: True Religion jeans; Tourbillon watches; La Maison du Chocolat; and Pylones, a French-owned purveyor of luxury household items in unusual colors.

For the ordinary resident, even the affluent one, retail is a serious problem, and it grew worse even during the boom years of the past decade. "I live just about geographic dead center of the Financial District," longtime resident Ro Sheffe said toward the end of the boom in 2008, "and the three delis we had in 2000 are all gone. One is a high-end cosmetics store, one is high-end condos, one is Gucci couture. After nine o'clock at night [when the drugstores close], if I want a carton of milk, I have to walk nine blocks. In 2000, I could walk down the street."

Others express serious reservations about the "population explosion" that has brought the baby strollers into the heart of the district.

Very little of it has been the result of families moving into the neighborhood; the vast majority of children are born to people who came to the Financial District to live as singles or couples, and then married and started families later. There is nothing wrong with this, but it points up the fact that few married couples who already have children find the district an appealing place to move to. In the view of some critics, this is not the way a "real" community should work.

To say all this is not to deny that what has taken place in the Financial District in recent years is a remarkable transformation, and a significant triumph of modern urbanism. It is merely to accept that it is an imperfect transformation, and that the flaws it exhibits will not be easy to correct anytime soon.

SIX MILES EAST of Wall Street, in a corner of Brooklyn that outsiders seldom visit and some have never heard of, an even more unusual urban transformation was taking place. It was the transformation of large portions of Bushwick, a singularly unattractive industrial territory with aging apartment buildings tucked alongside abandoned factories, into a magnet for artists, a home to increasing numbers of recent college graduates, and a destination even for young Europeans seeking a neighborhood that is edgy, hip, and hypertolerant.

Bushwick is not in the midst of any standard gentrification process. A 2007 census estimate placed the population at 129,000, with nearly 90 percent of it Latino or African American. It is a large, minority-dominated chunk of Brooklyn, one in which more than 30 percent of the population receives some form of public assistance. Bushwick is the seventh-poorest community in New York City.

The young and hip newcomers to Bushwick are not joining with the established residents to create a melting pot. They constitute a white subculture within a relatively stable Latino and black majority culture, for the most part interacting and socializing with one another in lofts and a few cafés and bars, and allowing the majority to go about its business as it did before. Newcomers lament the absence of retail shopping opportunities in Bushwick, but they are misstating the situation. What they are lamenting, whether they know it or not, is the absence of wine-and-cheese shops and high-end stores selling household goods. They are mildly annoyed at having to procure these items in nearby Williamsburg. But there is plenty of shopping in Bushwick. Anyone who walks down Knickerbocker Avenue almost any day of the week finds vibrancy in the street and on the sidewalks, and endless opportunities to buy shoes, inexpensive costume jewelry, and samples of virtually every Latin American cuisine. A developer who has been building new condos and rental units for the Anglo arrivals lamented one day in 2009 that "Bushwick is starved for retail." But it is a starvation amidst a kind of plenty, as he admitted a moment afterward. "No one in Bushwick," the developer said, "could ever want for low-priced tamales or tortas."

The really remarkable thing about Bushwick—and perhaps a lesson for struggling neighborhoods in other parts of the country—is just how much attention an influx of at most three thousand self-identified artists was able to attract in a community of more than one hundred thousand people. "More than anywhere else in the city they are here," says Deborah Brown, a painter in her fifties who has maintained a studio in Bushwick for the past decade. "Right now in art schools and colleges, people are hearing, 'Bushwick is where I want to be.' Bushwick has this street cred that if you live here, you're cool."

In the fall of 2009, sponsors of an art festival in Stavanger, Norway, invited street artists from Bushwick (graffiti taggers, in other words) to come and demonstrate their techniques. Not long before, an issue of the British Airways in-flight magazine had cited the "thriving underground arts scene" that Bushwick had managed to create. "We get a lot of calls from Europe," says Kevin Lindamood, a local entrepreneur who rents out loft space to artists in what was once a textile factory.

In June 2009, the first Bushwick biennial art fair in the center of the neighborhood provided a glimpse of Bushwick at its edgiest. Some 115 studio artists and more than a dozen public galleries demonstrated their work. One of the participants called it a "huge clusterfuck art happening." One gallery exhibited a huge sculpture of a very chunky couple copulating on a piece of ground painted in plaid. Another one showed a painting that it called *Afterbirth,* described by a critic as "a rendering in tasteful salmons, dirty pinks, and peach of bloody female genitalia, a placenta, a gray baby, and a dripping penis." Still another exhibitor not only presented a lifelike rendering of a sleazy S and M den, but invited passersby to come in and take part.

Art fairs in Bushwick are not events calculated to appeal to main-stream tastes. They look for all the world like celebrations designed to shock conservative sensibilities, except that there is scarcely anyone with such sensibilities around to be shocked. These are in reality proj-ects through which a small coterie of local artists seek to display their sheer edginess to one another.

There is no disputing that Bushwick has brought together a sizable community of people who consider themselves—and some who are considered by others—to be serious artists. But it is nothing like the SoHo of the 1970s or the Chelsea of the 1990s. There is little in the way of commercial art sales. Most of the studios are in lofts and living rooms; most of the public galleries are open only on weekends. Very few artists make significant money selling anything, conventional or unconventional, to the outside world. It is very much a self-contained community. Some of its residents occasionally describe one another as hipsters, invoking 1950s terminology that would no doubt please Norman Mailer were he around to hear them.

Who are these pioneers of Bushwick? To all appearances and personal testimony, they are not all (or even mostly) artists, but twenty-first-century products of the hippest liberal arts colleges—Wesleyan and Vassar, Bard and Sarah Lawrence. They live doubled up in small lofts and crammed into larger ones that sleep as many as eight or nine people. Many of them carved out an alternative mode of life for themselves as undergraduates, and they are eager to find a place to re-create it in their postcollege years. They are aspiring film-makers, video producers, and creators of fabricated music acts—for every actual art gallery in Bushwick, there seem to be several record-ing studios. The newcomers can live cheaply in Bushwick, at least in New York terms. Instead of paying hundreds of dollars more a square foot for a fashionable ersatz loft in Chelsea or on the Lower East Side of Manhattan, they can pay $500 a square foot in Bushwick for unre-touched loft space in a genuine industrial building, often with the marks of its former existence in plain sight.

In the mysterious way that such a process typically proceeds, the flourishing of the Bushwick art scene has brought in other urbanites in their twenties and thirties, some of whom hold down eminently conventional jobs in Manhattan, to come and live among them. In 2000, the white population of Bushwick was about 4 percent. In 2007, it was 9 percent—in demographic terms, still a drop in the bucket. The change occurred mostly in districts that were almost exclusively rental, rather than in the visually more attractive precincts where struggling minority home owners had more incentive to hang on. But in certain well-defined parts of the neighborhood, the signs of change were everywhere.

In the northeast section of the community, close to the Queens border, the middle years of the past decade saw an increasing pace of condo development on land that once housed breweries and textile sweatshops. Some of it is brownfield land requiring extensive environmental remediation before it can be developed for residential use. But at least until the real estate recession hit in 2008, there was no shortage of developers and real estate agents willing to build and promote it. Sometimes they went to extra effort to make medium-rise condos that respected the neighborhood's history, with metal paneling rather than glass for the exterior. "They didn't want a glass tower in Bushwick," one developer explained in 2009.

Some of the developers are going further to appeal to upper-middle-class tastes. Across the street from the Jefferson stop on the L subway line, on a block where a trendy pub and a coffeehouse attract musicians, painters, writers, and dancers, a new residential project managed to lure a wine shop and an organic grocery. At Flushing and Knickerbocker avenues, in the old commercial heart of the neighborhood, another new development contains sixty rental apartments and space for twenty-one stores. Both these projects were leased, with relative success, in the still-recession-plagued early months of 2009.

· · ·

EVEN CONSIDERING all of this—the appeal to artists, the old industrial properties available for cheap residential use—it is hard to avoid a fundamental question: Why would people who have a choice want to move to Bushwick in the first place?

Even with the arrival of some relatively affluent newcomers, it remains a very poor neighborhood. It has hundreds of apartment buildings in acute need of repair, some of them in blatant violation of city housing codes. Many of the apartment buildings are plagued by bedbugs, the result of the purchase of infested reconditioned mattresses. The asthma rate, due to the vestigial presence of the old industrial properties, is higher than in almost any other neighborhood in any of the five boroughs.

Of course, not everyone lives this way, but anybody who moves to Bushwick faces an irony of local life: There are really two distinct parts of the neighborhood—the southern section centered on Broadway and Bushwick avenues, on the edge of Bedford-Stuyvesant, and the northern section, closest to Queens. The southern area actually has some attractive residential streets lined with trees and early twentieth-century brownstones, but it is also the more dangerous part of the community and the place where African American renters run the risk of having landlords raise their rents without warning, in the hope that they will move out and the unit can be rented to a white newcomer at a much higher price. The northern and eastern parts of Bushwick, along Myrtle and Wyckoff avenues and adjoining the Ridgewood section of Queens, are safer and confront relatively few displacement issues, because so much of the land was industrial rather than residential. But these streets are not pretty places to live. There are long, dreary blocks lined with abandoned textile factories and large strips of vacant land. One can buy or rent a townhouse on, say, Jefferson Street, restore it with painstaking care, and still have to look across the street at a long row of old storage sheds crammed with used mattresses, refrigerators, and air conditioners.

Even some of those who have been part of Bushwick's revival in recent years seem to wonder why the whole phenomenon has taken place. "I think it's bizarre that there are people who think we move here because Bushwick is wonderful," the writer and activist Jeremy

Sapienza declared in 2008. "No. We move here because it's CHEAP. Why is it cheap? Because it's dirty, it's (comparatively) crime-ridden, it's run-down. Bushwick is manifestly NOT wonderful."

BUSHWICK WAS NEVER what many people would call "wonderful," but for a century it was a comfortably safe working-class neighborhood where first German and then Italian immigrants raised families, and where many organized their social lives around St. Barbara's Church, a massive and spectacular baroque edifice that still towers over the neighborhood. The German immigrants came to Bushwick in large part because of its breweries—at one point, there were 121 of them in the community and Bushwick was known as the "beer capital" of the northeast. The largest of them, the Rheingold Brewery, occupied 6.7 acres and produced more than a third of all the beer consumed in New York State. The owners built mansions on Bushwick Avenue, which was known as "Brewers' Row."

Mae West and Jackie Gleason grew up on the Bushwick streets; Gleason used the address of his birthplace, 364 Chauncey Street, as the location of the apartment Ralph and Alice Kramden occupied in the *Honeymooners* television series, and the drab interiors portrayed on the show were designed to resemble the places where Gleason lived as a child.

Bushwick remained a stable neighborhood for more than a decade after nearby Bedford-Stuyvesant and Brownsville deteriorated. But most of the breweries closed in the 1950s and 1960s, and by 1970, Bushwick was as badly decayed as any neighborhood in New York. *The New York Times* reported that "in a five-year period in the late 1960s and early 1970s, Bushwick was transformed from a neatly maintained community of wood houses into what often approached a no-man's-land of abandoned buildings, empty lots, drugs, and arson." Between 1969 and 1977, one out of every eight buildings in the neighborhood was damaged or destroyed by fire. Not all the fires were intentional, but many of them were made worse by the fact that the narrow wooden houses were built with "cocklofts," or half attics, that joined one dwelling to the next and hastened the spread of flames.

But the worst was to come. On July 13, 1977, Bushwick suffered through the most disastrous episode in its entire history: the looting and arson that followed the legendary citywide power blackout. These crimes occurred in many parts of New York, but the devastation in Bushwick was by far the worst. By the time it ended, 134 stores had been looted and 44 buildings had been set on fire.

In the aftermath of the blackout rampage, the half-empty streets of Bushwick became more crime- and drug-ridden than before. Knickerbocker Avenue, so recently a thriving commercial thoroughfare, degenerated into an open-air drug-dealing mall known as "the Well" and tightly controlled by the ruthless and widely despised crime boss Carmine Galante, who was finally gunned down while having lunch on the patio of Joe and Mary's Restaurant at 205 Knickerbocker in 1979.

Nothing much improved in the 1980s. The crack epidemic led to a still higher surge of violent crime, with seventy-seven murders in the neighborhood in 1990 alone. Bushwick differed from the South Bronx only in its failure to achieve national notoriety, and in its relative obscurity even to the residents of the other boroughs of New York City. Hardly anyone set foot in Bushwick who didn't have to.

The following decade brought a few signs of hope. Vito Lopez, who was elected to the state assembly in 1984 and rose to become chairman of its housing committee, turned out to be a prodigy when it came to prying loose state money for low- and moderate-income housing, much of it promoted by Lopez's political power base, the Ridgewood Bushwick Senior Citizens Council, and the semiprivate New York Housing Partnership Development Corporation. The huge Rheingold Brewery site, once considered too badly contaminated for residential reuse, was cleared for a construction project that eventually yielded nearly three hundred homes, condominiums, low-income rental apartments, a day-care center, and a community center.

What these efforts proved, however, is that it is possible to construct large numbers of affordable housing units in a neighborhood, even attractive and comfortable ones, and still not substantially improve the area's economic fortunes. As the new century began, Bushwick was still pockmarked by whole swaths of vacant land and abandoned industrial buildings. Some 34 percent of its residents were living below the poverty line. The median household income was $31,531, near the bottom among all of the city's neighborhoods. As late as 1998, only two permits were issued for new private residential construction in the entire community.

And then, in a very short space of time, Bushwick began to change. The artists and self-styled artists started reclaiming the industrial lofts. Amid the housing bubble of the new decade, condo buildings began to rise. By 2003, the number of new private building permits had grown from 2 to 173. The population began to grow as well, from just over 100,000 in the first year of the decade to about 130,000 eight years later.

Why did all this happen? There is no simple explanation. The community was far safer in 2005 than it had been a decade earlier, but there were large portions of it—there still are—where young single women have reason to be nervous walking alone at night. Much of black and Latino Bushwick was actively hostile to gentrification and organized to fight it, unlike the underclass in Chicago's Sheffield that simply left when the rents went up. In 2006, antigentrification protesters staged a march in the southern part of Bushwick, with protesters shouting, "Fight, fight, fight, housing is a right," and one of the protest leaders urging white newcomers to "build this in your own neighborhood. Don't build it here."

In the northern part of the community, where safety was less of a concern, there was the undeniable fact that the newcomers were moving to a physically unappealing place, where any new resident, however well-appointed his condominium or apartment, still had to contend with abandoned factories, barbed wire, and vacant lots.

There is, alternatively, the simple argument from economics. Housing prices had risen astronomically in Manhattan in the 1990s, and by 2000 they were rising rapidly as well in Williamsburg, the part of Brooklyn just across the river from Manhattan's Lower East Side. Bushwick was right next to Williamsburg, and livable apartments were available there at barely half the Williamsburg cost. A fair portion of the newcomers to Bushwick came directly from Williamsburg, where they found themselves priced out of the housing market or felt the neighborhood's amenities were becoming too costly for their tastes. "People move here because somewhere else is more expensive," Bushwick tenant activist Angel Vera said in 2005. "That's the system."

No doubt there is some truth to this. But it doesn't entirely explain Bushwick, either. There were at least a dozen Brooklyn and Queens neighborhoods that were about as cheap as Bushwick in the early 2000s, were considerably safer, and didn't have Bushwick's abysmal reputation. Some of these places did prove moderately attractive to the white middle class, but more of them, such as Sunset Park in Brooklyn and Astoria in Queens, did better at attracting the latest generation of immigrants from around the world.

The missing pieces of the puzzle have to do mostly with time and transportation. Neighboring Williamsburg has always been directly across the river from Manhattan, but it was not until the 1990s that many people seemed to appreciate that they could get from Union Square in the heart of lower Manhattan to Bedford Station in Williamsburg on the L line in five minutes. Or, more important, that they could get there in five minutes without having to worry about being mugged. The decline in New York's crime rate has had many consequences, but one of the most important of them has been the safety of the trains and the willingness of middle-class people to ride them to work in the daytime and to restaurants at night. Once it became widely known that the L line was safe, the renovation of Williamsburg was all but assured.

Bushwick has more problems than Williamsburg, but it is right next door, and a fifteen-minute subway ride from Union Square is only a little less convenient than a five- or seven-minute ride. Once it became safe to travel to Bushwick, the short ride was a powerful temptation to young people who worked in Manhattan. Between 2003 and 2007, the New York Transit Authority spent $50 million to build a shiny new subway station at Myrtle and Wyckoff avenues in western Bushwick that is one of the showpieces of the entire transit system. Bushwick may not be a pretty place—it will not be one anytime soon—but it is possible to get there quickly and safely. That matters a lot to young people who work in Manhattan and consider their free time a commodity at least as important as money.

"The train is the entire reason this is happening," says loft entrepreneur Kevin Lindamood, echoing the flat pronouncement of real estate agent Ted McLaughlin that "these days, convenience trumps aesthetics." Deborah Brown, from her studio on Jefferson Street, puts it a little more colorfully. "I'm fine," she says, "with having no view, barbed wire across the street, and the subway right next to me." Which is exactly what she has.

In every community in America, residents talk about what the place will be like ten or fifteen years hence. But in Bushwick, this sometimes seems to be almost the only issue. There are those who believe that by 2020 Bushwick will be another Williamsburg, chic, middle-class, and only slightly edgy, and that this will be a good thing for the city. There are those who believe that this will indeed happen, but that it will result in the cruel displacement of the Hispanic and African American majority that has resided there for a generation. And there are those, like the policeman who wrote in a neighborhood blog, warning Bushwick that "its fifteen minutes of fame can disappear and disinvestment will leave it just another high-poverty neighborhood."

And there are those somewhere in the middle, including most of the local political establishment, who believe that Bushwick is destined in the coming years to become more white and less poor, but that in the process it will retain its current edgy quality, making it very different from Williamsburg or lower Manhattan. It will remain a more ethnically diverse place, for one thing. The dominant minority population in much of the neighborhood will not be disappearing anytime soon. "Gentrification can't be prevented," said Vito Lopez, the state assemblyman and the area's most powerful political figure. "So the question is: How much can you control it?"

It's TEMPTING to wonder what Jane Jacobs would think of present-day Bushwick if she were alive and meandering down its streets. More than likely, she would render a mixed verdict. In the southern half of the neighborhood, she would find the vitality she looked for, with adults socializing on the corners, mom-and-pop groceries and bodegas seemingly everywhere, and children playing unsupervised in the streets. But she would also find little of the diversity she favored; indeed, she would encounter an outright scorn for diversity, if that means a large influx of white middle-class residents and rising rents that threaten the poorer people residing there. In the northern half, she would see the creativity and the diverse mix of interesting young people she felt a neighborhood needs, but she would find the physical environment depressing: long, uninterrupted blocks lined with drab industrial buildings and very little street life of any kind at most hours of the day. Probably she would shrug and say that one can't expect miracles. Bushwick would never come to resemble the Greenwich Village of the 1950s that she considered a model of successful urban life.

THEN AGAIN, she wouldn't find the Greenwich Village of the 1950s if she returned to the Village now, and revisited the 500 block of Hudson

This block of Hudson Street in New York's Greenwich Village was the model for Jane Jacobs's idea of diverse and harmonious urban living in the 1950s. Jacobs's own house (in the center, with the large glass window) sold for more than $3 million in 2010.

Street, where she lived, raised her family, and wrote *The Death and Life of Great American Cities*.

The West Village that Jacobs knew has managed at the same time to move dramatically upscale and yet show tangible signs of trouble. The candy store that occupied the ground floor of a Hudson Street building is long gone, as are the tailor, barber, and hardware store that combined to make Hudson a thriving mixed-use street half a century ago. When Jacobs's own three-story redbrick townhouse at 555 Hudson went on the market for $3.5 million in the spring of 2009, it was vacant for several months, finally selling for $3.3 million to an owner who rented the first floor to a boutique glass store displaying cups for $45. Most of the local merchants who served as Jacobs's "eyes on the street," who watched over its activity and thereby kept it safe, do not have counterparts today. That is not because Hudson Street has been unlucky, but because locally owned candy stores, fruit markets, and hardware stores have largely disappeared throughout America, the victim of market forces that have made them economically unsustainable. The mom-and-pop stores still in business on Hudson are essentially convenience stores trying to provide as many different services as they can: The store two doors down from Jacobs's old townhouse offers faxing, copying, mailboxes, and film developing.

The coffeehouse and deli have disappeared, along with the Hudson Corner Café that served as a neighborhood gathering place for years. Da Andrea, the popular Italian restaurant that constituted another social center, moved in 2008 due to rising rents, as have the short-lived Hunan Pan, MaMa Buddha, and Monster Sushi. Hudson Street in 2009, in the midst of recession, had become a victim of its own success: Its properties had grown so expensive that hardly anyone could afford them. The one conspicuous survivor on the block is the White Horse Tavern, where Jacobs mingled with longshoremen who went there to drink after their day's (or night's) work at the nearby docks, and where Dylan Thomas claimed to have downed eighteen whiskeys at a sitting shortly before he died. The White Horse made it to the twenty-first century in part on tourist dollars, but it is almost unchanged from the 1950s: The floor inside is still made of old wooden planks, and one can sit comfortably at one of the sidewalk tables in the late afternoon, drink a glass of ale, and look for reminders of the street life that Jacobs cherished.

There is plenty of activity on the street, if not the intricate "sidewalk ballet" that Jacobs talked about. It includes children, but not children romping delightfully in the street; most of them are in strollers or walking back home with nannies after school or organized playtime. Of course, one rarely finds children playing on the street unsupervised in any affluent neighborhood in America these days; to find that, you have to go to much poorer places, like south Bushwick. There is a curious mixture of adults on Hudson Street, though, many of them riding bicycles and parking them at meters, and their appearance and demeanor seem like an odd throwback to the old days. There are elderly men with ponytails who look as if they might be returning from a Jack Kerouac poetry reading at the White Horse in 1957. They tend to wear black, even on an afternoon when the August sun is beating down and the temperature is in the nineties. If one watches the people walking down Hudson, and stares at the old brick buildings that have survived, and if one can forget about the absent longshoremen and the myriad of businesses that have come and gone, then it is almost possible to see Hudson Street as Jane Jacobs saw it half a century ago.

Or one can ponder all the elements now missing from fifty years ago and recall what Jacobs herself wrote in *Death and Life*: "We must understand that self-destruction of diversity is caused by success, not by failure."

ONE THING WE HAVE LEARNED about the modern city is that even the smartest of observers, trying to predict the possibilities for revival and change in almost any urban neighborhood, are likely to be wrong. Anybody making a list in 1960 of places in New York likely to become centers of renewed residential life would almost certainly have put Wall Street at the bottom, as Jacobs did. Anybody making a similar list in 1980 of places unlikely ever to attract young white professionals would have put crime-ridden, drug-plagued Bushwick at the very top. And yet both, in very different and complex ways, have emerged as symbols of the transformation of the American city in the early twenty-first century.

We have also learned that retail business, especially the kind of everyday retail business that newcomers to a neighborhood most want, is very difficult to attract or sustain. It is much easier to lure people of means to live in an area than it is to give them the locally oriented commerce that Jane Jacobs considered essential to a thriving community. Thus it is that one can find a Tiffany & Co. in the heart of the Financial District but not a delicatessen that stays open late at night. If the merchants one seeks are barbers, candy store owners, and independent hardware dealers, it is a fruitless effort. Modern market forces have made them obsolete, even in places where a townhouse costs $3.5 million. This does not make newly wealthy inner-city neighborhoods unattractive, but it is a limitation they must face and a problem that no city has fully solved.

Finally, we have learned from both the Financial District and Bushwick (as we did from Sheffield) that the relative importance of travel time compared to other commodities is increasing as the years go by. To repeat the succinct aphorism of the Bushwick real estate broker, "These days, convenience trumps aesthetics." This is likely to become even more important as a new urban generation emerges. It is an idea we will continue to pursue in the remaining chapters of the book.

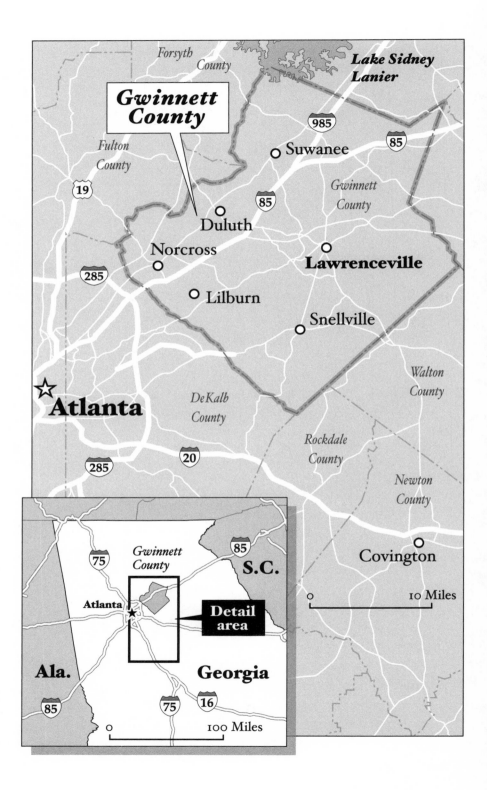

CHAPTER FOUR

THE NEW SUBURBIA

IT MAY SEEM FAR-FETCHED to compare the Hispanic construction workers of modern suburban Atlanta to the peasants from southern France who built Baron Haussmann's Parisian boulevards. But it reinforces an important point about the ways in which the American suburbs of the present mirror the European suburbs of 150 years ago: They are, in large part, the gateways to which newcomers come from far away to perform the entry-level work the society wishes to have performed.

The story of Hispanics in suburban Atlanta begins with the preparation for the 1996 Olympic Games. Those games, like every Olympic extravaganza, produced an enormous burden of immediate building needs. These included an eighty-five-thousand-seat Olympic stadium; temporary housing for more than ten thousand athletes; and a brand-new Centennial Park to serve as a gathering place for the two million spectators who were to attend the events.

Given the limited supply of workers and the time constraints, the Olympic organizers and the Atlanta building and development industry imported an army of laborers from the outside. Virtually all of these were Hispanics, some from the southwestern United States but most of them from Mexico. Few questions about legal status were asked. It was later estimated by the Urban Institute that at least 40 percent of the foreign-born workers in Georgia were undocumented.

Many of the people who built the Olympic facilities left after the games ended in August of 1996, but most stayed. The numerical increase was extraordinary. In 1990, Hispanics had comprised 1.7 percent of the entire population of Georgia. In the ensuing decade the numbers grew by 300 percent, and virtually all of this growth was in metropolitan Atlanta. By the time of the 2000 census, the Atlanta area as a whole was 7 percent Hispanic.

Relatively little of this post-Olympic increase came within Atlanta proper. The Hispanic population began to boom in DeKalb County, on the city's eastern border, and especially in Gwinnett County, the much larger and less developed territory just north of DeKalb. In the late 1990s, Gwinnett was in the midst of a spectacular residential building boom that would boost its overall population from 352,000 to 588,000 in the course of a decade. Much of this can reasonably be described as white flight, a response to the emergence of Atlanta's African American majority population and its control of city politics.

Gwinnett was a largely rural expanse of 437 square miles, 80 percent unincorporated, and in the 1990s it was being packed with subdivision after subdivision, cul-de-sacs and shopping centers and multicar garages. It was developed as a place of safety and homogeneity for white middle-class families, and for many years it was. In 1990, Gwinnett was 90 percent white. There was a black presence of roughly eighteen thousand people, but most of this was a legacy of the county's rural, cotton-growing past. Nearly everyone assumed the proportions would stay that way for a generation to come.

But labor was needed in large numbers to build the highways and the subdivisions, and this was work that the former Olympic laborers had the skills to perform, and were willing to perform at relatively low wage rates. Almost none of these workers lived in the new subdivisions, or anywhere near them. But they did gradually move into the county, into the closer-in towns such as Norcross and Duluth. They settled in modest apartment complexes built for the white working class in the 1960s and 1970s along and adjacent to Buford Highway, a ten-mile corridor running through both DeKalb and Gwinnett.

As late as the 1960s, old-timers will tell you, Gwinnett County didn't even consider itself part of the Atlanta area. It was farm country, and getting to the big city required a tedious journey over poorly maintained two-lane roads. No town in Gwinnett had more than four thousand people. When the county made news at all, it was usually for some form of crime or corruption, often relating to conditions at the infamous Buford Rock Quarry Prison for Incorrigibles, where in 1956 more than forty prisoners on a chain gang broke their own legs in a gruesome protest against abusive treatment. *TIME* magazine reported that the men "had been driven to their madness by the brutality of prison bosses."

The economic activity that drew the most notice was not agriculture but the transportation of moonshine liquor that was brought to hiding places in Gwinnett from stills in north Georgia, then transferred to other locations in the Atlanta area. Even completion of the early portions of Interstate 85 did little to alter the county's reputation for sleaziness: The highway became home to a string of chop shops trading in stolen auto parts. In 1964, proprietors of one of these chop shops murdered three policemen.

But in the mid-1960s, as the interstate stretched farther to cover most of the county, Atlanta began to discover Gwinnett not as a sleazy backwater but as a place with huge development potential. In 1965, the interstate had reached all but the eastern edge of the county. Two years later, I-85 was open from one end of Gwinnett to the other, creating a forty-five-mile corridor primed to attract legitimate businesses, at first mainly warehouses and distribution centers for manufacturers. But soon the dominant industry, as it turned out to be for the next thirty years, was residential construction. The first major subdivision, Cardinal Lake Estates, near Duluth, opened in 1959 with four hundred ranch houses surrounding a forty-acre lake and clubhouse. It continues to thrive half a century later with a population that is largely Korean. Similar projects followed. "Gwinnett County, which has suffered under national notoriety," the *Atlanta Constitution* wrote in 1966, "someday may be the prestige area of metropolitan Atlanta."

Gwinnett was a developer's dream: mile after mile of land that was empty, cheap, flat, and easy to build on. It was one massive greenfield. There was no real political establishment, few old families nervous about change, and few large landowners determined to drive hard bargains. The small-scale farmers who sold out to developers were almost incredulous about their good fortune. Some of them became millionaires literally overnight.

In 1971, the new Technology Park opened on the outskirts of Norcross, with transistor manufacturers comprising most of the original tenants. Two years later, the crucial breakthrough occurred. Western Electric, the Bell Telephone manufacturing subsidiary, opened a plant not far from Technology Park, with a workforce that would eventually reach nearly four thousand. Gwinnett had begun to acquire the physical character it has today: a vast expanse of low-rise residential subdivisions interspersed with business parks along the main thoroughfares. And the population had begun its relentless climb: to 352,000 in 1990, 588,000 in 2000, and 808,167 in 2010.

The developers who built the subdivisions that housed all these people were not surprised in the least by the extent of the county's growth. It was what they had planned for and invested in. But they were not prepared for the demographic changes that accompanied the growth. In 1990, there had been only 8,470 Hispanics in the entire county; in 2000, thanks to the Olympic Games and post-Olympic construction boom, there were 64,137. The black population continued to rise as well, and by 2000 also represented more than 10 percent of the overall numbers. Some perceptive planners had understood that this would happen. What they did not expect was that in the 1990s, and even more in the first decade of the new century, Gwinnett would become a magnet for newcomers from faraway places.

The Hispanic influx was merely the precursor of a much larger immigration of the foreign-born from seemingly all parts of the world, from India, Vietnam, and Korea, from sub-Saharan Africa, from refugee camps in eastern Europe. It has altered the face of Gwinnett County more quickly and more massively than that of any suburban jurisdiction of comparable size anywhere in the United States. When data from the Census Bureau's American Community Survey were released in September of 2008, they showed a degree of change that many of the white residents could scarcely comprehend. Gwinnett had become a majority-minority county, with a white Anglo population of 49.93 percent. The 2010 census confirmed this transformation. Census Bureau figures also showed that of all foreign-born newcomers to the Atlanta area, only a small percentage were settling in the city. The rest were becoming suburbanites. And the largest percentage of them were becoming Gwinnett residents: nearly a quarter of them by 2005, almost certainly more than that by now.

Many of the small towns in Gwinnett, such as Norcross, Lilburn, and Duluth, still have quaint old downtown main streets, built across from railroad stations in the early decades of the twentieth century, now sporting wine bars and bookstores and coffeehouses. These downtowns continue to be upper-middle-class Anglo enclaves—one rarely sees any immigrants there at all. But walk three hundred yards back from the pleasantly gentrified main streets, and you are in another world entirely: Buford Highway, where virtually all the faces belong to people from somewhere far away.

White residents were generally slow to catch on to what was happening in Gwinnett, but some perceptive outsiders picked up on it almost as soon as it began happening. "Six lanes of black hardtop," Tom Wolfe called Buford Highway in *A Man in Full,* his 1998 novel about Atlanta, "bounded by blasted heaths of concrete and hard-baked dirt studded with low tilt-up concrete buildings and wires strung with fluttering Day Glo pennants, signs that rose far above the buildings on aluminum stanchions, and every other device that might catch the eye of someone driving along a highway at 60 miles an hour beneath a broiling Georgia sun. Across the road . . . the Pung Mie Chinese Restaurant, but also Collision City and an astonishing array of pawnshops."

That could stand as an evocative description of Buford Highway more than a decade later, with a little bit of updating. The signs are now displayed in Asian languages as often as they are in Spanish, and the collision shops and pawnshops—still present—have been augmented by Vietnamese nail salons and Korean-owned businesses whose clientele is largely Spanish speaking.

Buford Highway, built for automobiles and almost entirely lacking in sidewalks, has ironically grown dense with pedestrians, mostly Asian and Hispanic women who are not afraid to walk long distances down the six-lane road. They are buying groceries and carrying them back home, crossing the street at crosswalks that are sometimes as much as a mile apart. The creators of Buford Highway had no interest

Strip malls, owned and patronized by immigrants, have become thriving commercial centers in suburban Atlanta's Gwinnett County, which had virtually no immigrant population in 1990.

in making it pedestrian-friendly, but the pedestrians have persevered despite them.

Today, strip malls are becoming abandoned relics all over America, but the ones on Buford Highway are mostly thriving, with vacancies among their modest-size storefronts comparatively rare. Meanwhile, just down the road, Gwinnett Place, the quintessential regional mall that was Georgia's largest shopping center when it opened in 1984, and whose gross sales placed it among the top 5 percent of malls in the United States, was by 2009 pockmarked with vacancies, including a big and embarrassing one at the conspicuous corner anchor spot where Rich's department store once served huge numbers of middle-class Anglo families. By 2011, the Rich's store (later briefly Macy's) had become a multistory Asian emporium called Mega Mart, specializing in fresh groceries appealing to Asians and fashions and merchandise from Korea.

On and around the asphalt lanes of Buford Highway, low-slung garden apartments still house Hispanic families and groups of unrelated Hispanic laborers. Much of the demand for construction labor ceased with the real estate recession in 2008, and many of the male breadwinners left the area, but many of them also left wives and children living in poverty in the apartment courts or in "extended stay" motels, where families can join together and rent dilapidated rooms by the week, sometimes staying a year or more and continuing to send their children to the Gwinnett public schools.

There are probably as many as three thousand people living in extended-stay conditions in the towns of western Gwinnett County; some count them as homeless, though the county commission regards their presence as a matter of personal choice. The county school system as a whole is now about two-thirds minority, and some of the elementary schools, such as Beaver Ridge, near the Buford strip, are virtually 100 percent black and Hispanic, with most of the black enrollment coming not from African Americans but from new arrivals who have left Ghana, Nigeria, or Gambia for the opportunities of the Atlanta suburbs. In the close-in towns such as Lilburn and Norcross, which contain large apartment complexes, some of the schools are reporting a 50 percent student turnover between the start of the academic year in August and its conclusion in late May. "It's almost like migrant workers," says Bucky Johnson, the Norcross mayor. "We don't mind having our share. We've gotten the lion's share."

All this was happening as the city of Atlanta underwent equally dramatic demographic change. The 2010 census for the city itself showed a decrease in the African American population of more than 10 percent, to a bare 54 percent majority, coupled with an increase in the Anglo white population of 17 percent. Meanwhile, foreign newcomers were bypassing Atlanta itself and moving directly to the suburbs.

By 2008, the Hispanic population of Gwinnett County was 17.5 percent, and much more in Norcross and Duluth. Then the increase slowed down, or even went mildly into reverse. By the end of the year, the real estate recession had taken its toll on the proliferation of subdivisions, and there was little construction work to be found. "Latinos are leaving the state of Georgia because there is no construction here," reported Letycia Pastrana, a longtime Latina activist and director of the Gwinnett Village Community Alliance. Indeed, the 2010 census showed a total population in Gwinnett County of a little more than eight hundred thousand residents, and a modest Hispanic increase.

There were no reliable numbers documenting how many Hispanic immigrants had left the county, or where they went. It was known that some of the male laborers had returned to Mexico, and others had gone to the Mississippi Gulf Coast to build the casinos put up rapidly in the aftermath of Hurricane Katrina. But the departing Mexican immigrants were replaced in part by an influx of new arrivals from Colombia, Bolivia, and several Central American countries. So while there is unlikely to be a significant increase in the overall Hispanic population in Gwinnett in the near future, the numbers are likely to stay relatively stable.

The white middle class moved to Gwinnett in large part to be safe from urban violence, and through the 1980s and 1990s it was in fact one of the most crime-free places in America. The countywide incidence of crime is still lower than the national average, but in the past several years, the influx of illegal immigrants has created an underclass that has raised the crime rate and brought the previously unknown presence of loitering day laborers into several of the small cities. Whenever there is even a small amount of construction work to be had, day laborers cluster outside strip malls in Gwinnett just as they do in other parts of the country. In 2008, one Norcross resident wrote an angry letter to the *Atlanta Journal-Constitution* lamenting what he felt had happened to his town. "Illegal immigrants have already broken several laws to get to my neighborhood," he said, "and I can attest that their penchant for lawbreaking did not stop at our borders. We have had murders, home invasion, and burglaries galore." There are outposts of the Mexican drug trade in Gwinnett, as well as a growing number of meth labs operating out of private dwellings. Longtime residents tend to associate these developments with illegal immigration.

It's dangerous to place much faith in the anger of one resident or anecdotal citizen fears, but no one really disputes that Gwinnett has acquired a crime problem in the past five years. It has also begun to confront the realities of poverty and homelessness. In 1990, the countywide poverty rate was 4 percent. By mid-2009, it had more than doubled to 9 percent, and 11 percent among children. "We are leading the region in the growth of poverty," says Ellen Gerstein, of the Gwinnett Coalition for Health and Human Services.

The issue of what to do about illegal immigrants poses a huge challenge for the five-member Gwinnett County Commission. This governmental body seems in a way to be an anachronism. All five members are conservative white Republicans; no Democrat or member of any minority group has been elected to countywide office in Gwinnett in the past twenty-five years. And all the current members are facing decisions that their careers and background have not really prepared them for.

Some of these, of course, concern illegal immigration. Georgia has one of the toughest laws against illegal immigrants anywhere in the country, providing in certain cases for their deportation, but it has not been strictly enforced so far. Some Georgia counties, among them Cobb, just west of Gwinnett, have signed up for the 287-G federal program that trains local police to crack down on the undocumented. The regional undercurrent of hostitility to immigrants is not to be underestimated.

Some of Gwinnett's small towns have passed their own ordinances to deal with what many residents consider public nuisances. Lilburn limits occupancy in any dwelling to one person for every seventy square feet of bedroom space, in an attempt to end the clustering of as many as a dozen single male Hispanic immigrants within one house. The city of Duluth allows no more than three unrelated persons to live together.

But the county commission, with far more power at its disposal, has treaded fairly lightly on immigration issues. This is in part because it is caught between two constituencies. The Republican commissioners have traditionally been close allies of the Gwinnett Chamber of Commerce, which has been phenomenally successful at attracting new business even amid demographic turmoil. And the chamber is unabashedly pro-diversity and pro-immigration. "If you don't enjoy and embrace diversity," says Nick Masino, the chamber's vice president, "then get out of the Southeast. Go to Nebraska."

The commission doesn't like to disappoint the business community. But if it sticks too close to the Chamber of Commerce line, it risks stoking up resentment against illegal immigrants that continues to exist among white middle-class residents. There are regular protests from activists such as Bob Griggs, publisher of the *Gwinnett Gazette*, who told his readers in 2009 that "illegal immigration costs cities, counties, and the state government an estimated $1.6 billion annually." The commissioners can't be sure at any moment how far they might be from a full-fledged populist revolt.

In early 2011, the state of Georgia passed one of the nation's strictest laws targeting illegal immigrants. It remains to be seen what effect this will have on politics in Gwinnett County.

IT WOULD BE a mistake to feel too sorry for Gwinnett County. Even in recessionary times, it has continued to be a magnet for businesses from around the world. In June 2009, NCR, the former National Cash Register Company, now largely a maker of ATMs and grocery checkout machines, announced that it would be moving its global headquarters and more than fifteen hundred jobs from Dayton, Ohio, to Duluth, in Gwinnett County. It was the second Fortune 500 relocation to the county in two years (the other was Asbury Automotive, a dealers' group, which moved from New York in July 2008).

Meanwhile, Gwinnett is pressing hard to attract Asian corporations, touting its large Asian population and overall diversity as a reason to do business there. Asian immigrants are nearly all legally documented residents, and the county school system, for all the demographic upheaval, remains among the more respected and high-performing large systems in the nation. According to the 2000 census, Gwinnett was the seventy-first-richest among the 3,140 counties in America on a measure of household income. By 2010, the median household income had grown to nearly $60,000.

In short, Gwinnett County is doing quite well in a number of different ways. But it is nothing like the place that its white middle-class home owners counted on when they moved there by the hundreds of thousands in the last quarter of the twentieth century. What the county has acquired is not merely diversity but what some scholars call hyperdiversity: a multiethnic presence infinitely more complicated than that confronting other places that have simply attracted growing populations of Hispanics and African Americans. If you want evidence of this, consider the schedule of services on a typical Sunday in 2008 at Lilburn's First Baptist Church: Regular service, 8:00 a.m; Chinese, 10:00; Hispanic, 11:00; Korean, 11:30; Vietnamese, 2:00 p.m; Arabic, 5:30; Indian, 6:00 p.m.

NO PLACE the size of Gwinnett County has changed quite the way Gwinnett has over the past twenty years, but suburbs all over America are moving in the same direction. In 1970, a majority of foreign-born newcomers to this country were settling in cities. By 1980, more were settling in the suburbs, although relatively few demographers were paying much attention. Today, the numbers aren't even close. In 2005, it is estimated, 4.4 million immigrants went to suburbs and 2.8 million to cities. This is far less dramatic than what has happened in metropolitan Atlanta, but it is a powerful statistic nevertheless.

It essentially violates the theories of immigration and living patterns that were developed by Ernest Burgess and the Chicago school of sociologists in the early twentieth century and were rarely questioned for decades after that: Foreigners came to this country, found marginal places to live in the center of big cities, close to the industrial core, and then gradually moved farther out as their savings enabled them to purchase or rent property separated from the noise, dirt, smells, and dangers of the inner city. This theory applied to New York, where the newly arrived residents of the Lower East Side moved out to the Bronx along the subway line, and then, a generation later, to Long Island or New Jersey. It applied on the other side of the continent, in Los Angeles, where immigrant enclaves such as Boyle Heights and East L.A. saw successive waves of the foreign-born move in, up, and then farther from the center.

As we have seen, inner-city neighborhoods such as Sheffield in Chicago and lower Manhattan in New York are becoming attractive to the affluent, and considerably more expensive than most of the metropolitan periphery. In most successful large cities, it is simply no financial bargain for newcomers to live downtown anymore. Most of the jobs they seek are in the suburbs anyway. At this point, more than two-thirds of all the manufacturing in America takes place outside city borders.

It does not require much more than this to explain why most of the conflicts over immigration now occur in suburban jurisdictions, often ones relatively distant from the big-city borders. It was in Herndon, Virginia, some twenty-five miles from the center of Washington, D.C., that voters unseated a mayor in 2007 because he had created a publicly funded gathering place for Hispanic day laborers. He hoped to bring them in from the street corners and strip-mall parking lots where they had been assembling each morning in search of short-term employment. The idea actually worked: 120 job seekers came in from the streets to use the facility, but a majority of local residents found the center to be an inappropriate gift to people who had entered the country illegally. As one voter complained, "Herndon is acquiring a reputation as a sanctuary, a place that is actually sheltering illegal aliens."

This was too much for a community that considered itself to be part of affluent exurbia and to a great extent was. Herndon had become an oddly dichotomous town, with wealth management consultants operating out of large Colonial homes around the corner from *pupuserías* where not only the customers but the employees spoke no English. The shuttering of the public day labor center did nothing to change this: By mid-2008, the laborers were back congregating in front of 7-Eleven stores and auto body shops in the center of town, as many as fifty at a time on an average morning. Only the slowdown in residential construction reduced those numbers significantly in the years after that. Herndon remains a place deeply split between a foreign-born population approaching 40 percent and a tenuous Anglo majority seeking to preserve its original exurban aspirations.

Few American suburbs have experienced the turmoil of Herndon, or that of Prince William County, on the south side of the D.C. metro area, but in the past decade, most suburbs have witnessed changes they never expected to see. Asian Indians have become so numerous in Plano, an upscale exurban community some twenty miles north of central Dallas, that there has been a proliferation of weekend cricket leagues and the establishment of an Asian Women's Lions Club. The suburbs east of Portland, Oregon, are now home to cul-de-sacs in which every resident is a Bosnian. The Hmong and Lao refugees who settled in St. Paul, Minnesota, in the 1980s have spread out into more affordable suburban territory, following the jobs, 80 percent of which are now located more than five miles from the center of either St. Paul or Minneapolis. Given these numbers, it is no surprise that Susan Hardwick, an immigration scholar at the University of Oregon, talks about the United States making a transition to a "suburban immigrant nation." What is surprising is that all this is happening much faster than demographers predicted a decade ago.

MORE AND MORE, Gwinnett County has come to be a magnet for newly arrived Asian immigrants. The first to come in large numbers were Vietnamese, many of them supporters of the fallen anti-Communist regime in Saigon, admitted as refugees under federal laws of asylum. Some had been senior officials of the South Vietnamese government, and had spent much of the previous two decades in jungle detention camps. Many more spoke French than English. Churches all over metropolitan Atlanta sponsored them, but large numbers eventually found their way to Gwinnett. They were not, at least at first, an economically successful immigrant group. Many had to settle for entry-level factory jobs, working on auto windshields and air-conditioning units. It wasn't work to which most of these newcomers, in their forties and fifties, were very well suited. But there weren't many other options. "You really have no choice," says Lam Ngo, a Vietnamese Realtor and community leader, "when you don't have the language and your résumé just says you were a bureaucrat and served prison time."

At first, many of the Vietnamese settled on the other side of the county border in Chamblee or Doraville, along the MARTA train route, where modest apartments had been found for them. But as the new century began, many of the Vietnamese had found businesses to operate in Gwinnett, most notably the nail-painting salons that seemed to be on every block of Buford Highway. These businesses involved virtually no start-up costs, other than leasing a storefront, often a vacant one in an old Buford Highway strip mall. Few of the customers of the salons were Vietnamese, but just about all the work- force was. Painting nails was a job that required good manual dexterity but little English proficiency. There was no shortage of young Viet- namese women who qualified. "We are taking over the county," one Vietnamese activist joked, "one nail at a time."

The Vietnamese also proved to be resolute home buyers, investing in part for speculation and in part because of their large family size: At one point, Vietnamese in the Atlanta region as a whole had an average household size of 4.18, compared to 2.68 for all ethnic groups combined. Vietnamese community leaders have estimated that 60 per- cent of all the Vietnamese immigrants in the Atlanta area now live in Gwinnett County.

In the wake of the Vietnamese came an influx of Indians and Paki- stanis, most of them arriving in the Atlanta area to study at local col- leges. Many found jobs afterward at the new tech center. Like the Vietnamese, these people were literate and well educated, but their literacy was in English, they possessed skills that were in demand, and they tended to draw good salaries. By 2008, Indians formed the largest Asian immigrant group throughout the region. Among men age twenty-five and over, 71 percent possessed bachelor's degrees, and 38 percent graduate degrees. Today, they make up a dramatically dis- proportionate share of the county's medical profession.

Gwinnett is home not only to the largest Indian community in metropolitan Atlanta, but to 31 percent of all the Indian immigrants in the entire state of Georgia. Many of them can afford to live almost anywhere in the county, and there are few easily identifiable Indian enclaves. They are generally mixed in rather inconspicuously with the rest of the ethnic population. But one Asian cluster is clearly develop- ing in the Gwinnett town of Lilburn, where in 2006 a Hindu sect known as BAPS, which stands for Bochasanwasi Shri Akshar Purush- ottam Swaminarayan Sanstha, built an immense temple, known as a mandir, on the outskirts of town. Seventy-two feet high and an eighth of a mile long, containing thirty thousand square feet of floor space,

The Hindu temple that rises suddenly and dramatically on Rockbridge Road in Gwinnett County is a graphic reminder of how a once overwhelmingly white enclave has changed its complexion in just a few years.

it is an amazing sight as one drives by. It is as if someone attempted to construct a rival to the Taj Mahal on an ordinary road in the Atlanta suburbs. Its building blocks of limestone, sandstone, and marble were carved in India and shipped to Lilburn to be assembled like an immense jigsaw puzzle. Its main staircase alone is seventy-three feet wide.

There is something undeniably incongruous about the BAPS mandir, situated as it is next to a Walgreens and a string of dilapidated bungalows. But in three years, it had become a focal point of Hindu life in Georgia and indeed in the entire South. In the words of Charles Bannister, the former county commission chairman, who lives in Lilburn, "They are buying houses and moving closer to [the mandir] all the time."

The mandir is in part responsible for an episode that startled much of Gwinnett County in the fall of 2009: Parkview High School in Lil-

burn was unable to field a ninth-grade football team. That is no major
tragedy; many schools have never even played ninth-grade football.
But Parkview is different. It has long been the sports powerhouse of
Gwinnett, the winner of four state football championships in a dozen
years. In 2006, *Sports Illustrated* named it the fifth-strongest athletic
high school in the entire United States. Ninth grade has traditionally
been the time when much of the aspiring varsity talent first displays
itself to the school's fans.

The failure to make up a team was a piece of gossip all over the
county within a few days. But few of the roughly twelve thousand
residents of Lilburn itself were puzzled about why this had happened
to Parkview. Locals knew how much the school had changed in the
previous five years. What had long been a mostly white institution
with an African American minority had become a miniature United
Nations, with the white and black cohorts nearly equaled by students
from dozens of countries all over Asia and Latin America. Asians, most
of them from India, now made up a fifth of the student body. They
were winning math competitions, boosting the school's SAT scores,
and enhancing its overall academic reputation. But very few of them
were playing football. The school "has regressed some in that respect,"
admitted former commission chairman Bannister. "Academically, it
hasn't."

But if the Indians are having a notable influence on school life in
Gwinnett, the most remarkable immigrant story in the county is that
of the Koreans. They are not the most numerous of the foreign-born,
nor the most conspicuous. But their effect on the county's economic
life promises only to grow stronger in the years ahead.

They did not come to the Atlanta suburbs in search of menial work,
the way many of the Hispanics did, or to find jobs as high-tech professionals, as many Indians did, or as refugees from persecution, like the
Vietnamese. They came, more than anything else, to make substantial amounts of money as business entrepreneurs. This they have done
with remarkable skill.

The growing importance of Koreans in Gwinnett County traces
back to the ambitions of Il Yeon Kwon, an entrepreneur who began
his career in the Saudi Arabia of the 1980s as a driver for the Korean

automaker Hyundai. There was a sizable Korean presence in Saudi Arabia at the time, and not a single restaurant or store that offered this population Korean food. Kwon switched his efforts from driving cars to feeding his countrymen, and did so well so quickly that he decided to apply the same formula in the United States. He started with a three-thousand-square-foot supermarket in New York, in Woodside, Queens, where a significant number of Koreans lived, and was equally successful.

But it was not until the beginning years of this century that he turned his attention to suburban Atlanta. In 2004 he opened his H Mart store on Pleasant Hill Road in Duluth, a massive store with sixty-five thousand square feet of space. There was already a substantial Korean presence in Gwinnett, but the store and the satellites it spawned quickly brought in a whole influx of newcomers. For some Koreans living in diverse parts of the United States, the clincher seemed to be the moment they learned that H Mart carried fresh octopus. "That one shop brought people from Korea, not just L.A. and Chicago," says Moses Choi, a prominent Korean businessman in Duluth. "Koreans have two degrees of separation, not six. Word of mouth spreads faster."

More than any of the other immigrant groups in Gwinnett, Koreans pooled resources and immediately began buying businesses. Strip malls are thriving in much of Gwinnett County, because Korean immigrants were willing to invest in them and maintain them. The billiard parlors and cell phone stores along Buford Highway in Norcross, patronized mostly by Hispanics, are owned almost entirely by Koreans. A large share of the beauty supplies sold to African Americans and Hispanics in the United States comes from small-scale Korean-owned factories along the Buford corridor. Many Koreans refinanced their homes to buy these businesses and strip malls, and they continued to buy them even in the depths of recession.

But the strip malls pale in comparison to Kwon's five massive H Mart supermarkets. Their produce, seafood, and prices are attractive enough that many have acquired a substantial Anglo clientele. One of the largest supermarkets is built around a horseshoe-shaped open-air mall, and the smaller restaurants and specialty stores that line that mall are thriving as well. The even larger Mega Mart opened in 2010 in the once-vibrant but now aging and troubled Gwinnett Place Mall, the 1980s retail blockbuster plagued by a declining Anglo customer base.

Meanwhile, there are four Korean-language daily newspapers in Gwinnett County, and two radio stations. On one day in 2009, the largest of the newspapers carried fifty-eight pages of advertising. Several of the old-line suburban banks in Gwinnett are now Korean banks: North Atlanta Bank is part of the Seoul-based Shinhan banking empire. When it comes to banking, unlike grocery shopping, virtually all the customers are Koreans.

Duluth, where the first H Mart opened, is rapidly becoming a Korean town. Another large contingent lives in Suwanee, the wealthiest town in the county, where the public schools turn out the highest achievement scores. By and large, though, the Koreans, like the Indians, have tended to spread out all around the county, rather than clustering together.

None of this takes into account the single largest minority group in Gwinnett County: African Americans. There has been a modest black population in the rural parts of the county for a century, but those numbers have grown substantially in the past two decades, and today nearly 40 percent of Gwinnett's minorities are African American or immigrants from Africa. There is an underclass black presence in Lawrenceville, Buford, and a few of the other larger towns, but much of the population growth has been rooted in middle-class flight from Atlanta, and is increasingly dispersed throughout the county.

The high-income enclave of Suwanee is home to a growing number of affluent African American families. Duluth's residents include a disproportionate share of the area's best-known black athletes and entertainers. In general, the African American community has had little social or political interaction with the foreign-born and has made few efforts to gain political power. "We're not as politically active as we should be," admits Herman Pennamon Jr., the community relations manager for Georgia Power and a longtime player in black leadership circles. "The minority community is not engaged." One senses that the current cohort of overwhelmingly Anglo Republican county leadership can't last much longer. But significant change will probably have to involve the more active participation of the black community.

. . .

ANY FAST-CHANGING community spends a sizable amount of its time wondering what it will be like a decade hence. That is why "visioning exercises" or their equivalent take place all over the nation. But in Gwinnett County, these questions take on more drama than they do in most places. The county has been altered so much in two decades—changed beyond comprehension, in the minds of some residents—that the future of Gwinnett seems to be an inescapable topic no matter where in the county you go.

One thing appears almost certain: Gwinnett will change physically. It is not only a sprawl county, it is utterly horizontal, more so than almost any of its large suburban counterparts in America. In 2009, there were only two buildings anywhere in the county more than ten stories tall, and you could drive for miles without seeing anything higher than four stories. Until 2005, it was actually illegal to build a structure of more than twenty-five floors, but that had little impact, because hardly any developers wanted to create them. Land was so cheap, and so flat and easy to build on, that businesses in search of extra space simply built longer and wider rather than taller.

But this will change. Gwinnett will continue to grow, and it is unlikely to grow through the construction of more sprawling subdivisions in the near future. Too many of the current ones are partially empty or unfinished. There is a nickname for some of the developments that became stuck in recessionary limbo: They are called pipe farms, for the small white utility pipes that stick a few feet out of the ground and represent the only visible prospect of future occupancy.

The Chamber of Commerce and the Gwinnett Village Community Improvement District, two of the leading players, have committed themselves to a much denser future. This means not only skyscrapers along Interstate 85, the traffic-clogged spine of the county, but mixed-use projects in the center of Norcross and Lilburn and Duluth. The county government seems to accept this in principle, although a fair number of the long-term residents still don't.

But much depends on transportation. Currently, Gwinnett County has what must be the single worst public transportation system of any large county in America. Until 2000, it had no public system at all. The county's voters twice refused to participate in MARTA, Atlanta's regional transit network. Express buses to downtown Atlanta do exist, but otherwise about all you can do without a car in Gwinnett is take an infrequent bus to the end-of-the-line MARTA stop at Doraville.

The Gwinnett Village Community Improvement District has drawn up plans for a new light-rail system that would reach many of the towns, and whose stations would be surrounded by mixed-use developments and buildings much taller than any of those existing now. Whether voters will support this remains an open question. The momentum for it in the business community may well make it happen despite voter doubts. But it will also depend in part on the makeup of the county commission.

Explanations for preservation of the status quo are not hard to find. For one thing, political participation among the burgeoning ethnic communities at both city and county levels continues to be low. "We don't have a lot of diversity in our civic organizations," says Diana Preston, the mayor of Lilburn. "For that matter, we don't have that many organizations." The county has set up a variety of boards to deal with immigrant social service needs, and there is often a minimum percentage requirement for immigrant participation, but the organizers have had difficulty recruiting immigrants to join the boards and stay on them.

Some consider the emergence of the new ethnic groups as key political players to be merely a matter of time. In most immigrant communities in America, it is the second generation that begins to take politics seriously. That doesn't imply as long a wait in Gwinnett as it might seem; among some of the groups, the second generation is already approaching adulthood. "It's about time for the Asian community to have some role in the government," declares Vietnamese community leader Lam Ngo. Korean activist Moses Choi insists that this is not only important, but inevitable. "It will change the landscape," he says, "and it will change politics."

But there are complications. It is not the same thing as African Americans rising to political power in Atlanta in the 1970s. There are literally dozens of distinct ethnic groups in Gwinnett, and most of them have little to do with each other in the settings where political ties might be forged. "Each minority kind of keeps to themselves," says Norcross Mayor Johnson. "They do business with one another, but when they want to go to church, they want to go to church with people who look like them." The Hispanics and the Asians have very little in common, and even among the Asians, there is a general absence of common ground. The idea of Koreans, Vietnamese, and Indians creating a political coalition seems, at best, premature.

The groups do work together on some questions that pose immediate concern to all of them. In 2009, when the Georgia legislature considered a bill to require that all drivers' tests be conducted in English, a consortium of immigrant organizations joined forces to help derail it. But that was the exception, not the rule. When it comes to immigrants achieving a role in county government that equates to their population in the county, there are few signs of progress as yet.

But the most intriguing question of all is the question of Gwinnett's demographic future. It is a question of whether the close division of white and nonwhite is sustainable—whether a new round of white flight will take place, into more distant counties such as Jackson or Forsyth, leaving behind a minority-dominated Gwinnett.

The white-flight scenario is unconvincing, for several reasons. One is that many of the remaining white home owners are older people who will choose to age in place, rather than taking up new roots in an even more distant exurban county. Another is that this sort of flight means choosing to live many miles away from jobs and amenities, not only those in Atlanta but even those in Gwinnett itself. At present, some 58 percent of the people who live in Gwinnett work in the county. Relocating farther out would mean, in many cases, reestablishing the painfully long commutes that Gwinnett residents have struggled in recent years to avoid. In short, there are few practical locations to flee to.

"Nobody moves out now for white flight," says Bucky Johnson, speaking with perhaps a touch of exaggeration but with an air of resolute confidence. Or in the words of Chuck Warbington, who runs the quasi-public Gwinnett Village Community Improvement District, "the rubber band of suburban sprawl has stretched about as far as it can go."

The politicians tend to envision—and statistics would seem to suggest—a different sort of future. This would involve significant white gentrification based on the urban density and transit options being planned for the small close-in cities; a leveling-off of the Hispanic population based on the unlikelihood of a new construction boom; and a steady increase in the number of Asians, especially from India and Korea. These demographics would be different in important ways not only from those of 1990, but from those of 2010.

Of course, nobody really knows. The only certainty is continued change. "Gwinnett County," says housing developer Marina Peed, "isn't really a melting pot. It's more like a petri dish. It's a real social experiment."

5 Miles

Lake Erie

Euclid

90

East
Cleveland

Cleveland

Downtown

*Case
Western
Reserve
Univ.*

Cleveland
Heights

480

77

Shaker
Heights

271

71

Cuyahoga

*271
490*

Cleveland

Detail
area

OHIO

50 Miles

480

Columbus
☆

Cincinnati

River

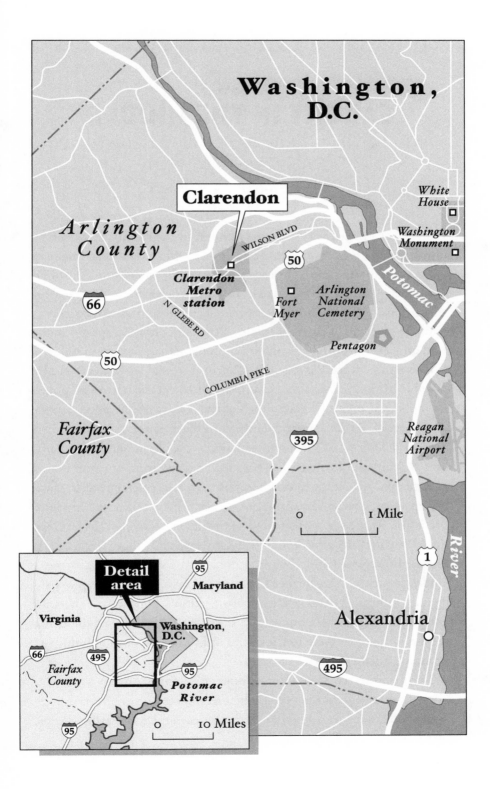

Washington, D.C.

Clarendon

Arlington County

WILSON BLVD

50

□ **Clarendon Metro station**

N GLEBE RD

66

□ Fort Myer

Arlington National Cemetery

Potomac

□ *White House*

□ *Washington Monument*

50

COLUMBIA PIKE

Pentagon

Fairfax County

395

Reagan National Airport

0 ————— 1 Mile

1

River

Alexandria ○

Detail area

95

Maryland

Virginia

66

495

Washington, D.C.

Fairfax County

95

Potomac River

95

495

0 ————— 10 Miles

CHAPTER FIVE

CAUGHT IN THE MIDDLE

IF GWINNETT COUNTY is an experiment in the twenty-first-century suburban future, then Cleveland Heights, Ohio, is an experiment of a radically different form. It tests whether an inner suburb next to an economically stagnant industrial city, a town built in the 1920s for affluent businessmen and their families, can hold on a century later as a strange pastiche of the very wealthy, the very poor, an aging middle class, and a burgeoning population of bohemians, young and old.

Cleveland Heights is a small suburb of 46,121 people, practically walkable from its eastern to its western borders at the narrowest point, but in its way, it encapsulates much of the history of the oldest American suburbia. At its southern end, along Fairmount Boulevard, it is lined with Tudor and Georgian mansions, still elegant and well maintained, although the ownership base has changed from one dominated by industrial managers to one composed to a large extent of medical doctors, professors, and a sprinkling of performers from the Cleveland Orchestra. At the far opposite end of town, along the blocks closest to the dilapidated neighborhoods of East Cleveland, there are nearly a thousand foreclosed and vacant homes and rows of prewar apartment buildings occupied by former Cleveland public housing tenants paying rent with the federal government's Section 8 housing vouchers. In between are Cape Cod bungalows built in the 1950s for blue-collar workers whose jobs were in Cleveland or in the neighboring industrial suburb of Euclid.

The commercial middle of Cleveland Heights can be a bit of a shock to those who haven't seen it before. Where one might be expecting a 1920s main thoroughfare of heavy car and foot traffic, shops, and restaurants, there is an immense sea of asphalt parking lot and a sprawling mall filled with big-box stores: Walmart, Home Depot, Best Buy. It is called Severance Town Center, and it includes the Cleveland Heights City Hall on its outside edge, but it is not a community center in any meaningful suburban sense. It is difficult even to get from one end of the project to the other without driving. To anyone who believes in the virtues of human-scale commercial life, Severance Town Center is a hideous eyesore. There is no other way to put it.

But a few blocks south of this asphalt jungle, one reaches Coventry Street and enters bohemia. The street itself, day and night, is a parade of millennials with tattoos and nose rings, baby boomers of both sexes with long gray ponytails, and young African American men driving by with hip-hop blaring from their car stereos. There are clusters of bookstores, mostly used and occult, and a vegetarian-friendly restaurant so popular that its patrons spill out onto the sidewalk as they wait half an hour for a table.

This is the volume of street life, if not the exact style, that one associates with the older American suburbs built for streetcar commuters in the 1920s. Cleveland Heights has it. There just isn't enough—at least, not in the place where one might go looking for it, the center of town. But the coexistence of Severance Town Center and Coventry Street is part of what makes Cleveland Heights so intriguing. It is suburban territory of every era and every style, perched rather awkwardly on one small municipal parcel of eight square miles. The question is whether it can survive in that form.

How exactly do you define a first-ring or inner suburb? There have been several plausible attempts. Bernadette Hanlon of the University of Maryland says, rather concisely, that an inner suburb is a place that is adjacent to a city and another suburb and in which a majority of the housing stock dates from before 1969. Cleveland State professor Tom Bier has a more nuanced description: a suburb that is almost completely built out, with no room for physical expansion; little or no growth in property value; housing that is at least fifty years old; and heavy unmet infrastructure maintenance needs. Cleveland Heights meets that definition very well.

.   .   .

CLEVELAND HEIGHTS is in the uncomfortable center of demographic inversion. Nine miles from downtown Cleveland; served by relatively good public transportation (although with declining levels of service in the last couple of years); immediately adjacent to the region's largest concentration of universities, hospitals, and museums, nearly all of which are experiencing job growth; blessed with an abundant stock of large, attractive prewar single-family homes; dotted with small neighborhood shopping streets along the lines of Coventry—Cleveland Heights might seem poised to get rich in the way that Sheffield got rich in Chicago in the 1980s and 1990s. Urbanites would find the place attractive, and the poor would be pushed farther out. And it may happen somewhere down the road, as a result of challenges and problems that are an inevitable part of demographic inversion.

One of those is race. The nature of Cleveland Heights' racial challenge has changed enormously in the past several decades. In the 1960s, it was based on a fear of blockbusting, massive white flight, as occurred in the suburb of East Cleveland immediately to the north—and on liberal concerns about discrimination against black families wishing to move into town. An African American arts center was firebombed in the mid-1960s. Those problems were taken care of. There was no massive white flight, thanks in large part to the quality of much of the housing stock, and church groups and other activist organizations put an end to the problem of discrimination in sales.

Cleveland Heights lost about 8 percent of its population in the last decade. It was 50 percent white in the 2010 census, a decline from 52 percent in 2000, and 42 percent black, a number almost unchanged from the previous decade. There is a demographic divide of huge proportions. On the one hand, there are the apartment buildings on the north side of town, bordering on East Cleveland, filled with black Section 8 tenants. On the other hand, the bulk of foreclosures that hit Cleveland Heights beginning in 2008 occurred among African American home owners, who had been persuaded to sign contracts on the modest working-class bungalows. Many have left. So there are forces working in both directions on the racial makeup of the area.

The real race problem in Cleveland Heights is not in housing, however, but in education. Although the overall city population is almost exactly half white, the public schools, including Cleveland Heights High School, are approximately 80 percent black. In the system as a whole, 52 percent of the students are classified as disadvantaged. It is not an easy task to persuade middle-class families of any race to settle in the community and send their children to the public schools, even at the lower levels. Of those families in Cleveland Heights that do have school-age children, about a quarter use parochial or other private education. They can afford to escape the racial tensions that pervade the public school system.

FOR MOST of the long history of American suburbia, the concept of the inner suburb was utterly unknown. There was the city itself, and then there was all of the territory beyond it. Only in the late 1980s did a collection of scholars and activists begin to argue that communities like Cleveland Heights had more in common with the central city than with the auto-dependent places that had sprung up in the previous twenty years along interstate highways. "The cycle of decline has recently caught up with the suburbs," the urban historian Kenneth Jackson warned in 1987. "Half a century after Levittown," the critic Herbert Muschamp wrote a decade later, "the dream is coming apart at the seams. . . . The first ring is in a state of emergency similar to that suffered by the cities the suburbanites fled."

White flight was a good deal of the emergency, as in some of the suburbs directly adjoining Cleveland and bordering on Cleveland Heights. Economic resources were a large part of it: Most inner suburbs, with little industry or large-scale commercial activity, were heavily dependent on residential property taxes. A decline in residential property values, as occurred in many of these places, was likely to be devastating. Moreover, in comparison with the inner city and the burgeoning exurbs, the inner suburbs received little help from any outside source: county, state, or federal. In a rational system of metropolitan triage, inner suburbs would have claimed a much larger share of outside assistance, as they stood on a precipice between renewal and decay, unlike the exurbs, which needed no immediate help; and the inner cities, many of which seemed beyond repair. But the exurbs got federal highway money to spread even farther into the countryside, and the inner cities were the beneficiary of a whole array of federal programs. "It's absurd," claimed Tom Bier, the urban scholar at Cleveland State. "Unless you are a slum, their attitude is, 'We won't help you.' You actually have to fall apart to the point where it's evident you are a disaster case." In reality, though, inner suburbs differ among themselves almost as much as they do from inner cities and outer suburbs. Even before urban demographers paid much specific attention to inner suburbs or their distinctive set of problems, they were interested in the way urban populations flowed through metropolitan areas over time. Elaborate theories were developed to explain this. Bernadette Hanlon provides a rich account of them in her excellent 2010 book, *Once the American Dream.*

In the 1960s and 1970s, there was what was called persistence theory. It held that the socioeconomic character of suburbs scarcely changed at all. As the upper middle class traded their postwar suburban homes for larger places farther from the city, they were replaced by newcomers who looked very much like them, transfers from corporate jobs elsewhere in the country, or families making their first move beyond the city borders. Similarly, factory workers moved out from their first-tier postwar bungalows only to be replaced by other blue-collar workers graduating from city apartment life.

Competing directly with this idea was the concept of "life cycle" change. The economic status of a given suburb gradually declined as its most affluent residents moved farther out and their housing "filtered" down to a less affluent but still economically stable class of newcomers. Some of these neighborhoods were attractive to a mixture of artists, gays, and others who found the edginess appealing and began what amounted to a revival in the attractiveness of the entire area. But a larger number, for one reason or another—often the modest quality and visual appeal of the housing stock—were not so fortunate. Rather than begin the economic and demographic life cycle all over again, these neighborhoods endured a period of pervasive price decline.

Finally, as an alternative to both of these ideas, there were arguments based on social stratification: Suburban status remained essentially frozen in place as the richer suburbs enacted zoning laws and other restrictions designed to keep the less affluent from moving in or multifamily apartment housing from being built. The poorer suburbanites remained "landlocked" in their poorer communities, just as many of them had been in the inner city a generation earlier.

One could, and still can, find support for each of these notions, even within a territory as circumscribed as the Cleveland area, but none is subtle enough to pick up on the complex qualities of inner suburbia. At the upper end of the spectrum, there are suburbs built for a corporate and professional class before World War II, usually filled with large Georgian or Tudor homes, generally situated on the edge of a big city, designed around public transportation and the existence of a village square. Even in a recessionary economy, these suburbs command intimidatingly high housing prices, are doing quite well economically, and need relatively little help from other levels of government. Most of them are overwhelmingly white. Brookline, Massachusetts, is an example of this type of fortunate inner suburb; so is Winnetka, Illinois, on the shore of Lake Michigan north of Chicago. So are some of the inner suburbs of Westchester County, on the northern outskirts of New York City.

At the most unfortunate end of the spectrum are the very poorest of the inner suburbs, usually on the edge of the city closest to what was the African American ghetto half a century ago. They tend to house a transient population, nearly all of it composed of minorities, and possess a housing stock dominated by apartment buildings, many of whose tenants left now-demolished high-rise public housing within the inner city. These are the real trouble spots of inner suburbia, circa 2010: havens for crime, underperforming schools, and general physical deterioration. In the Cleveland area, East Cleveland is an example of this sort of suburb.

In between are two kinds of surviving but vulnerable inner suburb. One is the enclave of tract homes, à la Levittown, built for the salesmen, engineers, and lower-level corporate executives who made up so much of the suburban postwar middle class. Their populations have turned over numerous times in the past half century, sometimes maintaining a consistent middle-class status, but sometimes sliding down a few notches on the socioeconomic ladder as new buyers replace the old ones. Middle-class African Americans wishing to flee the more troubled communities in the first category often settle here.

The other troubled variant of postwar inner suburbia is the industrial working-class suburb, mass-produced after World War II for upwardly mobile blue-collar workers employed in factories nearby. The most serious problems faced by these suburbs are easy to describe, although they are profoundly difficult to solve. They include a disappearing manufacturing base, a supply of bungalow housing whose units are too small for the tastes of most modern buyers, and an aging population incapable of paying for the services that the suburban government is expected to perform. In many cases, they are centers of foreclosure for homes financed with subprime mortgages in the past decade.

There is no bright line separating any of these categories. But one must understand their diversity to make sense of what is happening in inner suburbs right now. Generalizations about them are risky, but one can confidently be made: Increasingly, inner suburbs are doing really well or really badly—they tend to look either like wealthy Brookline or Winnetka, on the one hand, or like East Cleveland and most of the close-in industrial suburbs of Los Angeles on the other. The middle range is shrinking. In 1960, the average income gap between America's richest and poorest inner suburbs was about 2.1 to 1. Now it is about 3.4 to 1.

CLEVELAND HEIGHTS, more than almost any other community in America, manages to do a convincing imitation of all the different types of inner suburbs at the same time. It has the stately Colonial homes. It has the run-down apartment buildings housing tenants who have fled the larger city. And it has the blue-collar bungalows that are in need of repair, no longer convenient to factory work, and difficult to sell. It even has them in an almost equal division of thirds.

One can walk down the tree-lined, curving sidewalks of Fairmount Boulevard and envision the most pristine outposts of American suburbia, the Brooklines and the Winnetkas. One can travel just a few miles

The inner suburb of Cleveland Heights, sandwiched between a trou-bled big city and its sprawling outer suburbs, retains neighborhoods of prewar elegance that house a twenty-first-century professional elite.

north and look at dangerous apartment buildings where few who had a choice would want their children to grow up. Or one can drive through the bungalow neighborhoods and sympathize with the elderly home owners who are hanging on but who wonder what happened to the stable town they settled in during the heady years after the war.

The bungalows themselves are a large part of why Cleveland Heights sits perched uneasily on a precipice of demographic inversion. Some built in the 1920s, some in the 1950s, they are for the most part two-story, two-family houses, with the space for each family closer to the eight hundred square feet of Levittown in 1950 than to the twenty-two hundred square feet of the average home sold in the last decade. Careful studies by William H. Lucy and David Phillips of the University of Virginia have shown that it is the suburbs with the highest proportion of these houses—all past the fifty-year mark in their history, most of them needing an expensive and likely unaffordable new roof for the second time—that have shown the greatest income decline since 1980. Cleveland Heights simply has too many of these houses.

The problem is not without remedy. Small postwar houses can be retrofitted, strengthened in their construction, and made larger to meet twenty-first-century sensibilities. Several cities and inner suburbs across the country have had some success providing home owners with modest subsidies to perform this sort of modernization.

But these successes are occurring in suburbs whose metropolitan areas are thriving—or are at least stable in hard economic times. New jobs are being added to replace the manufacturing jobs that have been lost; young people come to the metropolitan area to fill those jobs and, as often as not, look for places to live that are close to their central places of work. As they do this, the center of the city becomes too expensive for the newest arrivals, and they settle in the neighborhoods just beyond and in the inner suburbs slightly farther away that are on convenient lines of transportation. These recently fading parts of town acquire a cachet, as Sheffield did in Chicago in the 1980s, and the poorer people who formerly lived in these communities move farther out to obtain cheaper housing. Demographic inversion has taken place.

It's not impossible to imagine this happening in Cleveland and Cleveland Heights. But it requires jobs—new ones in the postindustrial economy in numbers sufficient to replace the old ones in manufacturing. Cleveland has not been able to produce these jobs. In fact, the whole area has been losing them at an alarming pace. As the economist George Zeller reported from census data in mid-2010, in the years since 2000, Cleveland and surrounding Cuyahoga County had lost more than 130,000 jobs. There was little sign that well-paying jobs were emerging to replace them, as had happened in Chicago in the 1980s and 1990s.

It remains possible, of course, that in the aftermath of the recession, Cleveland will be able to gain back many of the jobs it has lost. That would go a long way toward ensuring the stability of Cleveland Heights and many of the suburbs that surround it. But at this point, it is difficult to make that prediction.

One perverse symbol of greater Cleveland's economic trouble is its absence of traffic congestion. To the drivers who still commute into town every day, that is a pleasant thing. But it is not good for the central city and most of the inner suburbs. In Cleveland, a commuter can nearly always make it in from the most distant exurb in half an hour or less. There is little incentive to move closer to the center to escape the traffic. That is not Cleveland Heights' fault, but it is part of Cleveland Heights' problem.

Given the difficulties of its housing stock and the stagnation of its metropolitan area, Cleveland Heights has done the best it can to sustain itself and establish an identity that can make it attractive to the kinds of newcomers it wants. It changed its city motto from "A City for a Lifetime" to "Home to the Arts." It plays up the fact that more than a third of the musicians in the Cleveland Orchestra live within the suburb's borders. It treats its fragile racial balance as a virtue rather than a challenge. "This is the model community to see how diversity works," boasts Jennifer Kuzma, the suburb's director of development.

Cleveland Heights has done everything it can to make a selling point of its history of funkiness. It has made a pitch to lure young academics to the offbeat sidewalks of Coventry and the environmental consciousness it actively promotes. It has been willing to try every stratagem imaginable to sell itself to outsiders, including an active campaign to promote the town to Hasidic Jews in Brooklyn who may be tempted to flee the grimy streets of Williamsburg or Crown Heights. This last effort has actually been fairly successful. Not only does Cleveland Heights now have a conspicuous contingent of Hasidim, but of Hasidim who have been relatively comfortable living in the mostly black areas on the north side of town.

While nurturing its free-spirited, tolerant attitudes, Cleveland Heights has been preoccupied with crime. It has more than one hundred police officers on duty, more than twice as many as some nearby suburbs with only slightly smaller populations. It has five patrolmen who spend much of their time on foot keeping an eye on the apartment buildings that border blighted East Cleveland. When budget cuts led to the elimination of these foot patrols, they were quickly restored. This too seems to be having its effect. The violent crime rate has often been lower than in some of the neighboring suburban jurisdictions.

Cleveland Heights has a reputation for being tougher on speeders and other minor law violators than any town on the east side of Cleveland. Whether the heavy-duty law enforcement will be possible to maintain amid sharply reduced help from the state of Ohio remains to be seen.

But the violence that threatens Cleveland Heights the most is violence within its school system. When a riot takes place at a basketball game at Cleveland Heights High School, as it did in 2008, everyone in metropolitan Cleveland seems to hear about it. Something of the same phenomenon occurs when a decline in test scores places the school on a Department of Education "watch list," as has happened periodically over the past decade. It remains true, of course, that each year students from local schools, including the public high school, are admitted to the most prestigious colleges in the country. But that is not the image that most Cleveland-area families with small children carry around in their heads.

Still, racial tension may be only the second-greatest burden. The property tax rates are the third highest in the entire state of Ohio. Moving into Cleveland Heights is not an economically easy decision for anyone, married or single. Voters in Cleveland Heights rejected an increased local income tax in 2008.

When it comes to fiscal problems, there is something that all the inner suburbs in the area, not just Cleveland Heights, can actually do: They can work together. In Cuyahoga County, the inner suburbs as commonly defined make up 39 percent of the county population. The city of Cleveland itself comprises only 33 percent. And in fact, Cleveland Heights and other towns have made heroic efforts to join forces for mutual economic benefit. Starting in 1996, when city councilman Ken Montlack and others organized the First Suburbs Consortium, they have labored to control their budgets by sharing costs and lobbying the county and the state legislature to pay attention to the needs of inner suburbs in general.

In many little ways, this has worked well. In 2006, a study by the Brookings Institution declared the First Suburbs Consortium to be a role model for inner suburbs nationwide. There are now sixteen suburbs in the FSC, on both the east and west sides of Cleveland. When the organization started, it represented communities with about four hundred thousand people. Now the number is close to six hundred thousand, and the FSC suburbs have received modest grants from both the state and the county to conduct joint operations. Each suburb pays only $3,000 of its own money to be an FSC member. The consortium engages in joint marketing for economic development, with common advertising and a common website, touting the locational advantages of suburban Cleveland to both businesses and potential residents.

The FSC does a lot of other things that make economic sense. It operates multicommunity procurement programs, recreation centers, and joint law-enforcement technology sharing. Three suburbs, including Cleveland Heights, run a common police dispatching operation.

But this is small potatoes. What might really bail out Cleveland's inner suburbs would be something closer to an actual merger, so that what is still currently a staggering level of duplication would be reduced, expenses trimmed, and taxes cut accordingly. No one thinks this is likely to happen in the foreseeable future. The individual suburbs simply have too much invested emotionally in their own cultures, their own identities and sense of place. It will be hard for them to cooperate much more than they have already done, no matter what the advantages might be. As Ken Montlack says, "Everybody talks about regionalism as an altruistic notion of collaboration." But moving beyond talk can be almost impossible.

And so Cleveland Heights sits on a fragile fault line of demographic inversion. It has its location, its shady streets, and big, comfortable houses that almost anyone would want to live in. And it is afflicted by painfully high taxes, obsolete working-class bungalows, a violence-prone transient population, and schools with a troubled reputation. Right now, the burdens seem to outweigh the advantages.

Of course, if the city of Cleveland itself could stage a twenty-first-century comeback, things would be different in Cleveland Heights. But that is another story.

THIS OTHER STORY can be told, at least in part, by exploring a different inner suburb in another part of the country, one that went through a similar period of uncertainty and came out on the positive side of demographic inversion—the side that attracts rather than repels affluent newcomers. Arlington, Virginia, is an inner suburb of Washington, D.C., just across the Potomac River, one that resembles Cleveland Heights in some ways and is distinct from it in others. Governmentally, it is a different creature; Arlington is a county unto itself, not part of a behemoth like Cuyahoga. It has more than four times as many people as Cleveland Heights, but it is still a small place—at twenty-six square miles, the geographically smallest county in the entire United States. It, too, came into existence a little more than eighty years ago, underwent massive demographic changes in the 1970s and 1980s, and has a significant minority population. It includes a substantial number of modest-size brick bungalows and ramblers built in the years after World War II. But, unlike Cleveland Heights, Arlington has emerged as a thriving twenty-first-century exemplar of inner-suburban revival.

For most of the past century, Arlington's economic life has been centered in Clarendon, in a commercial corridor along Wilson Boulevard, a couple of miles west of the Potomac. Like Cleveland Heights, Clarendon was suburbia, vintage 1925. Crowded with clanging streetcars and lined with small stores packed in close to the sidewalk, it always felt more like a neighborhood retail district in a big city than it did like a modern suburb. People got off the streetcar and stopped at the bank, the shoe store, the dime store, the cleaners. It was a downtown scaled to pedestrians rather than automobiles.

Even with the arrival of the car culture in the postwar years, Clarendon and central Arlington hung on reasonably well. Most of the leading retailers were still doing business as late as 1970. Then came the Metro. The idea behind the immense subway project was to save old commercial corridors, but its initial effect was to destroy this one. The dirt and noise and sheer inconvenience that accompanied nearly five years of Metro construction drove away virtually all the businesses that had not already fallen victim to the coming of the large suburban malls farther out from the city. By 1980, Clarendon (and much of Arlington) was a commercial wasteland, offering little that anyone wanted to buy and attracting virtually no customers from outside its borders. Scarcely anyone from the rest of the metropolitan area showed much interest in moving there.

But Clarendon in particular did have an unnoticed asset that ultimately saved the day. It had dozens of small, empty stores, vacated during the Metro construction, that landlords were willing to rent dirt-cheap. And to everyone's surprise, there were people who wanted them: Vietnamese merchants, mostly refugees from the collapse of Saigon in the mid-1970s, had resettled in the Washington area. One by one, Wilson Boulevard acquired Vietnamese restaurants, bakeries, bookstores, and dress shops. People began to call the Clarendon corridor "Little Saigon."

For the first few years, most of the customers as well as the proprietors were Asian. But the restaurants began to attract patrons of all nationalities, and soon there were new restaurants of all kinds—Cuban, Indian, Moroccan, Iranian, Cajun, Tex-Mex—opening up so fast it was hard to keep track of them. Restaurant reviewers began doing weekend guides to the Clarendon dining scene. Trend-spotting Washingtonians began taking out-of-town guests to see this interesting little cluster of cafés just across the river.

The restaurants brought forth coffeehouses, gourmet grocery shopping, and nightclubs, with a thriving entertainment scene. On a Friday evening in Clarendon, sidewalks that were empty in 1990 were packed a few years later with people eating at outdoor cafés, waiting in line for homemade ice cream, or checking out the live music choices for later that night. The only thing they had trouble finding was a parking space.

The press couldn't seem to write enough about this comeback. "It's the combination of trendy nightspots and prime real estate," *The Washington Post* explained a few years ago, "that has made Clarendon among the most chic places to live in the Washington area." *Washingtonian* magazine reported that the "bar scene has become so hot, it's even luring city-dwellers."

The revival of Clarendon was critical to a revival of the county as a whole. Thousands of young professionals decided they wanted to live near the big city, if not necessarily in the middle of it. Develop-

Arlington's Clarendon neighborhood, a commercial district near Washington, D.C., which thrived in the 1950s and then went into decline, has attracted new residents and visitors and become a model for successful inner-suburban revival.

ers responded to that demand with an open-air "lifestyle" shopping center, seeking to emulate some of the qualities of the old walkable Clarendon shopping district, and with dozens of new condominium buildings lining the transit corridor that ran straight through Clarendon to the western end of the county.

While Cleveland Heights was losing population, Arlington was gaining it. In 2008 and 2009, Arlington was one of the ten fastest-growing places in the country with populations greater than 100,000. By the time of the 2010 census, it was up to 207,627 people, an increase of nearly 10 percent during a period when Cleveland Heights was losing 8 percent. Most of the newcomers found work to do as well. In January 2011, as unemployment in the nation hovered around 9 percent, unemployment in Arlington County stood at 4.1 percent. Three-bedroom brick Colonials in Clarendon and in other parts of the county were selling for nearly a million dollars. And the school system, which in the 1970s seemed poised to resegregate the way some of those in suburban Cleveland have, was split almost evenly between white and minority students.

The ultimate desirability of Arlington's trendiness is a question on which reasonable people may differ. Most longtime Clarendon residents, having lived through some discouraging days in the past, generally seem pleased, if a little puzzled, by what has happened to them. Some are worried that the increased traffic and congestion will prove too high a price to pay for popularity. But that's not the issue that I'm posing at the moment. The question is: Why do some inner suburbs make it over the hump while others struggle and some fail utterly?

Nobody in local government predicted Clarendon's comeback as a restaurant, nightclub, and condominium district. That would have seemed ludicrous as late as the mid-1990s. But even had someone on the county planning staff conceived such an idea, it's difficult to see what they could have done to bring it about. The recent history of urban planning is dotted with examples of places that have created formal "entertainment districts," and sometimes backed that decision up with generous subsidies to entrepreneurs. The number of proven long-term successes remains small.

Clarendon, on the other hand, didn't declare itself to be anything in particular. It became an entertainment district without really trying, and certainly without spending a fortune in public money to become one.

That's not to say that government doesn't play a significant role in these situations. Arlington County did several important things. It helped to create a public-private partnership, the Clarendon Alliance, that recruited small businesses to the area and helped them succeed once they arrived. County zoning was flexible enough to allow for sidewalk cafés and other small-scale experiments, and to permit businesses located near the subway stop to dispense with parking-space requirements they would have been hard-pressed to meet. In general, the county had the good sense to stay loose and let the whole process unfold.

One thing that didn't save Clarendon was quaintness or architectural distinction. It doesn't have any. In contrast to the Colonial-style

grace and symmetry that mark such Washington tourist enclaves as
Georgetown and Alexandria (or the elegance of Fairmount Boulevard
in Cleveland Heights, for that matter), Clarendon is a jumble of building styles from different eras that have little to say to one another. The
polite word to use is "eclectic," but "mishmash" wouldn't be too far
from the truth.

Nor was Arlington rescued by the formal implementation of a civic
or governmental master plan. Such a plan does exist—it has existed
for the past twenty-five years, ever since the county government and
citizen activists drew up a detailed blueprint envisioning Clarendon as
a pedestrian-oriented "urban village" of the twenty-first century. The
framers of that document saw the grubby old prewar storefronts being
torn down and replaced by brand-new mixed-use developments of
much greater density, building to a high-rise crescendo at the subway
station in the center of the community. In the past few years, that has
begun to happen. But in the beginning, it was the old buildings, the
walkability and human scale of the neighborhood, that were the ingre-
dients of revival.

It was immigration that brought those old buildings to life. And
that's a reminder of one crucial difference: Cleveland Heights has
never attracted immigrants in any significant numbers. Arlington has
been a magnet for them, from the influx of Vietnamese store owners
and restaurateurs in the 1970s to the flood of Hispanic newcomers in
the decade of the 1980s. Over the years, this has brought its share of
tensions, especially in the school system, which had to cope with a
large cohort of pupils whose English-language skills were limited or
nonexistent. But in the long run, the immigrants were a boon to a
community whose future once seemed as precarious as that of Cleveland Heights does now. The vacant storefronts brought the Vietnamese in and set the whole process in motion. It may seem a bit ironic
that the way to bring in more affluent white newcomers is to lay down
a base of poorer people from other countries. But that is exactly what
happened in Arlington.

More important than immigration, though, was transportation.
Cleveland Heights isn't bad in this respect; it has decent bus connec-

tions to downtown Cleveland. But Arlington has a subway line, and its entire central corridor is dotted with stations, some of them less than a mile apart. Long before the revival began, Arlington County made the most fateful decision of all: It put a subway stop smack in the middle of Clarendon. Metro construction killed off the Clarendon that had existed for more than fifty years, but without the subway, the new Clarendon almost certainly would never have been born. That's not because the vast majority of neighborhood residents do all their traveling by means of mass transit. As in virtually all suburbs, old and new alike, most trips to work or shopping continue to be made by car. But one county survey a few years ago found that a quarter of the residents of the central corridor that includes Clarendon did not own a car at all. That is an exceptionally high number for an inner suburb anywhere in the country except the environs of New York City.

As an increasing number of cities and suburbs are finding out, a transit line is frequently a developmental magnet with powers of attraction far beyond its daily commuting numbers. In the words of Tom Downs, the veteran transportation planner, spoken many years ago, "It isn't the train that matters; it's the tracks." Once the infrastructure is in place, established businesses suddenly find themselves willing to take a chance on an older neighborhood, confident that its future is based on something more permanent than speeches and architectural drawings. That was what happened in Arlington.

Immigration brought Clarendon to life. Transportation gave it concentrated residential development. But behind all of Clarendon's (and Arlington's) good fortune was a metropolitan area dominated by an industry that everyone realized was never going to move out: the federal government. Washington, D.C., has been a troubled city for the past half century, with high crime rates, underperforming schools, and, until recently, a steadily declining population. But the presence of the federal government has kept the metropolitan area healthy in both good economic times and bad. Even though the size of the federal workforce as a whole decreased during the past decade, the regional job base held its own. This not only benefited the District of Columbia itself (which actually registered a gain in population between 2000 and 2010), but brought in young professionals, government employees and private-sector workers alike, for whom inner suburbia seemed like a convenient and appealing residential choice.

America's inner suburbs come in all shapes and sizes. But the keys to their success at this point in history are immigration, transportation, and a surrounding metropolitan area healthy enough to attract a steady supply of newcomers. Those that have all of these are going to do fine. Those that don't have any of them are going to be in trouble. Those in the middle, like Cleveland Heights, possess opportunities but are also destined to struggle.

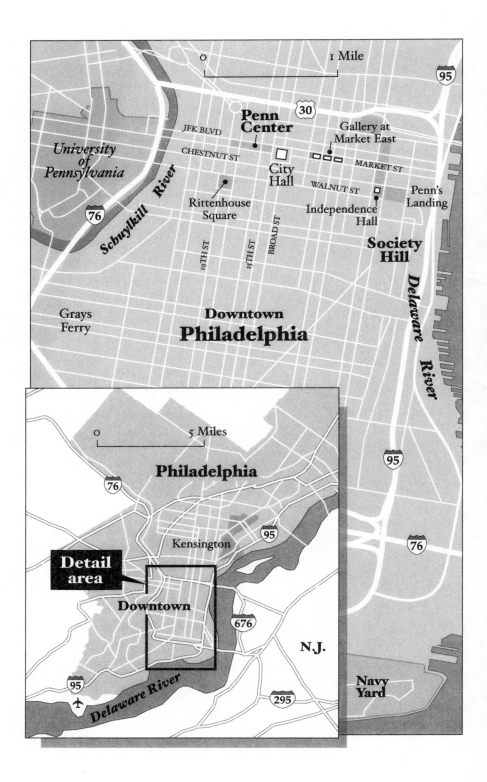

1 Mile

Penn
Center

Gallery at
Market East

JFK BLVD

CHESTNUT ST

City
Hall

MARKET ST

University
of
Pennsylvania

WALNUT ST

Penn's
Landing

Rittenhouse
Square

Independence
Hall

Society
Hill

19TH ST

15TH ST

BROAD ST

Grays
Ferry

Downtown
Philadelphia

Schuylkill River

Delaware River

5 Miles

Philadelphia

Kensington

Detail
area

Downtown

N.J.

Navy
Yard

Delaware River

CHAPTER SIX

UNEASY COEXISTENCE

Two notable events took place in Philadelphia in late February 2009. They had nothing to do with each other, but taken together, they suggest why Philadelphia offers many hints about the American city of the future—and presents so many obstacles to its realization.

One of the events was the opening of a spectacular new Cézanne exhibit at the city's major art museum. In honor of the exhibit, three gourmet restaurants in or near Center City announced that they were creating special menus that featured dishes from the artist's native Provence. One of the restaurants, Zinc, offered squid flash-seared with Pernod, and apple pastry in lavender caramel sauce for dessert.

On the night those dishes were being introduced at Zinc, a somber ritual was being enacted eight miles north on Broad Street. Some three hundred police were marching in columns four abreast from Archbishop Ryan High School to the Givnish Funeral Home on Academy Road in northeast Philadelphia. They were marching to honor fellow policeman John Pawlowski, murdered six days earlier by a thief who had accosted a taxi driver. Pawlowski was the fifth police officer in the city to be killed in the line of duty in just one year.

It is hard to know exactly what to make of such a place. There are cities in America, such as Boston, Chicago, and New York, that are, despite serious problems, glamorous and exciting and a magnet for tourists from all over the world. Others, such as Detroit, are so badly blighted that it is hard to imagine anyone wanting to visit them. Somehow, Philadelphia manages to be both those things at once. Its residents sometimes refer to it jokingly as Bostroit—a city that is healthy on the inside and decaying badly on the periphery.

To say that Center City is healthy may actually be to understate the case a little bit. A four-block walk down Walnut Street, from the Bellevue hotel at Broad Street to Rittenhouse Square at Eighteenth, is a stroll past amenities comparable to those of Michigan Avenue or Fifth Avenue, but on a much less intimidating scale. Walnut Street is not a canyon. It's a collection of low-slung century-old buildings with ground-floor retail that oozes wealth: Tiffany, Burberry, Godiva, Ralph Lauren; a sprinkling of spas and luxury salons; and an assortment of restaurants offering haute cuisine. One can take in the shops, stop to sip a Bacardi mojito at the sidewalk café outside Alma de Cuba, then order truffle-stuffed lamb loin with sweetbread tempura at Le Bec-Fin, the most elegant restaurant in town and one of the most famous on the East Coast.

Virtually all the storefronts are occupied: 90 percent of them even in the trough of recession at the end of the last decade. And Walnut Street is not only plush, it is thronged with people throughout the daytime and the evening as well. A 2009 survey found that 2,468

Walnut Street in Center City Philadelphia is an elegant thoroughfare with high-end restaurants and expensive shopping, and a lunchtime pedestrian count of more than two thousand a day.

people walked by the corner of Walnut and Sixteenth during the average lunch hour. Precise comparisons to downtown neighborhoods of other cities are difficult to make, but this is an impressive number by almost any standard. Many of the passersby couldn't afford to buy the items in the shopwindows, but many could. A significant number of Center City pedestrians are conventioneers or foreign tourists. In 2010, they frequented 305 Center City restaurants classified as "fine dining" establishments and watched the passing parade from an array of 213 sidewalk cafés with seating for 3,556.

Philadelphia's downtown is not only an interesting place to visit, it is a place where increasing numbers of affluent people want to live. More than twelve thousand new condominium and luxury apartment units were built or retrofitted in Center City in the last decade, and while the recession forced a pause in the construction of new ones, it didn't cause the population to drop. There were exactly eight residential foreclosures in Center City in 2008; the apartment vacancy rate was 4.4 percent. By one measure, Center City had a full-time residential population of ninety-two thousand. Allowing for variation in geographical definitions of city centers, this is a number that places Philadelphia behind only New York and Chicago in the size of its downtown residential cohort.

Urban scholars sometimes define a successfully renewed central city as one in which at least one downtown census tract has a median income higher than the average for its entire metropolitan region. In 2010, the census tract including the blocks on Walnut Street closest to Rittenhouse Square had a median income that stood at 183 percent of the regional average.

But while Center City is doing as well as comparable areas of downtown Chicago or New York (better in some places), it is an island of affluence more than an engine of citywide improvement. Venture just a few blocks north or west of the cafés and hotels and well-lit streets, and you are in a dangerous place.

In fact, a very dangerous place. Virtually every year in the past decade, Philadelphia has suffered from more violent crime per capita than any of the other ten largest cities in America. In 2006, it recorded 406 homicides. New York City, with a population more than five

times as large, recorded fewer than 600. In 2009, with a new administration focused intensely on crime, Philadelphia managed to reduce
the homicide count significantly, to 302, and held it to 306 in 2010. At
the same time, however, San Diego, with nearly the same number of
people, came in at 41 in 2009 and only 29 in 2010.

The vast majority of killings in Philadelphia aren't random attacks
on innocent people. They tend to involve drug dealers shooting one
another in lawless neighborhoods. If those neighborhoods were somehow farther in the distance, on the outskirts of town, it might be
easier for those in the center to ignore them. As it is, they are just
a little too close for Center City to put out of mind. A walk down
any of the streets of Kensington, Frankford, or southwest Philadelphia, row-house neighborhoods built for working-class families that
long ago abandoned them, is a walk through squalor that exceeds
what one finds in even the poorest neighborhoods of New York and
Chicago.

If, as this book maintains, American cities are coming to resemble
their European predecessors of a century ago rather than their American counterparts of the past generation, then Philadelphia represents a
striking piece of evidence. It is a fashionable center surrounded on two
of its four sides by a periphery of seemingly endless poverty. The one
distinctive element is that the periphery is much closer to the center
than it is almost anywhere else. Philadelphia, says Feather Houstoun,
president of the city's William Penn Foundation, "is as close to a European city as you can get in the United States." That statement is true
in a way that neither Houstoun nor almost anybody else would wish.
Center City is a pleasant playground that might as well have a medieval moat around large parts of it.

To be fair to Philadelphia, there has been a significant amount of
gentrification in recent years in some of the areas surrounding Center
City, especially in the once overwhelmingly Italian neighborhood of
South Philly. There has been a noticeable influx of middle-class newcomers even in some districts north of the center. But the fact remains
that demographic inversion in Philadelphia is still plagued by the existence of a partially abandoned no-man's-land, some of it not too many
blocks away from the pleasant sidewalk cafés of Walnut Street.

. . .

IT'S IMPORTANT to remember that Philadelphia, like a handful of the oldest American cities, has always possessed a significant downtown residential culture. For most of the city's history, this was largely a working-class culture, tied to jobs along the docks of the Delaware River. The narrow streets at the end of Center City are the same ones that Benjamin Franklin walked in the eighteenth century as a printer and irrepressible civic activist.

As late as World War II, this culture was more or less intact. But in the postwar years, in Philadelphia as in virtually every corner of urban America, downtown began to fall apart. Residents, corporations, and retail businesses all left for the suburbs. The docks were no longer economically important.

Philadelphia responded to its urban decline more boldly than most other cities. Under the leadership of urban planner Edmund Bacon, it developed two huge projects on Market Street: Penn Center, a nest of eleven towers containing five million square feet of office space along with retail units on the site of a demolished railroad station; and, a few blocks away, the Gallery at Market East, an indoor festival-style mall with 125 retail units and eating places.

Edmund Bacon was so widely admired that *TIME* magazine ran an elaborate spread on Penn Center while it was still in the construction stage. The project ultimately did slow down the exodus of office jobs to the suburbs, but only to a modest degree. Between 1956 and 1974, Philadelphia lost seven of its fifteen Fortune 500 headquarters. Penn Center never really made it as a shopping destination, and the Gallery, meant to be a gathering place for Philadelphians of all ages and classes, slid inexorably downscale. Its retail courtyards pointed inward, with nothing to face Market Street in many places but a blank brick wall. It sucked life out of the streets instead of fostering it. Workers and shoppers parked in attached garages and went home promptly once their working day or shopping trip ended.

By 1990, both projects were recognized as failures, or at least as inadequate to accomplish any serious reversal of the city's fortunes. City Hall, the fulcrum of Philadelphia's urban life for virtually the entire twentieth century, was encircled by hundreds of thousands of square feet of empty office space, and a plaza frequented mostly by homeless people. "Center City is being despoiled," *The Philadelphia Inquirer* editorialized in 1989, "by litterers tossing candy wrappers, panhandlers shaking plastic cups, muggers snatching shoulder bags, shoplifters fingering the merchandise, and street people doing their business in public stairwells." No market-rate housing had been built in Center City in the previous twenty years.

Only two pockets of affluence remained, on the fringes of the center. On the western side, closest to the University of Pennsylvania, parklike Rittenhouse Square retained its dignity, held its property values during the leanest years for downtown Philadelphia, and remained a residential enclave for what was left of the old white Protestant elite. On the opposite edge, near Independence Hall and the river, the city recruited architect I. M. Pei in the early 1960s to build Society Hill Towers, three modernist residential high-rise buildings of thirty-two stories, with 624 luxury apartments. The towers project was a commercial success (it converted to condominiums in 1979) and sparked the revival of the larger Society Hill neighborhood around it. Society Hill became a gentrified district of eighteenth-century redbrick townhouses and new ones designed to blend in. By the 1990s, Society Hill had been a fashionable residence for young professionals for thirty years. But it was an aberration. By and large, Center City continued to be a dreary place to live and work.

That changed very quickly, however, in the closing years of the decade. It changed in part because of demographic trends but also because of an experiment in tax policy. Understanding this requires a brief digression into the intricacies of Philadelphia's perverse revenue code.

Philadelphia derives less of its budget from property taxes than any other large American city. Instead, it collects roughly 60 percent of its money from a wage tax, established in 1939, that imposes a heavy burden on the paychecks of employees and employers working within the city. In other words, it takes in funds from mobile sources—individual residents and proprietors who can flee the city anytime they wish—and treads lightly on the immobile source, the homes and apartments that stay rooted to their urban locations. The main reason there was no residential development in Center City for two decades was that the wage tax depressed the demand for houses, condos, or even rentals within the city limits, and especially downtown, where construction costs were highest.

Repealing the wage tax was politically impossible, because home owners still living in the city would not accept the higher property taxes that it would require. But in 1997, the administration of Mayor Ed Rendell did the next best thing: It enacted a ten-year tax abatement on virtually anything built in Center City. New condominium projects or conversions of old office buildings to residential use would be taxed for a decade as if they were still unimproved property. All of a sudden developers could open up high-end residential units and price them low enough that the benefits outweighed the burden of the wage tax.

The impact was dramatic. By 2004, fifty-three office buildings had gone residential. Their estimated value was $110 million. The value of their tax abatements was $29 million. In the old CIGNA insurance building, a twenty-story Art Deco structure on Arch Street north of City Hall, all the residents combined were paying a little more than $200,000 total in property taxes on the units they owned. Without the abatement, the figure would have been close to $1 million.

Not everyone thought tax abatements were such a wonderful idea. Although the abatements were extended citywide in 2000, they primarily benefited the development industry and affluent professionals who bought into the buildings the developers built or renovated. They did next to nothing for owners of smaller existing properties, especially the row-house home owners who still populated many of the city's outlying districts. As the program entered its second decade, there were continuing debates in City Hall over ways it could be made more equitable, such as focusing the subsidy on neighborhoods rather than downtown. But on one issue there was no real disagreement: The policy had been instrumental in creating a Center City where people who had choices wanted to live, shop, and work. "Without tax abatements," says John Kromer, who was Rendell's housing director, "Center City would have improved, but it's hard to imagine it becoming the success that it became. . . . You could buy a condominium within a newly restored, historically noteworthy building in the Rittenhouse Square area, and pay a fraction of the taxes you would have paid" for a similar property in another city.

Tax abatements made the new Center City not only attractive but affordable, but this too was a double-edged sword. Because it was subsidized, it didn't price very many customers out of the market. It wasn't expensive enough to generate the excess demand that had pushed newcomers into outlying neighborhoods of New York and Chicago and served to revitalize large portions of those cities. As the first decade of the new century unfolded, most of Philadelphia (62 percent, according to one study) was still mired in blight. In the words of John DiIulio, a University of Pennsylvania political scientist and lifelong Philadelphian, "Center City has never looked better. The old neighborhoods have never looked worse. End of story."

Every big city has dangerous neighborhoods, but Philadelphia is one of the few in which those places still form a barrier against the expansion of central-city affluence. The physical decay and social disintegration of communities only a short distance from downtown are an immense obstacle. Not far from Center City, a whole ring of neighborhoods looks to be simply too far gone to attract professionals and office workers who might otherwise be tempted by the convenience. "These areas hem in the city," says one longtime observer. "There's a feeling of pushing against the frontier that you don't have in other cities. . . . There's some places in North Philadelphia that it's hard to imagine anyone doing anything with in our lifetime."

IF YOU RIDE the Broad Street subway north just a couple of stops past Temple University, you'll find yourself in a world of abandoned houses, rotting factories, and drug-gang turf wars. "For miles on end," the Metropolitan Philadelphia Policy Center reported in 2001, "the fabric of the city has worn clear through, creating a landscape of rubble punctuated by a few houses. One of Philadelphia's greatest assets during its twentieth-century heyday was the abundance of small homes for working people. But the exodus of people and prosperity to the suburbs during the past fifty years has left the city with a huge surplus of houses and few resources to maintain them."

One can simply look at the jobs-to-residents ratio and get a glimpse of the problem. Boston has almost an equal number of people and jobs. Even Pittsburgh, which suffered through the collapse of the steel industry, its economic lifeline, has close to an equal number. Philadelphia has a population of 1.4 million and a little more than six hundred thousand jobs. And the greatest effect of that imbalance has been felt in the old row-house neighborhoods that spread north and west from Center City.

Philadelphia's neighborhoods were not merely places to live; they were all-purpose communities wound tightly around manufacturing employment. They were lunch-pail neighborhoods. The breadwinners in those small homes walked to their factory jobs in the morning, carried their sustenance with them, and walked back home again later in the afternoon to open a beer and glance at the evening paper. The factories closed up in a period of just a few decades: In 1950, 45 percent of the city's jobs were in manufacturing; by 1980, according to Pew's Philadelphia Research Initiative, that figure was down to 20 percent. In 2008, it was less than 4 percent. As the factories closed up, the working-class home owners departed as well, leaving behind obsolete enclaves that no longer could support most of those who remained. The people who stayed behind were primarily older people too settled or too infirm or exhausted to move, and younger people who made their living primarily through illicit activities.

Kensington is a classic example. Its residents worked at the Navy Yard, just to the east along the Delaware River, and the winding down of the Navy Yard in the 1990s was in many ways the act that sealed Kensington's fate. But the neighborhood's breadwinners also made Phillies cigars, Stetson hats, and Disston saws. They held down skilled machine jobs in smaller plants that made things whose origin few consumers bothered to think about: zippers, tuxedos, patio furniture.

Kensington is a close-in neighborhood with easy transportation access to downtown and a scattering of houses that could be saved and sold. But both the neighborhood and the areas around it lack the job base to provide a stimulus for saving it. Emerging from the

Somerset El station in the heart of Kensington, one first sees the abandoned hulk of the five-story Orinoka Upholstery mill, whose business declined through the second half of the twentieth century, and which closed altogether in the 1990s. There are only a few factories left in Kensington now; ironically, some of them produce luxury hardware for the apartments and condos of Center City. Many of the abandoned industrial buildings serve now as drug markets. Drug dealers also own some of the functioning buildings on Kensington Avenue.

Southwest Philadelphia, in the shadow of Philadelphia International Airport, is in even worse shape—the most dilapidated neighborhood, many believe, in the entire city. It doesn't have the history that Kensington has. Its row houses were mostly built in the 1960s for workers who earned a living at the nearby General Electric plant and an ARCO oil refinery. Cut off geographically from most of the city, it always bore the burden of being a "white-trash" neighborhood, a place known as much for its waste dump and junkyards as for any sense of community it could develop. Still, says John DiIulio, who grew up there, "it was a paradise in its way. A working-class paradise."

That changed almost overnight when General Electric shut down in the 1980s. White residents fled, poorer African Americans replaced them, and southwest Philly became a textbook case of social disorganization, with scarcely anyone residing there who possessed any attachment to or roots in the community. Its reputation today is as a haven of violence and foreclosure. It seems moderately plausible to envision Kensington, in a future housing boom, making at least a partial comeback. It is harder to imagine in the case of southwest Philadelphia.

IRONICALLY, IT IS ONE OF PHILADELPHIA's most deeply entrenched sources of civic pride that has contributed most to the decay of its neighborhoods: its physical character as a row-house city. Philadelphia was never a city of apartments the way New York and Chicago were. It was a place where an ordinary working-class family could afford a small redbrick investment of its own, fifteen feet wide and no more than forty feet deep, but a badge of pride for anybody who worked on the ships at the Navy Yard or on the assembly line at General Electric.

Many of the city's banks, unlike those in other cities, were perfectly willing to lend money for the purchase of a home this small. And so people were home owners in Philadelphia who would have been renters almost anywhere else.

For decades, the row-house phenomenon contributed to the rootedness—one might say the parochialism—of many Philadelphia neighborhoods. Many longtime residents almost never ventured downtown, even if downtown was only three or four miles away. A city that was the most cosmopolitan in America in the eighteenth century evolved into perhaps the most provincial over the course of the twentieth. Whole communities linked themselves to individual industrial companies, or to individual unions that thrived there. A shipworkers' neighborhood and a carpenters' neighborhood could easily develop intense and long-lasting rivalries. A typical row-house block in Kensington might have as many as sixteen houses on it. The small size and sheer proximity of the living quarters—sixteen families each joined to one another by a common set of walls—made an undeniable contribution to community and solidarity. But when jobs disappeared and families began to leave, each block was left with a special set of vulnerabilities. An apartment building with thirty-six units is, in a certain sense, too big to fail. A landlord nearly always has an interest in keeping it in operation, even if at a low level of maintenance. A fifteen-by-forty-foot row house is an easy thing to abandon when all of one's friends are leaving the area and the resale value is next to nothing. In the words of Alan Greenberger, the city's economic development commissioner, "Lots of individual houses fail because the occupant is unable to deal with it. Then it spirals. The easiest thing to do is to leave it there until it deteriorates."

Walking down a block in Kensington today, one encounters what real estate brokers like to call the 60/40 problem. Sixty percent of the homes have been abandoned and are more than likely boarded up. Forty percent are still occupied. Each unit is individually owned, and even if a developer could be found who wanted to build on the block, the 40 percent of occupied houses would have to be acquired piece by piece, or the owners evicted by public action, which is in many cases politically impossible. This is a primary reason Kensington in particular, almost literally within the shadow of Center City, has attracted virtually no investment. It is just too hard to put a decent-size piece of land together.

"When you pass under the elevated train tracks just east of the Temple University campus," the journalist Rob Gurwitt wrote a few years ago, "you find yourself on streets whose gutters are lined with trash and broken glass. Although in the minds of most Philadelphians this area is just a uniform sea of blight, that's not the case; it's much more variegated than that. There are mostly vacant blocks, with one or two scruffy, vulnerable-looking houses still standing amid weed-grown fields. There are gap-toothed streets on which half the houses have been torn down and the lots are strewn with junk—old tires, a cardboard box with wood scraps sticking out, a few rusted paint cans—but the remaining houses are in decent shape. There are streets of aban-

A generation ago, Philadelphia's Kensington neighborhood provided stable row-house homes to thousands of blue-collar families whose breadwinners worked in nearby factories. Today, with those factories closed, the row-house blocks are lined with abandoned dwellings fit only for demolition—along with a scattering of home owners trying to hang on or waiting for renewal.

doned but intact row houses, their windows boarded up or jagged with broken glass. There's a street on which the corner houses are vacant but the rest of the block is made up of small, two-story row houses with undamaged cornices and carefully planted bushes and well-painted shutters that hang straight. You can even find entire blocks of neatly kept row houses, their bricks pointed, their brass address numbers gleaming." It is the houses with the straight shutters and the neatly planted bushes that are very difficult for the city to acquire, no matter how advanced the stage of decay around them.

THE RESULT of all this is an abandoned housing problem of staggering proportions. Philadelphia is, of course, far from the only major city in America to suffer from abandoned housing. On the East Coast, Baltimore's problem is almost as serious. In the Midwest, St. Louis has large swaths of abandoned territory, and Detroit, as is well-known, has them in virtually every section of the city. But those cities with a strong enough job base—Chicago, Boston, New York—and overall demand for places to live have a chance to escape from this condition. New York's South Bronx and portions of Brooklyn were wastelands in the 1980s; public and private subsidies and the overall scarcity of affordable places to live close to the center of the city revived many of these areas in the first decade of the new century.

But the sheer volume of abandoned housing in Philadelphia sometimes makes the problem there seem as intractable as Detroit's. In the middle of the past decade, the number of abandoned properties approached sixty thousand in a city of 1.5 million people. In a study of eighty-three cities conducted by the Brookings Institution, Philadelphia was found to have the largest proportion of abandoned properties: 36.5 for every one thousand residential units. This is a major reason crime was slow to decline in Philadelphia the way it had in other large American cities. Boston and Chicago have crime to worry about, but they do not have huge swaths of abandoned territory for criminals to use as a breeding ground. Most of the residential buildings in these cities, even the blighted ones, have somebody who wants to live in them. In this respect, Philadelphia is simply different. It resembles Detroit more than it does the successful American cities of the twenty-first century.

And the crime statistics have consistently borne this out. Throughout the past decade, as murder rates were going down in most cities, they remained stubbornly high in Philadelphia—as witnessed by the 406 homicides recorded in 2006. Since then, the numbers have come down roughly in tandem with those in the rest of the country, but the level of violence on Philadelphia's partially abandoned streets continues to be an embarrassment and a civic preoccupation. In 2010, the number of major crimes stood at 76,334—it had been over 100,000—but the city's prison population remained over 8,000. New York, with more than five times as many people, had a prison population of less than 14,000.

None of this has had a major impact on Center City. As a local demographer points out, "No one sitting in a sidewalk café ever gets gunned down. . . . But the perception of crime is still a huge problem." It is one more barrier that keeps the vibrancy of the center confined within a narrow (although gradually expanding) enclave.

Crime and abandoned housing are interrelated problems that sometimes seem intractable in Philadelphia. The crucial role played by abandoned housing in maintaining Philadelphia's "Bostroit" demographic has been a preoccupation of the city's leaders for more than a decade. Former mayor John Street took over in 1999 determined to focus on the estimated sixty thousand abandoned properties that were the most obvious obstacle to the city's broad-scale renewal. Deciding that the problem could never be dealt with on a piecemeal, block-by-block basis, he won passage of a $295 million city bond issue aimed at tearing down fourteen thousand abandoned buildings and replacing them with sixteen thousand new homes. He called it the Neighborhood Transformation Initiative.

"If you were to aggregate all the vacant land in Philadelphia," Street's chief of staff said at the time, "you would have a landmass the size of Center City. Some of the neighborhoods are so devastated that you look around and realize, if you just took down the two or three buildings left standing, you would have acres. And we might really be positioned to do something with this land if we just get a handle on it."

Outside experts who came to look at the Neighborhood Transformation Initiative were impressed. "What you generally see is tinkering around the edges as Rome burns," said Bruce Katz, director of the Metropolitan Policy Program at the Brookings Institution. "This is not your run-of-the-mill initiative here. It is highly unusual and very ambitious, and extremely smart in the way it has been designed. . . . It treats land as one of the fundamentals."

In the end, though, Street's initiative was little more than an ambitious failure. By the time of the mayor's departure in 2007, twenty-one thousand new housing units had been created in Philadelphia, but many of these were condos in Center City and had nothing to do with the slum-clearance program. Only about five thousand existing buildings were demolished. Most of the bond money was spent on previously existing housing programs, largely to replace federal funding that had dried up.

What the Neighborhood Transformation Initiative was really good at was removing cars. By 2007, the initiative reported that it had taken 289,000 abandoned automobiles off Philadelphia's streets. One might wonder how any city, even one of Philadelphia's size, could possibly have that many junk-heap cars on the street. But that is beside the point. The bottom line is that Philadelphia has nearly as many uninhabitable neighborhoods today as it did a decade ago.

PHILADELPHIA'S ROW-HOUSE neighborhoods might have remained mostly intact had one thing happened: the arrival of immigrants. If the city, in the last quarter of the old century, had attracted a large cadre of newcomers from foreign countries, they might have been willing to settle in the houses at bargain prices, accept the safety concerns, and nurse the buildings themselves back to decent physical condition. But no such event occurred.

Philadelphia was once a city of immigrants, attracting Irish and Germans in the eighteenth and nineteenth centuries and Italians in the early twentieth—in 1910, a quarter of its population was foreign-born. But it did not become a magnet for immigrants in the years after immigration restrictions were lifted in 1965. While Los Angeles, New

York, and Chicago were being remade during those years as multi-ethnic communities, Philadelphia remained through the 1990s a place where demography and politics were almost entirely a matter of black and white.

The number of new arrivals picked up considerably during the last decade, with the immigrant population of the area as a whole growing by 113,000 in the first six years of the new century. Indeed, it has been estimated that three-quarters of the region's job growth in those years was the direct result of immigration.

Most of the recent immigrants have settled in the suburbs, but a fair number congregated within the city itself: Nepalese in the neighborhoods around the University of Pennsylvania; Russians in the northeast; Liberians and Ghanaians in parts of west Philadelphia; and Mexicans in South Philly, where they have turned the legendary Italian Market into what should more properly be called the Italian/Hispanic Market.

But when it comes to reviving the most troubled neighborhoods, it has been too little and too late. In 2007, Philadelphia ranked tenth among the ten most populous American cities in the percentage of its population that was foreign-born, with only 9 percent. Among Eastern cities of any significant size, only Baltimore ranked lower. New York City, by comparison, was 37 percent foreign-born. And even though the numbers have picked up, what matters most is that during the years when the row-house neighborhoods were losing their original home owners, there was no significant immigrant cohort available to revive them. When the immigrants did start coming, early in the new century, many of these neighborhoods were simply too far gone for any purchaser, native or immigrant, to reclaim them.

Why did Philadelphia fail to attract the immigrants who could have done it so much good? One explanation is that in recent times, immigrant magnets have all possessed hub airports and regularly scheduled international flights, and Philadelphia has been stuck with a regional airport with few flights to anyplace outside the United States. For Asians or Latin Americans seeking to relocate, Philadelphia has simply been hard to get to. The cities that attracted the largest share of immigrants between 1970 and 2000 were all cities with decent air connections. When Atlanta's Hartsfield-Jackson airport inaugurated nonstop service to Rio de Janeiro, traffic on the route reached fifty thousand passengers within one year, and the majority of these were Brazilians seeking to settle in the United States. Philadelphia offered no such service, to Rio or virtually any other foreign capital. As of 2010, there was still no direct service from Philadelphia's airport to anywhere in Asia.

But immigration is not primarily a matter of travel connections. Until very recently, Philadelphia not only didn't lure in many immigrants, it didn't seem to want them very much. In the words of Feather Houstoun, of the William Penn Foundation, "Philadelphia has traditionally not been very tolerant of immigrants." When a member of the city council tried a few years ago to create an Office of Immigration, arguing that the city was losing out on an important source of economic vitality, the move attracted noisy political opposition from nativist council colleagues and had to be abandoned. The current mayor, Michael Nutter, ran for office on a pledge to bring more immigrants to Philadelphia as a way of increasing the number of jobs, and later issued an executive order maintaining that all immigrants, even undocumented ones, were to receive city services. But none of this will do much to revive the neighborhoods that needed help so badly in the 1970s, 1980s, and 1990s.

There is another explanation for the slow rate of immigration in the crucial decades of the late twentieth century, and it may in the end be the most important one. Immigrants create jobs, but they also show up in places that are already creating jobs, and Philadelphia simply has not done this very well in the past thirty years. During that period, Chicago actually lost more manufacturing jobs than Philadelphia—almost six hundred thousand of them. But Chicago essentially replaced these with other jobs; Philadelphia did not. As the Metropolitan Philadelphia Policy Center complained in 2001, "We simply don't have enough economic vitality to draw immigrant entrepreneurs in large numbers."

Philadelphia has enough well-paying jobs in Center City to keep that part of town affluent and lively, but the hollowing out of the manufacturing sector in the 1970s and 1980s was a calamity from which Philadelphia, unlike other major cities, has been unable to recover. As the University of Pennsylvania's David Thornburgh puts it, "The game is not keeping people; it's bringing people in. Not enough people have wanted to come here."

THAT, OF COURSE, begs the question of why people have not wanted to come to Philadelphia. It is a bit of a cause-and-effect question: Have newcomers been repelled by all the blighted neighborhoods, or did the neighborhoods become as blighted as they did because the newcomers were so few? This is not an easy question to resolve.

One of the first points to make in partial explanation of Philadelphia's lackluster economic development is that it is not really the heart of any region or segment of the economy. As economic development commissioner Alan Greenberger said in 2010, "New York considers itself the capital of the known universe. Boston is the capital of New England; Chicago is the capital of the Midwest. Philadelphia isn't the capital of anything." The one economic engine that seemed to make Philadelphia a commercial powerhouse, its port, has long since ceased to play that role. Today, the port of Philadelphia is only the fifth-busiest on the East Coast, behind New York, Boston, Baltimore, and Norfolk. In Greenberger's view, the failure of Philadelphia to establish itself in modern times as the "capital" of anything has had an impact that stretches well beyond the problem of job creation. While the remnant of a corporate elite still exists, it is not robust enough, many Philadelphians feel, to support massive revitalization projects on the order of Millennium Park, the joint public and private initiative that has reinforced Chicago's status as a global city in the new century. "We don't have the economic juice to do things other cities do," Greenberger argues. In other words, too little private economic development means a lack of ambition in the public realm. And the lack of ambition discourages the attraction of new private players, in a spiral of negative feedback that is very difficult to escape from.

But this argument can be taken only so far. If Philadelphia has ceased to be the capital of anything, it is arguably the best-located city on the eastern seaboard: squarely in the middle of the most populous corridor in the United States, halfway between Washington and New York, and a comparatively short distance from Boston. Philadelphia is so close to so many capitals of different kinds, one wonders why it really needs to be the capital of anything itself. It is a short ride from virtually everything. Not being a capital city may have slowed down the pace of economic development, but the mere fact of Philadelphia's physical centrality seems to have been sufficient to attract and keep the affluent population that has revived Center City in the past decade.

So if we are looking for reasons Philadelphia has been unable to break out of its "Bostroit" box, it is necessary to seek out other factors as well. It is necessary to look at factors that pertain more directly to government and public policy.

ANY DISCUSSION of Philadelphia's economic development problems has to focus on the wage tax. No one in public life defends it, but it has remained on the books since 1939, when the Pennsylvania legislature allowed jurisdictions in the state to impose it as a temporary means of managing Depression-era fiscal shortfalls. Residents of Philadelphia who work in the city currently pay 3.928 percent of their earned income to the city, deducted automatically from their paychecks. Nonresidents who work in the city pay about 3.5 percent. These rates reflect modest reductions enacted during the past decade, but as we've seen, the tax remains the single largest source of public revenue, making Philadelphia unique among major American cities. In a city where an unusually large percentage of voters are owners of small row houses, the property tax is almost impossible to increase. Mayor Nutter found that out in 2009, his first year in office, when he sought to trade a wage tax reduction for a modest property tax increase, and ended up having to trade it for a sales tax increase instead.

So the wage tax remains even though it is a flat-out incentive for employers to move outside the city. Philadelphia law firms and other Center City businesses routinely locate their back-office operations in the suburbs to avoid it, costing the city job growth it badly needs. As political scientist David Thornburgh puts it, "Our employment trajectory has been shaped by our tax structure."

But it isn't just the structure that holds Philadelphia back: It's the amount of tax that its residents and workers pay. In 2009, according to the Philadelphia Research Initiative, a family of three making $50,000 a year paid 17.3 percent of its income in taxation. This compared to 8.5 percent in New York, 7.8 percent in Boston, and 7.1 percent in Chicago. Philadelphians were paying these taxes to support a system of public employee benefits that strains the city budget even in prosperous times.

The amount of its budget that Philadelphia spends on pensions for its former employees has long exceeded that of almost every other large American city. This is a function of very generous contracts agreed to by a whole succession of mayors in order to buy labor peace, but it is also a function of the sheer number of workers. In 1955, with a population of more than 2 million, the city had 24,560 employees. In 2000, the population was 31 percent smaller, but the number of employees had increased.

Philadelphia's two most serious fiscal burdens—the wage tax and the benefits—could probably be solved by reform-minded leadership that possessed the concentrated political power to make responsible decisions in the face of popular opposition. For a variety of complex reasons, Philadelphia has not had that in recent years, and may not have it in the foreseeable future.

When it comes to politics, Philadelphia has the worst of both worlds: It is a machine city without a boss available to run the machine. "It's a ridiculously weak executive form of government," says John DiIulio. "It's not that the problems should be worse than other places. It's the leadership."

The machine seems to function on residual energy, and in anachronistic fashion. The city council has ten members elected by district who treat their districts as virtual fiefdoms, and who have the effective power to veto any project within their constituency that they or their constituents don't like. When a program is proposed, its benefits usually have to be spread around all the council districts in order for it to be enacted. This is one reason Mayor Street's Neighborhood Transformation Initiative was largely a disappointment: Instead of targeting a small number of neighborhoods that needed it most, it had to be extended virtually citywide, thus diluting its impact on any one part of Philadelphia.

The parochialism of Philadelphia politics is merely one more reflection of the widely felt parochialism of its culture, the native orneriness that not only sets races and classes against one another, but casts seemingly similar communities as rivals rather than cooperating entities. Janet Rothenberg Pack, a public policy professor at the University of Pennsylvania, wrote a few years ago that "Philadelphia is remarkable in terms of its provincialism. It's a city of neighborhoods but the neighborhoods don't like each other." Alan Greenberger, the economic development commissioner, put it a little differently. "Being aggravated and contentious is part of who we are," he said. One would be foolish to blame all of Philadelphia's troubles, or even most of them, on its parochialism and insularity. But it matters.

Philadelphia is still the only large American city in which no one is surprised when parade watchers boo Santa Claus, where fans boo their sports teams for failing to win a second consecutive championship, or where grandmothers at the stadium insult spectators who happen to be wearing the wrong jersey. These are small things, taken alone, but when added together, they contribute to a reputation that ultimately has its bearing on the level of investment and needed in-migration that the city cannot fully succeed without. The cities that are gaining ground in the postindustrial world are cosmopolitan and diverse, and for the most part tolerant. Philadelphia, despite its vibrant center and cultural richness, has yet to make that crucial transition. "I've lived in the Midwest, California, and Florida," the newspaper columnist Monica Yant Kinney wrote late in 2010, "but in no other place have people fixated as much on the hyperlocal specifics of where one rests her head. . . . As long as Philadelphia remains an island—unlike, say Cook County, which envelops Chicago and thirty suburban townships—territorial grudges linger."

It would be foolish to pretend that all successful big cities in America have fully overcome such grudges. And it seems quite possible that Philadelphia, with a much more diverse population cohort in 2012 than it had in 2000, will make steady progress toward surmounting them. In the meantime, however, parochialism is a problem that affects not only the city's social climate but its economic prospects.

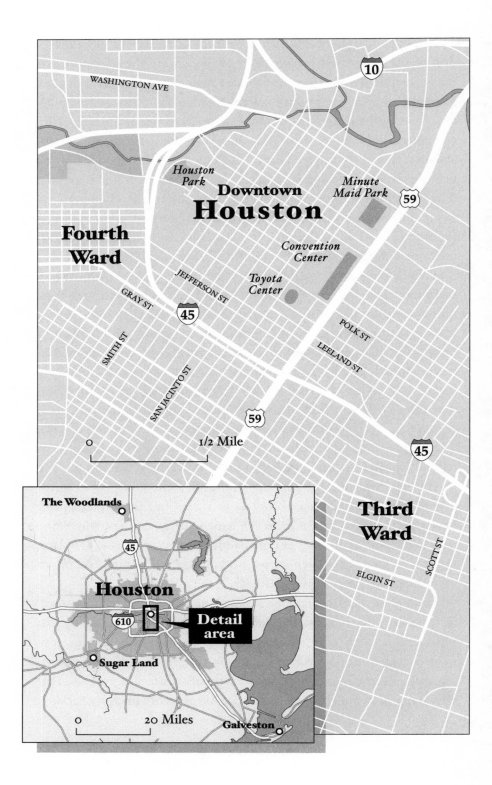

WASHINGTON AVE

Houston
Park

Downtown
Houston

Minute
Maid Park

**Fourth
Ward**

Convention
Center

Toyota
Center

JEFFERSON ST

GRAY ST

SMITH ST

SAN JACINTO ST

POLK ST

LEELAND ST

0   1/2 Mile

The Woodlands

Houston

Detail
area

Sugar Land

0   20 Miles

Galveston

**Third
Ward**

ELGIN ST

SCOTT ST

CHAPTER SEVEN

THE URBAN SQUEEZE

AT THE CORNER of Dowling and Elgin streets, in the middle of Houston's Third Ward, is a small green plot of land called Emancipation Park. It has been there since 1872. Emancipation Park was the place where ex-slaves gathered for a celebration every year on June 19, the anniversary of the day in 1865 when they learned they had been set free. They sang and danced and ate smoked meat and drank red soda water. Many of the freed slaves lived in the neighborhood; they could buy ten acres of farmland for a relative pittance, although not many had anything resembling the means to afford it. Emancipation Park was a gathering place through the decades, as black businesses and institutions grew up around it. In the 1940s, Cab Calloway sang "Minnie the Moocher" at the El Dorado Club, just adjacent to the park.

Farther up the street on Dowling were all the symbols of what was called the "parallel black economy": churches, insurance companies, funeral homes, movie theaters, beauty and barber colleges, and photography studios. At Twenty-fourth and Dowling was the headquarters of the Grand Court Order of Calanthe, an organization whose cornerstone reveals that it is "Dedicated to Negro Womanhood."

The park, the Calanthe clubhouse, and the El Dorado Club building are unusual in one respect: They are still there. Most of the tangible institutions of segregation-era black life exist only as photographs and dim memories now, their remains part of the landscape of vacant lots that take up more space in this part of the Third Ward than the buildings that remain. The vast expanses of empty land give the Third Ward almost a rural Southern quality. It is possible to see the remnants of the old neighborhood as a precious heritage that needs to be preserved

This commercial building in Houston's close-in Third Ward, once a social center for the city's black community, is one among many dilapidated structures that have been vulnerable to the onslaught of new residential development and middle-class gentrification.

at all costs; it is also possible to see them as a nearly empty wasteland afflicted by poverty, crime, and drugs, and far more in need of massive redevelopment than of any nostalgic commitment to the past.

Between the vacant lots are shotgun shacks, rickety wooden houses unlike anything one sees in the dilapidated sections of any city outside the South. Many of them were originally built as servants' quarters to house the black maids and laborers who worked in the homes of the affluent at the southern end of the district, in the MacGregor neighborhood along Brays Bayou. Few of these structures are more than twelve feet wide, and the lots are rarely more than thirty feet wide. The rooms lead straight back from the front door, with a living room first, then a bedroom and a kitchen and usually a bathroom at the rear. They are nearly all owned by absentee landlords, some the descendants of original owners who have long since moved away and do not want to spend money on repairs. But despite their condition, they provide shelter for renters who cannot afford to rent anywhere else. Their one notably desirable feature is cross-ventilation, created by the absence of hallways, that sends a breeze moving straight through the house during the sweltering summer months.

Historic though it may be, the upper Third Ward is an important part of Houston's future not because of its past or present, but because of what it might become. It lies in the shadow of Houston's downtown, which contains a forest of oil company skyscrapers, an immense convention center, theaters and concert halls, municipal parks, and a baseball stadium. Not many people live within the strict confines of downtown—that is in part because, unlike in Chicago or New York, there are few old office buildings to convert to residential use. In the words of Bob Eury, the downtown economic development manager, "We're supply-constrained down here. The downtown was basically abandoned. There was a hollowing out of the core. We tore it all down." But 140,000 people work downtown every day, most of them members of Houston's multiracial middle class, and they have moved at a rapid pace into the neighborhoods that surround the inner core on the north and west, and now gradually in the eastern corner as well. Most of them live in neighborhoods that are less convenient to their jobs than a home in the Third Ward would be—if the vacant land sprouted townhouses and the remaining shotgun shacks were sold to developers. Right now, the Third Ward has approximately fifteen hundred newcomers living in recently erected two- and three-story townhouse buildings. It is quite possible that there could be twenty or thirty thousand new residents if the ward acquired the momentum of a building boom. That would be a majority of the ward's population. As former Houston mayor Bill White once said, "The Third Ward is the epicenter of gentrification."

But despite the pent-up demand, it is not gentrifying rapidly at the moment. The reason is not the residual effects of the recession. The reason is Garnet Coleman, the Texas state representative who represents the area and is determined not to let it happen.

Garnet Coleman, who is fifty years old, has represented the Third Ward and adjoining parts of central Houston since he was thirty. He was born to social prestige and political influence in Houston's black community. His father, John B. Coleman, was a widely respected physician and banker. The building where Garnet Coleman's office sits, on Almeda Avenue at the southern end of the old Third Ward commercial district, is the John B. Coleman Center.

As a state legislator in Austin, Garnet Coleman has been widely recognized for his efforts in health care, particularly for protecting funding for the Children's Health Insurance Program. But as a power broker in Houston politics, he has focused on a much different goal: keeping middle-class townhouses out of the upper Third Ward. His method is simple: buying land and holding on to it so it can't be developed. There is no one quite like him in any inner-city neighborhood in America.

To understand what Garnet Coleman is doing, it is necessary to try to see the Third Ward the way he sees it—as a place where his family has lived for a century, as a place whose few remaining landmarks are a shrine to African American culture, and, most important, as a place whose poor black residents will be forced to leave as shotgun property owners sell their land and the buildings are torn down one by one. There is nothing in Garnet Coleman's record or his public statements that suggests he is a racist. "I'm an egalitarian like everyone else," he told a reporter in 2009. "Talking about the racial aspect of all this, or saying this is born of race, is not something I feel absolutely comfortable with."

Coleman insists that he wants economic development in the Third Ward. He just wants it to build on what's been there—or the remains of what's been there—for the past hundred years. "If somebody's going to move into the Third Ward," he said in 2010, "I don't care who you are, just become a part of it. Don't come into the community, renovate your house, then act like the people who have been living there have no standing."

In fact, Coleman wants to discourage the arrival of a black affluent elite as much as he does a white one. He insists that young professional townhouse buyers have no desire to form close relationships with members of the existing community, merely a wish to live in a convenient place near urban amenities and wall themselves off from their neighbors. "Quite frankly, this is personal," he concedes. "We just don't want to be the only people who have to adjust to the world. We'd like the world to adapt to us a little bit."

Coleman's methods are both legally complex and economically simple. He isn't spending his own money to buy land. He's spending money that belongs to a tax increment financing district, which he sits on the board of. The special districts, known in Houston as Tax Increment Reinvestment Zones, receive a substantial amount of money from the city each year for the ostensible purpose of increasing the overall property value of city neighborhoods and reaping the financial benefits of the higher value. Tax increases generated by new development stay with the TIRZ for a period of twenty-five to thirty years, and bonds are sold to make improvements based on paying bondholders back with the added increment. The TIRZ districts have the right to build or support affordable housing in the communities where they are located, but they also have the right simply to acquire vacant land or abandoned properties and hold them for an indefinite period.

Coleman, as a major player in the Midtown TIRZ, has control of a large pot of money. As state representative, he has sway over the appointment of a substantial number of the TIRZ board members. In the past decade, the Midtown TIRZ has spent roughly $15 million to buy 1.5 million square feet of land in the northern section of the Third Ward, closest to downtown. The land is sold to churches and nonprofits with restrictive covenants that block any eventual sale to private developers. In most cases, the price is about $10 a square foot. The previous value of the land was $3 to $4 a square foot. If the land were available now on the open market, Coleman estimates, the value would be closer to $25. If he wanted to, he believes, he could sell it for even more and developers would simply sit on the land themselves, waiting for the right moment to promote a gentrified townhouse project.

"Our goals are two-pronged," he says. "One is to provide affordable housing; the other is to prevent gentrification. Has the affordable housing been built? No. But that was only part of the objective. If you ask me, we should just keep buying land and banking everything that we buy. This is a chess match. There aren't many tools left for communities to protect themselves."

At the start of the last decade, the Third Ward as a whole had a population of slightly more than fifteen thousand, of whom roughly twelve thousand were black and about one thousand were white. But Coleman has not focused his land banking on the entire ward—he's focused on the northern sections, represented most clearly by census tract 3123, concentrated north of Alabama Street. In 2000, census tract 3123 was still almost exclusively black—2,088 African Americans to only 67 white residents. Data from American Community Survey reports toward the end of the decade showed a considerable increase in the white population. But none of the figures count the land on which no structure remains standing at all. A 2000 census map of tract 3123 shows large blocks of land colored in gray, meaning that the land is undeveloped. Coleman has succeeded in keeping the amount of gentrification down in the Third Ward, but at the cost of increasing the amount of emptiness.

There are those who think Coleman, for all his acknowledged political and economic influence, is on a fool's errand—that the Third Ward is simply too close to downtown to prevent a demographic inversion, and that one will come relatively soon no matter how much land Coleman is able to bank. What Coleman is saying, says University of

Houston architecture professor Tom Diehl, "is, 'Give us our blight.' Eventually they are going to get booted out to the suburbs. There's no way to stop it."

Coleman is no fool. He knows that is possible. But he believes he can assemble enough land to stop the transformation—and the eviction of his constituents—for years, if not decades. "If we weren't banking land it would be over. It would all be filled in. Whole city blocks would be townhouses. There would be the equivalent of New York row houses."

ONE REASON Coleman can be fairly certain of his point is that something very similar happened in the 1990s, in the adjoining district of Houston's old inner city, the Fourth Ward.

Before the Third Ward became the center of Houston's African American life, that distinction belonged to the Fourth, a smaller enclave that sat just to the west of the downtown commercial district. The Fourth Ward was the home of Freedmen's Town, where slaves settled immediately after the Civil War as they moved north along the Brazos River from rural south Texas. Like the Third, the Fourth Ward was a neighborhood of shotgun houses and brick streets, the bricks handmade by the residents themselves, many of whom were skilled masons. A majority of its residents were black, and they formed the largest concentration of black residents anywhere in the Houston area. More than 80 percent of the city's black doctors lived there.

By the 1930s, however, the Fourth Ward had been eclipsed by the Third as a place for middle-class blacks to live, and it slid deeper into poverty and disrepair. Construction of Interstate 45 in the 1950s essentially cut the neighborhood in half, further consigning it to a status as downtown's ugly and unvisited backyard. By the 1980s, more than 50 percent of the residents were below the federal poverty line. To most Houstonians, the ward was known mainly as home to the decrepit and dangerous Allen Parkway Village housing project, 963 low-rise redbrick apartment units constructed as a home for defense workers during World War II. Forty years later, it was a haven of crime and crack addiction. The city spent years debating plans to tear it down and replace it with more livable housing units for the ward's dwindling number of residents.

Finally, in the 1990s, Mayor Bob Lanier and the federal Department of Housing and Urban Development agreed on a plan called Houston Renaissance, under which most of Allen Parkway Village would be bulldozed. Developers would replace a majority of the units with new subsidized housing designed to echo the area's shotgun architectural past. In return, they would be permitted to build market-rate townhouses on much of the rest of Fourth Ward land, reaping profits that would allow them to finance the subsidized component.

The intention was not to obliterate the Fourth Ward's history and existence as a neighborhood, but that is what happened. For all the blight, there were 530 formally designated historic structures left in the ward as late as 1984; today there are fewer than 30. Some subsidized units were built, but most of the shacks were replaced by modern red-brick townhouses on land bought cheaply by the development firm Perry Homes. These dwellings sold at market rates to downtown office workers and covered much more of the ward than the original Houston Renaissance plans had called for. Many of them were gated at the entrance. Critics complained that Perry Homes had simply grafted suburban-style tract housing onto a fragile but irreplaceable piece of Houston history.

Defenders of the transformation insisted that there was little in the Fourth Ward worth preserving. "When you look at what they were being displaced from," said loft developer Larry Davis, "the houses were totally run-down; they should have been torn down. The only culture displaced was a culture of needles and syringes." Some of the remaining residents felt the same way. "If it's historic, it needs to be restored. Don't just leave a crack house sitting there. A lot of the people in the historic preservation society don't live in this neighborhood," one of them told a reporter in 2007. "They are not having to deal with people using these homes for prostitution, drug dealing, and drug using."

For his part, Mayor Lanier vehemently insisted that bulldozing the Fourth Ward out of existence had never been what he wanted.

"Gentrification was never my goal," he said a few years ago. "If you restrict it to rich people, I think that would be a mistake. I like to see mixed-income presence." Nevertheless, the fact remains that virtually all of the Fourth Ward, including Freedmen's Town and hundreds of nineteenth-century shotgun houses, has ceased to exist. In 2000, there were only 635 black people living in the ward. The Fourth is precisely the kind of noncommunity that Mayor Lanier professed not to desire. And it is the specter that haunts Garnet Coleman as he continues using public funds to buy up land and prevent gentrification from spreading.

Of course, in the Third Ward, as in any neighborhood, it makes an enormous difference whether one is a renter or an owner. Those who own their properties potentially stand to benefit from a sustained increase in their value. But in the Third Ward, there simply aren't very many owners—and those who do own houses face the prospect of their property taxes rising so high that they will be forced to sell out and leave the neighborhood behind.

The city of Houston itself has developed programs to try to preserve affordable housing in the Third and Fourth wards and slow down the process of gentrification, but they haven't accomplished a great deal. One is LARA, the Land Assemblage Redevelopment Authority, which acquires tax-delinquent properties and sells them to local buyers at subsidized prices. The difficulty with LARA is that it competes with private developers, and the developers nearly always outbid the city. Some critics have suggested that LARA may even hasten gentrification by encouraging developers to bid on properties before the city can get them. In its first five years, LARA acquired fewer than thirty houses—a drop in the bucket.

More ambitious was Houston HOPE, launched with considerable fanfare by the White administration in 2004. Using a combination of city money and private philanthropy, Houston HOPE was designed to foreclose on delinquent properties rather than bidding for them in the open market, and work with developers to create new affordable projects for local ownership, with public money provided to help the buyers make down payments. The maximum sale price for the Houston HOPE units was $150,000, with up to $45,000 in down payment assistance to the purchasers. Over six years, Houston HOPE acquired 1,110 abandoned lots, with an average tax delinquency of eighteen years. It built 382 new homes and repaired more than 1,000 others. It assisted in the construction of projects in nine neighborhoods, aimed at replacing some of the units eliminated with the destruction of Allen Parkway Village. White called Houston HOPE "redevelopment that's the opposite of gentrification . . . It's good that there are people who want to live in the city limits, but we don't want to destroy the character of a neighborhood. Unless we do something aggressive, the market will build in concentric circles around the employment center."

But in the teeth of a national recession, Houston HOPE simply ran out of development opportunities. Early in 2010, faced with a decline in contributions from private sources, Houston HOPE ceased its lending and development programs altogether.

One community that did not participate actively in Houston HOPE was Garnet Coleman's Third Ward. Coleman does not believe in spending his TIRZ money to stimulate home buying. What he wants is to keep renters in their dwellings. One effort that Coleman has supported is Project Row Houses, a collection of apartment buildings designed to look like modern versions of the old shotgun houses. It's a small project, several dozen buildings created and developed by Rick Lowe, a local artist who builds the units and then rents them out at subsidized rates to existing neighborhood tenants, many of them senior citizens. One experiment is a collection of duplexes rented entirely to single mothers. There's no foreclosure problem at Project Row Houses, because there are no mortgages offered.

Lowe is fully on board with the elements of Coleman's strategy. "Every time one of these little old houses goes down through fire," he says, "or a landlord decides, 'I don't want to do this anymore,' it means there's one less opportunity for someone to ever live in those neighborhoods again." Still, he is under no illusions. "You will see basically in ten years a scattered hodgepodge of townhouses throughout all this area," he has predicted. "It's just going to happen. Hopefully the exception will be this little row house village we're doing."

· · ·

HOUSTON DIFFERS from other rapidly changing cities in several important ways. One is sheer geographical size. At 620 square miles, it is big enough to hold all of Portland, Baltimore, and Detroit within its city limits. It is less than half as dense as Los Angeles. When people talk about central Houston, they are usually referring not to downtown or even the close-in wards but to the area inside Interstate Highway 610, which functions as an inner beltway. But Interstate 610 is a giant rectangle stretching nearly seven miles from north to south and eight miles from east to west, holding a quarter of the city's 2.2 million people. No other large American city would refer to a "center" this vast.

Indeed, the heart of the oversize in-town area is relatively free of residents: Only 4,100 people lived in the downtown business core in 2009. There was one major new high-rise development, One Park Place, thirty-seven stories and 346 units in rose-colored brick masonry alongside the new and expensively outfitted Discovery Green park, which boasts theaters, ice skating, and restaurants; One Park Place was 60 percent occupied as of early 2010. But there was little of comparable scope on the drawing boards.

Where urban development is most obvious in Houston is in the neighborhoods that ring the downtown core, some historic in the way that the Third Ward is, but others, composed of unused industrial land, that do not require significant displacement of existing residents to generate new residential opportunities. Within just a two-mile radius of the city's historic commercial center, in 2010, there was a population of forty-four thousand. Within a four-mile arc there was a population of three hundred thousand.

What's striking is how many residents of the area say they want to live some form of urbanized existence. In a survey conducted early in 2010 by the Rice University Kinder Institute for Urban Research, 41 percent of the 750 respondents, including those currently well outside the 610 perimeter, said they would like to move to "a smaller home in a more urbanized area, within walking distance of shops and workplaces." The survey also showed that 57 percent opted for "a single-family home with a big yard, where you would need to drive almost everywhere you wanted to go." But in a city such as Houston, the percentages aren't as important as the absolute numbers. Forty-one percent of two million is a little more than eight hundred thousand people. What seems equally important in this survey is the comparison over time, especially among Anglos. In 1999, some 46 percent of Anglo city dwellers expressed a desire to move to the suburbs, while only 28 percent of suburbanites said they would like to move to the city. Today, those figures have evened out. Twenty-five percent of those in the city want to go to the suburbs; 23 percent of the suburbanites expressed a desire for urbanized living. Given the increasing appeal of an urban-centered life, freed from the long commutes and the auto dependency of a home far out on the periphery, it seems possible that those figures will shift further toward the center of the city in the years ahead. The likelihood that central Houston will ever be a pedestrian mecca, like neighborhoods in New York, Chicago, Philadelphia, or Boston, may be slim, given the heat that makes a stroll down the streets an unpleasant experience during so many months of the year. But whether or not there is a revival of all-day street life, there seems as much potential as in many other cities for urbanized existence of some variety.

THE FUTURE URBANIZED HOUSTON would not look much like big Northern cities. The downtown residential population is unlikely to increase very much; nor will the number of downtown jobs. Downtown currently holds about 23 percent of the office space in the Houston region, largely because major oil companies have made a downtown commitment, and because a new downtown energy complex has sprung up around the wind-power industry. But the percentage of Houston-area workers employed downtown is much smaller than that, and few expect that the overall downtown employment percentage will change very much in the coming years. Instead, Houston will have to urbanize around its satellite employment, retail, and residential centers, of which there are a large number, most of them inside the 610 loop but some at a considerable distance outside. According to Stephen Klineberg of Rice University, who conducts the annual survey of resident choices and opinions, Houston can actually be said to have five to eight downtowns, and eighteen centers of activity. Houston is, in the language of urban sociology, a "multicentered metropolitan region." And many of those quasi-urbanized centers remain comparatively cheap compared to similar urbanizing patches in other cities. As Klineberg says, "If the rich are going into downtown now, there are other centers that are still affordable."

For many students of Houston, the reason for the city's comparative affordability is a simple one: the absence of zoning laws. In fact, the commonly held image of Houston as a wide-open build-what-you-want-anywhere-you-want city is somewhat exaggerated: Chapter 42 of the city's municipal code provides for sewer controls, and for a developer of substantial properties, these can be used to serve the same limiting purpose as a formal zoning law. There are also deed restrictions, of the sort that Garnet Coleman has employed successfully in the Third Ward; these can be written by the developer himself, and can, for example, impose legally enforceable rules about the number of low- or moderate-income tenants or buyers a project must contain.

Even so, Houston's political leaders have traditionally believed that the absence of formal zoning makes it much easier for developers to operate. Mayor White once commented that "one reason Houston is affordable is that they don't have to pay lawyers several extra thousand per lot to go through a zoning."

Despite the existence of informal zoning by other municipal codes, several scholarly studies have pointed to the absence of zoning in its official sense as the main reason the city remained (relatively) affordable even in its most desirable districts during the height of the national real estate boom of the early 2000s.

In 2008, the Harvard economist Edward Glaeser published an essay in *City Journal* that attributed lower housing costs in Houston directly to the absence of official zoning laws and the relative simplicity of the permitting process. "The unavoidable fact," Glaeser wrote, "is that New York makes it a lot harder to build housing than Houston does. The permitting process in Manhattan is an arduous, unpredictable multiyear odyssey involving a dizzying array of regulations, environmental and otherwise, and a host of agencies. Then developers must deal with neighborhood activists and historical preservationists. Any effort to build in one of New York's more attractive, older communities would almost certainly face strong opposition from the Landmarks Preservation Commission. . . . Houston's builders have managed—better than in any other American city—to make the case to the public that restrictions on development will make the city less affordable to the less successful."

Not everyone agrees that the absence of zoning laws is a good thing for Houston. It is not hard to find planners who argue that, even though some controls do exist, it is an incongruous hodgepodge of a city, with townhouses and warehouses stacked next to one another because there is nothing in the statute books to prevent them from locating there. Planners in nearly all cities complain that the really important decisions are made by developers, not by planning professionals, but the case is far easier to make in Houston than almost anywhere else. In the words of architect and former mayoral candidate Peter Brown, "There are no tools to guide the growth of the city. . . . Not having zoning is a detriment when you're trying to determine what kind of city you will be." The reality in Houston is that if you want to build a small property or make substantial changes to an existing one, the process is easier than almost anywhere else in America. If you want to implement a master plan for the city or even a significant portion of it, there are enormous political and procedural obstacles. This is very nearly the opposite of what prevails in many American cities with a complex zoning code.

A cheaper, much messier city than nearly all its national counterparts: That is what the consensus seems to be, among those who watch it from the inside and those who observe from a distance. But one other point seems inescapable: A city without formal zoning is a city that changes faster than other cities do. It is much quicker to respond to even modest evolution of market demand. Developers in particular can react faster. "As long as they can put forth the required cash," says architecture professor Tom Diehl, "there are few prohibitions from getting dirt turned and foundations poured."

Among the changes that can occur faster in Houston is demographic inversion. The demand of the affluent to move closer to the center can be met quickly, through the construction of individual townhouses or condominiums without regard to any overall master plan for the site or the surrounding area. Small developers can do fill-ins without having to worry about the legality of a nonconforming use. As a report by the real estate analysis firm Metrostudy put it in 2006, "The type of development being done in riskier areas generally speaking tends to be small and somewhat opportunist. Find a site on a good corner, reasonable access, and they do a dozen townhouses."

While other cities hold seminars on the likely future of gentrification, Houston is in a position to gentrify virtually overnight. This is the main reason Garnet Coleman is buying up vacant land piece by piece in the Third Ward. Small-scale developers do not need to acquire large parcels or jump through bureaucratic hoops to start erecting homes for the affluent wherever there is an available piece of property. They can, to all intents and purposes, just show up and start digging.

The ease of building on small lots next to properties with radically different uses is what led to the accelerated population changes in the Fourth Ward in the 1990s. The Third Ward would have seen essentially the same process except for the amount of land banking that has taken place. Indeed, the southern parts of the Third Ward, closest to Houston's Museum District and to Texas Southern University, have seen a substantial transformation in the years since 2000. And over the course of a decade, without much attention being paid to it, central Houston in general has lost most of its white working class. The center of town has become an enclave of arriving Anglo professionals, a declining center for African Americans, and the home for a rapidly rising number of Hispanics taking over properties that African Americans have left. All of this has occurred, in large part, because it is so easy to create change one house at a time, instead of waiting for construction to be approved on large parcels.

Not all the changes are easy to document statistically, but they can be traced through changes in political behavior. The Anglos in the central-city townhouses have quickly become a dominant force in city elections. When Houston chose a new mayor, in November 2009, it is estimated that Anglos—mostly liberal Anglos—cast about 65 percent of the vote, even though the 2000 census had shown them to be only about 30 percent of the overall city population. Some of this was the result of a low turnout in which Anglos tended to vote more heavily, but a good deal of it also resulted from the rapid demographic changes of a build-to-market city. The winner of that mayoral election, Annise Parker, was the openly gay city auditor, and her sexual preference was a negligible factor in the campaign. Parker's election came as something of a shock to political observers from around the country who would not have expected Houston to make such a choice; it came as no surprise to those who had been watching the demographic changes in the city over the previous ten years.

To see the peculiar way in which central Houston is redeveloping itself, one need only walk around behind the immense George R. Brown Convention Center that borders Discovery Green. There one finds railroad tracks, warehouses, loading docks, huge amounts of vacant land, and, nestled in between, pockets of high-end townhouses built by Frank Liu, a Taiwanese-born real estate developer. He has made a specialty of squeezing homes for the professional class into blocks that look like wasteland on the outskirts of downtown and in the poorer neighborhoods immediately to the north.

Most of Liu's projects do not involve much displacement, if any, because rarely are there more than a handful of residents to displace. One of his largest parcels of unbuilt property is a Superfund pollution site. On Nagle Street, in the dingy backyard of the convention center, he is marketing a Mediterranean-style townhouse development with three-story condominiums, each more than two thousand square feet, complete with high ceilings, luxurious bathrooms, and huge picture windows.

To tell the truth, there isn't much to see out of the picture windows. The buyers are essentially purchasing property in a railroad yard. Liu makes a joke about this. "You've always loved trains," he tells some of the empty-nest suburbanites who make up a majority of the visitors on open-house days. "Congratulations! You get to be near the train." They are not near much of anything else. There is no grocery store within walking distance; for that matter, there is still no grocery store downtown, even on the more presentable west side of the convention center. It doesn't seem to make much difference. The demand persists anyway.

The area around Nagle Street never used to have a formal name; it was just the wasteland on the other side of the tracks from the convention center and the rest of downtown. Now it is called EaDo—East Downtown—and thanks to developers such as Frank Liu who are willing to build high-amenity homes on small and seemingly unpromising pockets of land, the population of EaDo is now roughly equal to the population of downtown itself. Even in the recessionary years that slowed the market in Houston and especially in its suburbs, new houses sold on Nagle Street. In the words of Bob Eury, of the Central Houston Civic Improvement organization, "You see people buying housing in Houston that you never would have imagined anyone buying."

The current population of the Nagle Street development, Liu estimates, is about 70 percent empty nesters and 30 percent young professional singles and couples. Almost no children live here. "The higher the price," Liu says, "the more empty nesters," who tend to ask about high-quality appliances, the amount of light streaming into the living room, elevator capability for future years, and sometimes smoking balconies for baby boom contemporaries who have not shed their tobacco habit. The young professional contingent places a higher priority on green features and energy savings.

There are twenty-seven units to one acre of land in this particular development—the empty nesters who buy there are often cutting the amount of their living space in half. But they don't seem to mind. "They've already fallen in love with intown," Liu says, citing an infatuation that even the most committed urbanites in most other American cities might find difficult to understand.

PERHAPS EVEN MORE dramatic than the infill going on in Houston's central neighborhoods is the urbanization of its more distant population centers built expressly for the automobile in the 1960s, 1970s, and

1980s. All over metropolitan Houston, far outside the 610 loop as well as within it, car-oriented suburban clusters are seeking ways to capture at least the trappings of urbanization.

The most prominent of these is The Woodlands, the massive conglomeration of nearly one hundred thousand people thirty miles north of downtown Houston that was conceived in the 1960s and 1970s as a virtual antidote to big-city life. Less than a decade ago, 80 percent of the people who lived in The Woodlands and worked in downtown Houston drove there. Today, by some estimates, that figure is closer to 30 percent. Large numbers drive to park-and-ride shuttle lots inside the Woodlands complex. Even more don't commute downtown at all—they earn their livings in the six-million-square-foot Woodlands commercial and retail complex. The majority of them seek recreation and entertainment opportunities along the 1.25-mile-long Woodlands Waterway, a linear park and transportation corridor whose promoters advertise it as a "pedestrian-friendly atmosphere" with "urban resi-

The Woodlands, a booming suburb that used to symbolize escape from Houston's problems, now seeks to market itself as an urbanized area centered on a waterway and surrounded by pedestrian-friendly places to live and shop.

dences like brownstones and lofts." The asphalt parking lots that used to line the center of The Woodlands are gradually being converted into a gridded street plan.

In Sugar Land, another freeway-created suburb of about eighty thousand people southwest of the city, something similar has happened in just the past five years. Sugar Land is now a suburban doughnut with a town center and city hall in the middle, and its advertising stresses that it has become an urbanized place—not the Sugar Land that Houstonians have in their heads. "Urban and Sugar Land were not always compatible words," one of the town brochures concedes. "Ten years ago Sugar Land was considered a quaint Houston suburb. Now it is working to provide an increasingly urban atmosphere for its increasing population." Tower Lofts, a ten-story luxury tower, is planned for the core of the town center itself.

The Woodlands and Sugar Land strike some visitors as ersatz urbanism, instant glitz without history, character, or meaningful community life. A loft apartment in downtown Sugar Land will never be confused with a house in one of Houston's leafy west-side neighborhoods. But the newly created streets are full of pedestrian traffic, and similar automobile suburbs all over metropolitan Houston are wondering whether they can emulate what Sugar Land and The Woodlands have created in a remarkably short time. "Everybody wants that," says David Crossley, who heads a group called Houston Tomorrow. "They look at Sugar Land and say, 'That's it.' . . . This concept is happening everywhere in Houston now. It's surprising how fast it has happened."

Or perhaps it isn't so surprising. If Stephen Klineberg's surveys are correct, and more than 40 percent of Houston-area residents really do want "a smaller home in a more urbanized area, within walking distance of shops and workplaces," then The Woodlands and Sugar Land and their emerging imitators are merely meeting a rapidly growing and inescapable demand. Only a tiny proportion of these people can live in the close-in neighborhoods west of downtown in the Mediterranean townhouses that Frank Liu is inserting on the vacant lots that surround the heart of the city. There simply isn't enough room for more. The only practical response to the demand is the urbanization of the suburbs.

From a classical urban standpoint, however, there remains one massive flaw in the suburban town concept: It is virtually impossible, at most hours, to get to any of these places without a car. How the area chooses to solve that problem—or whether it makes a meaningful attempt at all—will be a crucial part of the Houston story in the next few decades. No one is predicting that Houston residents, even those who live in rapidly urbanizing parts of the metropolitan area, will ever give up their dependence on automobiles. But in many places, the car-dependent life will be part of a much more complex mixture of living patterns and transportation uses than has existed for the past half century.

Like most cities, Houston once had an extensive streetcar system, but as in most of them, this essentially disappeared after World War II. From the 1950s through the 1980s, as Houston was ringing the entire metropolitan area with freeways, public transport was limited to an inadequate and generally unreliable bus network. In the early 2000s, a start was finally made on a light-rail system meant eventually to link the region's most important commercial and residential centers, then accessible for all practical purposes only by car. The first segment, seven miles of light-rail line running south from downtown to the city's huge medical center complex, opened in 2004 and has been both a success and a disappointment. Its average daily ridership of about forty-five thousand, mostly recreational or shopping users rather than commuters, has exceeded early projections. But the line has not led to transit-oriented residential development directly along the route, as many of the early planners had hoped. Much of the adjacent land has been bought up by speculators willing to pay as much as $50 a square foot to sit on the property pending future demand. So the first segment has not produced much new residential construction in the immediate vicinity of the new tracks.

Now, however, Houston is on the verge of constructing something much more ambitious: thirty miles of light-rail transit with sixty-five new stations, scheduled for completion sometime between 2013 and 2015. The vision of the city's urban planners is that these new transit lines, extending out into the most important satellite centers, will give those centers an urbanized quality that most of them so far lack.

"There will be more transit-oriented real estate in Houston opening all at once," predicts David Crossley, "than anywhere in the country."

Architecture professor Tom Diehl adopts an even more visionary tone. "The people who want to live close in are finally getting something now. The people who want to live on the freeway already have what they want. It's not like you'll step off the light rail and feel you're in Boston. I don't think people will call it a victory soon. But it will happen. You will ultimately have little urban pockets where you can get your urban fix."

It remains to be seen, of course, whether the much larger transit system now being built will generate the development that the first segment failed to generate, or will simply bid up the price of nearby land for speculators willing to do nothing with it for years. But it's fair to say that the belief in an extensive transit system, and the willingness to pay for it, is now an article of faith among the city's business establishment. None of the mayoral candidates in the 2009 election expressed any desire for a reconsideration of the plan to get the system built. "If I had to take one thing that would measure the success of Houston," said candidate Peter Brown, "it's transit linking mixed-use centers." Brown didn't win the election; he narrowly missed making the runoff against eventual winner Annise Parker. But none of the major candidates took issue with his essential vision. It may be difficult for Houston to make major additional investments in transit in the near future. Money is tight; the overwhelming sentiment seems to be to wait to see what effect transit has in the coming decade and make plans for the future based on that. But what Houston has already promised to do in creating a metropolis with a significant transit component, and what it is already in the process of accomplishing, seems remarkable in a city whose identification with the automobile has been all but total.

BEYOND THE TRANSIT QUESTION, Houston's civic leaders seem to share a conviction that, more than most, theirs is a city and a region that embodies the American urban future. It has an urban middle class expanding for several miles around the downtown; a diversity of population that includes roughly equal numbers of African Americans, Latinos, and Anglos; a relative racial harmony based on the desire for growth rather than a contention over social differences; a rapidly expanding eagerness for the more distant satellite centers to offer significant elements of urbanized life; and a transit system that will eventually link new centers and relax the auto dependency for which Houston has become famous all over the country. It may be an urban planner's pipe dream, or it may be the reality of the next few decades. Houston, says sociologist Stephen Klineberg, "is the most interesting city in America. Its diversity shows what the United States will look like in thirty years. Chicago was the city of the twentieth century. Houston is the city of the twenty-first."

Whether there will be a stable place in it for Garnet Coleman's people of the Third Ward remains very much in doubt.

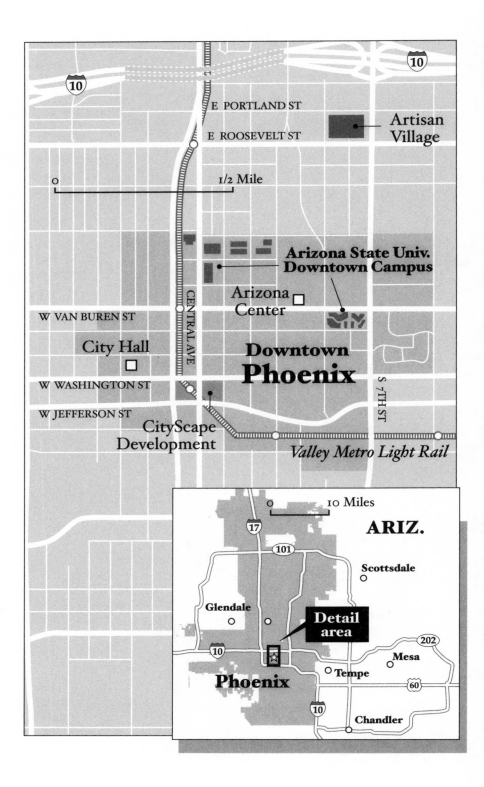

E PORTLAND ST

E ROOSEVELT ST

Artisan
Village

1/2 Mile

**Arizona State Univ.
Downtown Campus**

Arizona
Center

CENTRAL AVE

W VAN BUREN ST

City Hall

**Downtown
Phoenix**

S 7TH ST

W WASHINGTON ST

W JEFFERSON ST

CityScape
Development

Valley Metro Light Rail

10 Miles

ARIZ.

17

101

Scottsdale

Glendale

**Detail
area**

202

Mesa

10

Tempe

60

Phoenix

10

Chandler

CHAPTER EIGHT

CREATING A DOWNTOWN

IN THE FIRST DECADE of the new century, in cities all over the American South and Southwest, something puzzling happened. Separately, but more or less at the same time, leaders of these sprawl-based conurbations that had grown enormously in the past generation began to express deep longing for a downtown. Not a mishmash of office buildings, hotels, and stadiums—most of them already had that—but a city center comparable to ones that members of this political and business elite had seen on visits to older cities: New York, Boston, and Chicago, but especially older places closer to home—San Francisco, Seattle, Portland.

So it was that in a remarkably few years, Phoenix and Dallas and Charlotte did things they would have considered unthinkable a decade or two before. They spent billions of public dollars on light-rail transit systems; they drafted long-term "vision" documents that projected a future in which downtowns were friendly to pedestrians rather than just convenient for automobiles; they won voter support for striking new public buildings and placed them as close to the center of the city as they could.

Just what was it they were looking for? Two things, really. One was the downtown residential population that they were convinced older cities had and great cities needed. Intimately related to that was a desire for street life, a round-the-clock presence of locals and visitors that would project a sense of vibrancy to anyone who saw it.

Why did they want those things? That turns out to be a more complex question. For some, the reasons were relatively specific. They were tied closely to the desire to recruit and retain big corporations, and the sense that these companies were uneasy locating in a metropolis without a center. Motorola, crucial to the economic development of Phoenix in the postwar years, had all but pulled out in the early 2000s and relocated to Austin, Texas, where the center of the city bustled with life at all hours of the day and night. The perception in Phoenix business circles, whether entirely accurate or not, was that Motorola left because it wanted a place with a downtown. More specifically, it wanted a place with a sophisticated urban scene that would appeal to the bright young college graduates it hoped to employ.

This was a common refrain across the big Sun Belt cities. In the words of Michael Smith, Charlotte's director of downtown development, the bankers who dominated the town's economic strategy felt that they had to have downtown amenities "to attract hip young professionals." Virtually all of these Sun Belt cities agreed with the geographer Richard Florida's argument that future prosperity depended on the ability to lure the "creative class," and that this could be done only with a thriving urban culture.

More broadly, though, there was a perception that the twenty-first-century world was dividing rapidly into global cities and cities that were second-tier, no matter what their metropolitan size, and that rebuilding (or creating) a downtown was the only way to move into the first rank. "The common element of great cities," proclaimed Phoenix mayor Phil Gordon, "has always been a belief in the central core as the heart."

I listened to those leaders and I found myself thinking, oddly enough, of Pinocchio. After a long series of struggles, he wasn't doing all that badly as a wooden puppet. He had learned to tell the truth about himself. But he wanted desperately to be something more than he was: a "real" boy, made of flesh and blood and possessed of a heart just like the other boys he saw around him. There is a sense, at least, in which the great modern cities of America's South and West are in the grip of Pinocchio fever.

OF ALL THE PINOCCHIO CITIES in the United States, Phoenix is perhaps the strangest and most interesting case. Unlike most of its counterparts, it hadn't really abandoned its center in a rush to the sub-urbs; more accurately, it never possessed a center in the first place. One can find pictures of downtown Phoenix before World War II, pictures of relatively busy streets with coffee shops and men wearing bolo ties and department stores sitting comfortably on the main thoroughfares (including the store that made the Goldwater family rich and famous), but it is the downtown of a modest-size Western county seat. No one would confuse it with the core of a major urban center.

And a modest little town is just what Phoenix was in the first half of the twentieth century. In 1940, it had only sixty-five thousand peo-ple. Then, almost without warning, it began to grow inexorably, first with the coming of the aircraft industry during World War II, later with electronics companies such as Motorola in the 1950s. Especially important, the development of artificial air cooling made the place liv-able in the summer months and turned it into a magnet for newcom-ers from the North who were eager for a fresh start in a sunny climate. As early as the end of the 1940s, Phoenix had more window air condi-tioners per capita than any city in the United States.

All American cities sprawled outward in the decades after 1950, but Phoenix had more room to sprawl than nearly any of them, into flat, empty desert land where growth encountered no serious geographi-cal obstacles. The only real impediment was water, and although not everyone realized it, Phoenix actually had plenty of that, thanks to the Roosevelt Dam that had emptied the nearby Salt River early in the century, and then later to the Central Arizona Project that brought in water from the Colorado River and allowed home owners in the middle of a desert to have lawns as green and lush as if they were in Atlanta or Miami.

By the time of the 1960 census, due to both migration and annexa-tion, the city had surpassed four hundred thousand people; by 1980 it was approaching eight hundred thousand; early in the 1990s it crossed the million mark. And the older prewar suburbs were growing expo-nentially as well: Metropolitan Phoenix was home to three million people in 2000, and it is home to well over four and a half million today.

The newcomers of the 1950s bought into subdivisions lined with virtually identical one-story ranch houses, made of concrete block, topped by low-sloping roofs, and flanked by open-air carports that offered modest protection from 110-degree summers. The new arrivals of the 1970s bought a different product, typically a beige house with a stucco exterior and a wooden frame underneath, more likely two stories than one, with a red tile roof that emulated the Mediterranean look that developers and buyers both seemed to like. From the air, Phoenix looks like a vast carpet of red tile.

The subdivisions were bigger in the 1970s and 1980s than in the early postwar years: 180 homes on average, compared to just 30 in the 1950s. And the houses were larger as well: By 1980, the average single-family home in Phoenix was twenty-two hundred square feet. But the lots were getting smaller, so that more units could be built on a given parcel of land. In some of the less affluent new subdivisions, the distance between houses was so small that they looked crammed together. The carports were obsolete, replaced by huge attached garages that often took up more land frontage than the house itself. There was actually a word for the long, curving residential streets that sprang up in Phoenix in the 1970s and 1980s. They were called garagescapes.

And the proliferation of these stucco neighborhoods reflected more than living choice. They constituted, by the mid-1980s, the most important industry in metropolitan Phoenix. In the words of Susan Clark-Johnson of the Morrison Institute, an urban policy think tank at Arizona State University, "Real estate is to us what gambling is to Nevada. We're basically a one-industry place."

BUT EVEN AS PHOENIX built a successful economy around low-density growth and seemed to embody the very idea of it, the community's longtime residents and even some newcomers came to fear it as well. They liked the Valley of the Sun, but they had a feeling that something about it was out of control: Metropolitan Phoenix wasn't just growing; it was exploding, and no one in local leadership was placing any limits on the explosion. They saw the valley as a messy blob that reached farther into the desert every year. Where would it stop? Could it be stopped? Home owners who lived ten miles beyond the center developed a queasy feeling when subdivisions similar to theirs began popping up ten miles beyond them. And those who lived twenty miles out felt just the same way when the blob stretched ten miles farther, to Goodyear and Buckeye in the scruffy desert west of Phoenix, or to Apache Junction in the east, on the edge of the Goldfield Mountains.

It wasn't mainly a fear of congestion or traffic jams. Phoenicians did complain about those things, but in fact Phoenix has never had a really serious traffic problem. It didn't complete its freeway system until the mid-1980s, later than almost any other city, but it hardly mattered, because the main arterial streets were so wide and capacious that commuting around the city was relatively easy whatever route you chose. Basically it still is.

In part, fear of sprawl in Phoenix was related to pollution, reflected in the number of smog alerts that seemed to grow more frequent each summer. Beyond that, though, it was a much less tangible sense people had that the valley just wasn't the same oasis in the desert it had been when they arrived a decade or two before. To families who had bought stucco homes with red-tiled roofs in close-in Glendale in the 1960s, the prospect of thousands of new ones almost identical to theirs going up in the 1980s in Surprise, fifteen miles away, generated a vague but powerful unease about the future of the entire area.

And so even as it sprawled, Phoenix began debating what could be done to move its center of gravity back closer to the center, at least keeping the inexorable blob under control. New ideas kept popping up every few years.

In the 1960s, there was a belief among city leaders that a conventional downtown might be impossible, but that a measure of urbanity could be constructed by turning Central Avenue, a major arterial highway running north from the middle of town, into a fashionable boulevard of midrise office buildings and high-rise apartment buildings. To a certain extent, this strategy succeeded. Central Avenue looks pretty nice even today. But the main consequence of developing it was to empty out downtown even further. Central Avenue didn't bring many people into the city except to work at nine-to-five office jobs, and it all but eviscerated what was left of the old downtown.

In the 1970s, the city council decided that the way to at least make suburbanization more orderly was to promote a network of nine "urban villages," each with more than fifty thousand residents, in which the neighborhoods and subdivisions ringing the city could have separate identities, concentrated business districts, and a general sense of community that many felt was slipping away all over the valley. It was an intriguing idea, but it was also a huge flop. Only one or two of the proposed nine villages ever acquired anything like the semiurban core that had been envisioned. In 1986, a full decade after the project was started, a survey revealed that only a quarter of the villagers knew which village they lived in, and that less than a third of the area's residents even knew that the experiment had been attempted.

Finally, in the late 1980s, a consensus developed among civic leaders that something might actually be done for the downtown itself. And something was, on a large scale. It was Arizona Center, on the eastern edge of the ninety-square-block downtown district that came to be known as Copper Square. Arizona Center was a project of the Rouse Company, and it displayed one of the features that Rouse had been promoting successfully for years: notably, a courtyard planned to accommodate quirky and inviting craft shops and boutiques and restaurants, 150,000 square feet of retail in all, similar to the "festival mall" concept that had been successful in Boston, Baltimore, and a few other places.

Arizona Center generated considerable excitement among Phoenix's growing cadre of urbanists when it opened in the early 1990s, but ultimately it too proved a failure. All the action was on the inside of the courtyard; walking past it on the street, what you saw was mostly a blank brick wall. This was done for a reason; some of the city's more troubled neighborhoods were only a few blocks away, and it was felt that visitors needed a sense of protection. But security, if it was needed, came at a high price. Arizona Center wasn't an appealing place for locals or tourists to visit. Over the years, fewer and fewer merchants inside the enclave proved able to make a profit; gradually retail space gave way to office space, so that by the early 2000s Arizona Center was a collection of mostly occupied office buildings with a scattering of shops on the ground floor that catered to the office workers, not to tourists or visiting suburbanites.

. . .

THE DIFFICULTY of creating a significant retail presence downtown is one that has plagued cities much further along in the downtown development process than Phoenix. In the past 20 years, Charlotte has done something no other American city has done: It has ripped out its historic city center, put up a brand-new one, and made the rebuilt downtown into a functional, generally appealing economic and cultural enclave. Even the recession that has badly damaged the city's two big banks and economic drivers, Bank of America and Wachovia (and forced Wachovia to merge with Wells Fargo), has not diminished the entertainment vibrancy and affluent ambience of the downtown streets.

Many big cities, including a significant number in the South and West, tried wholesale urban renewal in the mid- to late twentieth century, nearly always with disastrous results. Charlotte, for now at least, seems to have beaten the odds.

It has done that for many reasons, but one above all: the presence of two of America's four biggest banking institutions. Bank of America and Wachovia wanted to stay in downtown Charlotte, they wanted it to be a showplace, and they paid for what they wanted. In most respects, they have gotten their money's worth. Even suffering from the ravages of a financial recession and plagued by more business failures than it would like to see, Charlotte has the most walkable big-city downtown in the Southeast.

There are some highly affluent stretches of downtown Charlotte— as you reach the corner of Fourth and Tryon close to the center of the new downtown, you'll notice a string of fashionable locally owned cafés. You can now do all sorts of interesting things in downtown Charlotte: work in a gleaming postmodern office tower, live in a stylish condo a few blocks from the office, dine and drink at a pleasant sidewalk café. All the things that the Phoenix business elite have been trying to accomplish for the better part of a generation now.

Only one major problem clouds the picture: There's almost nowhere to shop in downtown Charlotte. Thirty years ago, in a dilapidated central city that was plagued by poverty and petty crime, you could fight

Skyscrapers and outdoor dining, generated by investment from Charlotte's two giant banks, have given the city an urban ambience where scarcely any functional downtown existed thirty years ago.

your way through the chaos and buy a good many of the necessities of life on Tryon Street, one of the two major downtown thoroughfares. Today, you basically can't buy anything.

Charlotte's retail problem is striking because it contrasts so sharply with the ongoing revival, but it is a problem that afflicts most big cities in America, whether their downtowns are reviving, declining, or standing still. They all are having trouble attracting any significant retail presence to the traditional urban core. People move to the center of town, live in luxury apartments, wait in line at expensive restaurants, enjoy the late-night entertainment scene. But when they want to buy something—a screwdriver, a pair of socks, a tablecloth, a printer cartridge—they have to drive somewhere else in the city or to the suburbs, often to a mall several miles away.

Ironically, there's a wonderful old shopping arcade in downtown Charlotte—the Latta Arcade, built in 1914 to house cotton brokers, with two parallel rows of one-story office and retail shop units, all beneath a glass skylight. The arcade was restored in the 1980s and is on the National Register of Historic Places, and its spaces are almost entirely rented. But it's also another emblem of downtown Charlotte's problem: Among its notable businesses are a taco shop, an Indian carryout, and a hot dog stand. Other than one tiny jewelry store, no one sells anything much besides food.

Is there a solution? In Charlotte, the civic establishment is convinced there is. At Charlotte Center City Partners, one of the most active and entrepreneurial downtown development organizations in the country, they talk endlessly about "the retail problem." In 2007, the group completed a fourteen-month study of the issue, releasing a detailed statistical report citing possibilities for a retail revival. Among other things, the report pointed out that nearly seventy thousand people work in downtown Charlotte; that a majority of them make more than $50,000 a year; that four hundred thousand residents of the metropolitan area come downtown at least once a year, mostly to eat, watch sports, or go to a museum; and that six hundred thousand more come into town on business and stay in a downtown hotel. If that wasn't a sufficient base for retail shopping, the report concluded, then nothing was. It was just a matter of showing retailers what was out there.

Michael Smith, the president of Center City Partners, conceded that this was not necessarily an easy task. And the ensuing climate of recession, which hit Charlotte's big banks particularly hard, slowed down the pace of retail recruitment. But the desire on the city's part to solve the problem has not gone away. "We must solve the riddle of urban retail," Smith said in early 2010. "It's the last great frontier."

There is some shopping one flight above the street in downtown Charlotte, in a bizarrely laid-out string of second-floor retail corridors that go by the name of Overstreet Mall, but they don't resemble a mall as much as they do a maze with no clear entrances or exits. Unless you have an obsessive curiosity, I wouldn't suggest a visit to Overstreet Mall. It's so poorly designed and marked that you may have a hard time getting out.

Scarcely anybody in Charlotte likes Overstreet Mall, and not too many people shop there anymore. The consensus is that retail has to move back to the street, now that downtown is a healthy place with plenty of affluent passersby. So far, though, the city has had little luck persuading any major retailer to open up. "Retailers are not pioneers," says Michael Smith. I think you can call that an understatement. But without a significant retail presence on the downtown streets, downtown Charlotte, like all the other newly created Sun Belt downtowns, will continue to face questions about whether it's a "real" downtown or just a clever imitation.

BY THE LATE 1990S, it was clear that walled-off retail wasn't the answer to downtown Phoenix's problem. But still another new idea came along: entertainment, and specifically sports. The city had a highly successful professional basketball team, the Phoenix Suns, and a brand-new major-league baseball team, the Arizona Diamondbacks, and huge new stadiums were built for them at the southern end of downtown. Big-time sports were seen as the magnet that would draw people into the center of the city, not only generating evening street life but complementing the two theaters and concert hall that had managed to survive near the city center during the two previous decades. Entertainment was the magic word for Phoenix planners in the closing years of the 1990s. Arizona Center added a multiplex cinema with twenty-four screens to try to cash in on the trend.

But visiting planners came to town and warned that entertainment alone couldn't possibly create a downtown. The vast majority of people who came to Suns or Diamondbacks games simply parked their cars in the parking lots and went straight home when the game was over. In 1997, the urbanist critic William Fulton arrived and saw exactly what was happening. What needed to take place, he said, was for Phoenix and other cities like it "to use entertainment in the service of downtown revival—not simply to turn downtowns into theme parks. If downtowns succeed in the entertainment era, it will be because the drama of day-to-day life in the city remains just as compelling as the drama in the movie or the sports event."

In Phoenix, after Arizona Center failed to become the retail magnet that some of its promoters hoped it would become, attention focused on a different project. Unfortunately, this one was an abject failure. Patriots Square Park, a 2.2-acre public space right in the middle of downtown, at Central and Washington streets, was an ever-worsening embarrassment. Opened in 1976, and redone under a huge white canopy in 1988, Patriots Square Park was supposed to be the catalyst for outdoor concerts, parades, rallies, and laser light shows. But it was awkwardly designed and poorly shaded, and after just a few years it went unused virtually all the time. By the 1990s, it was essentially a shelter for homeless people.

By then, after more than a billion dollars of public money had been spent on projects in the central city, some prominent Phoenicians were very angry, not just about the failures downtown but about all that had happened in the metropolitan area. "For thirty years," the novelist Glendon Swarthout wrote, "we let the businessmen and politicians who ran the valley lead us down the path of unplanned growth. Crime, traffic, heat, air pollution, bankruptcies, unemployment, corruption—the quality of our lives is pathetically diminished, and what have we been given in compensation: professional sports."

As the new century began, however, the local leadership had finally realized what might have been obvious to them years before: The real reason downtown was such a flop was that no one lived there.

When other cities complain about the absence of "downtown residential," they usually mean that no more than a few thousand people out of at least half a million in the metropolitan area have chosen to make their homes in the center of the city. In Phoenix, at the turn of the new century, that would have been a large increase. The central area known as Copper Square housed perhaps 250 transients and a few dozen unusually intrepid urban pioneers. The downtown Phoenix strategic vision plan of 1994 declared that "housing is a vital part of downtown's renaissance—nothing else works without it." That plan set a goal of ten thousand residential units, a modest enough number in a metro area then approaching four million people, and vowed to realize it by 2014, two full decades in the future. As downtown planner Don Keuth was to put it later, "If you want to create a real downtown, you have to create a neighborhood."

The 1994 strategic plan made a point that local planners have been making ever since: that Phoenix couldn't have a "real" downtown until it developed some connectivity—some sense that the buildings and open spaces were linked together in a coherent way.

As things stood, most of the elements of a downtown existed, but they existed as freestanding entities, often connected by nothing more than a parcel of vacant land. Downtown Phoenix, the planner and critic Grady Gammage Jr. said, "looks like a truckful of buildings was dumped on the site." The strategic plan envisioned "a series of oases that could be linked to achieve greater synergy and connectivity." It saw shade, in the brutal summer climate of the Valley of the Sun, as perhaps the crucial unifying quality for the downtown area. "Use shade everywhere," the plan urged, "especially in connected and civic spaces, so that shaded spaces become Phoenix's signature."

The potential was certainly there: As of 1994 there were 135 acres of vacant land and surface parking in the immediate downtown area. But at the halfway point of the strategic plan, in 2004, virtually no progress had been made. The vacant lots and parking lots remained as they had been.

One reason downtown residential was so hard to do was that Phoenix, unlike, say, San Diego and Denver, lacked any real reservoir of historic buildings from which downtown residential booms typically take off. Only a tiny number of buildings in the center of the city dated from any period before World War II. "Our historic building stock," city planner Jason Harris lamented, "is dumpy old warehouses."

Even that was putting it generously. There were a few old structures down by the railroad tracks, built originally to store fruit, but the idea of turning them into a "warehouse district," with lofts as residential units, was simply ludicrous. "Phoenix had Quonset huts," recalls Don Keuth. "We put them all over the place. We didn't need a warehouse district." If Phoenix was going to acquire a "real" downtown, one with people living there and life on the streets, it wasn't going to do it by preservation or renovation.

And so Phoenix embarked on still another downtown revival, buoyed by Mayor Gordon's urbanist enthusiasm, the hot housing market of the early 2000s, and the presence of some wealthy developers who saw the high-rise condos along the waterfront in San Diego and Seattle and felt they could work the same magic in the Arizona desert.

By 2007, there were some exciting and very tall condo towers close to the center of the city, including one of thirty-four stories at 44 East Monroe Street, directly across from City Hall, and another of twenty-two stories, literally in the shadow of the baseball stadium, known as the Summit at Copper Square. Others were close to construction.

It remains open to argument whether these projects might have succeeded in the absence of a recession, but most Phoenix planners and real estate brokers think not: Pitched almost entirely at luxury-end buyers, and selling for as much as $450 a square foot to cover the high building costs of glass and concrete, they weren't the smartest way to introduce urban living to a metropolitan area that had almost no experience with it.

The only way the nearly four hundred units at 44 Monroe and at

Summit could have made money for the developers would have been if many of them were sold to extremely wealthy part-timers: highly paid athletes, wintering Europeans eager to take advantage of the cheap American dollar, businesspeople from affluent suburban Scottsdale or Paradise Valley who worked downtown and could afford a pied-à-terre close to the office. "There was a wildly optimistic view of what the market would accept," admits Tom Franz, the head of Greater Phoenix Leadership, an influential consortium of corporate leaders. Susan Clark-Johnson, of the Morrison Institute at Arizona State, puts it more colorfully: "We've got all these edifices to the egos of developers who saw nothing but rich people and marble countertops."

There is limited value, though, to guessing how the downtown high-rise condo projects would have fared had there been no recession. At the end of 2009, Summit was less than half occupied and moving toward foreclosure; 44 Monroe had thirteen occupants for its 165 condominium units. Perhaps most disappointingly, CityScape, an enormous project on the site of the old Patriots Square Park, designed as a complex of three high-rises—an office building, a hotel, and a residential tower—was going forward as offices and a hotel only. The residential tower had been postponed indefinitely.

Phoenix's failure to realize its downtown residential dreams was all the more frustrating because, in other ways, its central-city revival project was succeeding remarkably well. In December 2008, Phoenix opened the light-rail transit system that Mayor Gordon and the business community had persuaded the voters to approve by referendum earlier in the decade: a twenty-mile, $1.4 billion Valley Metro train network. Ultimately, $402 million in spending by Phoenix and the other participating jurisdictions bought $647 million in federal funds for just the first phase of the project.

Light-rail in Phoenix was an unexpected hit from the start. On opening day, there was a two-and-a-half-hour wait to board the trains at the eastern terminus in Mesa. The local congressman, Harry Mitchell, emphasized to curious onlookers that "this is not a Disneyland ride. This is the first phase of a light-rail system that will help us realize a shared vision of an economically vibrant urban corridor."

The official projection had been that the system would attract

The sleek new Phoenix light-rail system, built in part to revitalize a nondescript downtown, attracts relatively few commuters but an unexpectedly large number of recreation and entertainment seekers.

twenty-six thousand riders a day; it averaged thirty-three thousand from the beginning. Those numbers weren't necessarily conclusive evidence of anything; cities have learned to lowball their initial transit projections to achieve the public relations triumph of exceeding them. The real evidence in Phoenix is the experience of riding the trains. One can board at almost any time of day or evening and find the cars filled with riders from virtually every demographic category in the region: students, people going out to lunch or dinner, suburbanites coming in for sports events or bar hopping, tourists, lawyers with offices in the midtown corridor riding downtown to City Hall or the county courthouse. During much of the day, every car seems to be crowded with bicycles; one often has to maneuver around a cluster of bikes just to get to a seat. People who live along the transit line are riding bikes to the stations, loading them aboard the train, and riding them to their final destinations once they disembark.

The one major constituency that doesn't use light-rail in large numbers is the commuting population. Light-rail serves downtown Phoenix mainly as a recreational tool, but an effective one. At the end of the first year, it was difficult to find anyone other than free-market ideological zealots who didn't consider the costly experiment at least moderately successful. "Now that it's up," said city planner Carol Johnson, "everyone is asking when do we get it in our neighborhood."

The students riding Valley Metro, going back and forth from the main Arizona State University campus in suburban Tempe, were in many ways the most important component. Arizona State president Michael Crow, presiding over the unwieldiness of the nation's single most populous campus, with more than sixty-five thousand enrolled, saw downtown in terms almost as messianic as those of Mayor Gordon. He decided on a long-term plan to bring fifteen thousand of the students to a new downtown campus, a species of urban revival more ambitious than any other city had dared to try. "Our presence will be catalytic in nature," Crow predicted. The mayor was equally exultant. "ASU downtown is more than a few nuggets," he said. "It's a gold mine. We've hit the mother lode."

Voters approved spending $225 million in public money on the new campus in 2004, as part of a $900 million bond issue that also included money for police, fire, libraries, streets, and sewers. Whatever Phoenix residents might feel about their hyperenthusiastic mayor, there was no disputing that he was a genius when it came to packaging ballot measures for maximum appeal.

Creation of the new downtown campus was far from complete at the start of the new decade in 2010. Crow had moved the nursing, social work, and public policy programs into downtown Phoenix, and built a striking steel-and-glass building for the Walter Cronkite School of Journalism. More than eight thousand students were taking at least one class in downtown Phoenix every week. Many of these, especially in social work and nursing, were midcareer students who left immediately after class and played no real role in creating a downtown community. Still, there was a growing residential component. During the 2009–2010 school year, more than eight hundred students were living in the just-opened Taylor Place twin-tower dormitory at the north end of downtown.

The Arizona State campus was tangible evidence of the potential that a downtown university might possess for transforming the area nearby. But it was also, in an odd way, a reminder of how far the ultimate dream of a residential downtown, with a vibrant street life, was from realization. With eight hundred students living there, Taylor Place was the single biggest residential cluster in the central downtown core. But relatively few of the students seemed to venture much farther downtown. A distressing number of the students weren't sure exactly what existed there.

One might be tempted to conclude, after all the false starts in the drive to create residential life in downtown Phoenix, that there was no answer to the problem. Phoenicians simply didn't want to live there. Actually, though, there was a solution, or at least one that might well have worked had it been adequately tried and supported.

While the big-name developers from outside were investing heavily and ultimately losing out with high-rise towers, a third-generation Phoenix builder named Eric Brown was experimenting with a different idea: much smaller apartment buildings, stucco over frame, designed to human scale and generally affordable to the middle class. Brown put these structures up in and around downtown, wherever there was a vacant lot he could afford. He generally created twenty units to the acre, much less density than the high-rises, but much more density than downtown Phoenix had had before. By 2008, there were five of these projects in central Phoenix, including Artisan Village, just north of downtown, five acres of townhouses that included ten live-work units, with retail on the bottom and condominiums above reserved for the merchants.

None of Brown's projects was as striking as the tall towers, but they were generally pleasing to look at, and they had one crucial advantage: They sold. Virtually every unit was occupied, even during the leanest recession years, and those that were resold generally went for markups of as much as 50 percent. In fact, though, not many of them did go on the market for resale. "People weren't buying to flip," as Brown put it. His projects had the lowest turnover rates of anything being built in metropolitan Phoenix. Brown's admirers felt he might be laying the groundwork for a twenty-first-century Western equivalent of New York brownstone neighborhoods.

Brown's buildings varied slightly in height, but all of them were less than sixty feet, because sixty feet is the threshold that triggers much more onerous building code requirements for things like plumbing and fire prevention. The majority of the buildings were five stories, four for residential units, with a retail podium extending out on the ground floor. For Brown, this was not only a business decision but a matter of urban philosophy. "Life happens under five stories," he said. "Everything above is just a place to pack people."

IF ERIC BROWN sees an element of magic in the five-story building, he is not the first one. The boulevards that Haussmann built in Paris were lined with five-story buildings; so was most of the Ringstrasse in nineteenth-century Vienna. Of course, there were nonaesthetic reasons for that uniformity—in the days before elevators, five sets of stairs were about as much as anybody could be expected to climb, and the absence of steel-frame construction made building much taller than that difficult anyway.

So Paris and Vienna became five-story cities. And many consequences flowed from that. People on fifth-floor balconies could lean over their flower boxes and watch the action on the street below. The pedestrians could wave or talk to those above. Residence and street were integrated in a way entirely different from anything that prevailed at the time in neighborhoods of single-story townhouses, or later in neighborhoods where the apartment buildings were skyscrapers.

Is the charm of five-story scale replicable in a twenty-first-century American city? Is it replicable, most incongruously of all, in a place like Phoenix? One is tempted to say the idea is absurd—but there is the fact that the handful of five-story experiments that Eric Brown built there remained fully occupied through the hardest of recession years, while the ambitious skyscraper condominiums went unsold.

Brown is not the only developer or civic leader who envisions a successful midrise downtown in Phoenix mixing residences, retail, and offices. But before anything like that could happen, the city would have to deal with a mundane but serious problem: parking. Phoenicians are almost as preoccupied with where they park their cars as with where they park themselves. In the suburbs, the general rule is four or five parking spaces for every thousand square feet of living space; in the high-rise downtown condominiums and office buildings, it is three per thousand square feet. A five-story residence can provide lots of amenities, but copious parking is not one of them. So before Phoenix can begin to consider seriously the vision of Eric Brown and others who think like him, it will have to recover from its parking obsession.

That will not be easy. "The less frequently you use your car," says Grady Gammage, "the more paranoid you are about where it goes. If we followed the lead of other cities and prohibited new parking in downtown, the likely result would be no new development downtown."

The creativity of Eric Brown's solution suggests one important thing about Phoenix: With an ample supply of empty land in the center and very little of historical value to protect, it has the ability, in theory at least, to build a downtown that would possess many of the traditional urbanist virtues—street life, compactness, casual sociability—and yet would not resemble the downtowns of older cities. The civic leadership clearly believes this is possible, even if it has little sense of what the ultimate result might be. Don Keuth of the Phoenix Community Alliance believes his city has the potential to create a brand-new form of urbanism that could serve as a model for desert cities all over the world. He thinks a density of ten to twelve units an acre is entirely feasible. "In ten years," Keuth says, "this could be one of the great downtowns of the United States. I'm not sure what it will look like."

No one else is sure, either. But no serious observer of life in the Valley of the Sun minimizes the likely resistance to anything very dramatic. The reluctance to ease up on parking requirements, trivial as it may seem, is a good symbol of that resistance. So is the disgust some newly arrived downtown condo dwellers expressed when they found a hotel garbage Dumpster not far from their doorsteps. (No one on Wall Street would have given it a second thought, no matter how much they had paid for their living space.) And so is the way drivers respond to even a small increase in the number of downtown pedestrians who impede their progress. Some are surprised when they learn they are supposed to yield the right of way. "This isn't an urban city," Keuth admits. "It wasn't set up to be an urban place. We're literally creating it from scratch."

But by 2010, Phoenix did have one quality that it shared with all other large American cities—a cohort of people in their twenties and early thirties who seemed to be tiring of exurban life. "We have all these people who came here after World War Two," said city planning manager Carol Johnson, "who are terrified we're going to take their green lawns away from them with density. But their children don't feel that way. They want a more urban experience."

Indeed, when the Gallup Poll surveyed young people in Arizona (most of them in the Phoenix area) in 2009, only 11 percent gave their community top grades as a place to live. A full 29 percent said they would move to another city or state if they had the choice. "When I think about Chicago," an Arizona State junior told Gallup, "I think about twenty-four/seven energy. And great food. When I think about Austin, I think young people and music. . . . Will I be here in five years? No."

One survey response does not prove anything. But it suggests what the elite in Phoenix worries about, and why it has embarked so many times on the difficult project of trying to create recognizable urban life. In the words of Grady Gammage Jr., "There is something genuinely vital about a city that we are lacking here. And we want that. We worry about the image of Phoenix being all golf courses and old people."

In the end, leaders in postwar cities such as Phoenix crave urbanity not only because they have enjoyed it in Portland or San Francisco, but because they believe the future of their region depends on it. If only there were a hip music scene; if only they could have a safe, vibrant street life that extended beyond working hours; if only they could have thirty thousand people living downtown—if they could have all these things, they could be twenty-first-century cities with hearts instead of huge twentieth-century population clusters aging before their time. As Don Keuth likes to put it, "We're not a global city. But we can be. We just have to think about how to get there."

It's Pinocchio's dream translated to urban scale.

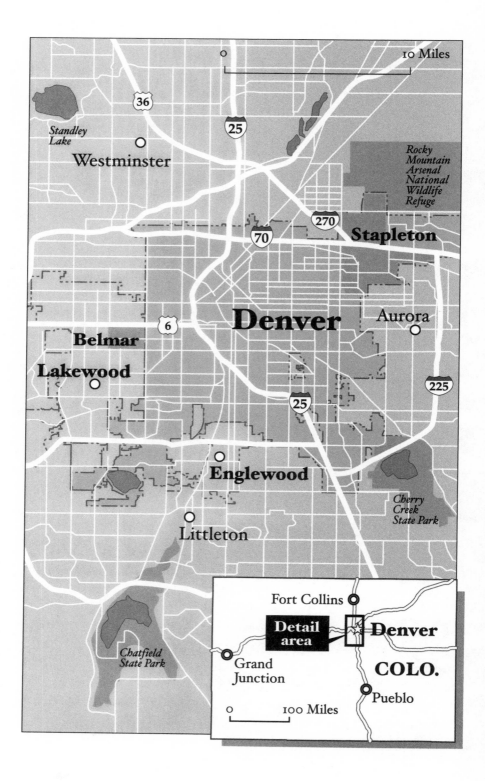

10 Miles

Standley
Lake

36

25

Rocky
Mountain
Arsenal
National
Wildlife
Refuge

Westminster

270

70

Stapleton

Denver

Aurora

6

Belmar

Lakewood

225

25

Englewood

Cherry
Creek
State Park

Littleton

Chatfield
State Park

Fort Collins

Detail
area

Denver

Grand
Junction

COLO.

Pueblo

0   100 Miles

CHAPTER NINE

URBANIZING THE SUBURBS

WHERE DO THE MILLENNIALS want to live? In many ways, this is the demographic question that will determine the face of metropolitan America in the next twenty years. The strands of opinion on this issue have hardened into what amounts to an ideological debate. On one side stand the prosuburban, largely free-market scholars who believe that once the economic downturn ends, America will resume its twentieth-century thrust outward and seek ever-newer greenfield homes on plots of land farther and farther from the city, transporting themselves back and forth by means of the automobile.

They have some statistics to back them up. One study by a real estate consulting firm in 2009 reported that only 17 percent of Generation Y (the "millennials," born roughly between 1980 and 1995) expressed a preference for urban living, most likely a rental apartment, over a suburban mode of life. But there are equally compelling, and strikingly different, results on the other side. A competing study by the consulting firm RCLCO, in 2008, revealed an almost precisely opposite result: 77 percent of Generation Y wanted to live some variant of the urban life.

"Generation Y's attitudes toward home ownership have been changed by the housing crisis and the recession," the Urban Land Institute found in commenting on the RCLCO study. "The number of people trapped by underwater homes that cannot be sold and the millions of foreclosures are tempering their interest in buying their own homes and they will be renters by necessity rather than by choice for years ahead." In many if not most cases, that means urbanized rather than traditional suburban rentals.

Between 1990 and 2007, the Urban Land Institute found, central cities increased their share of housing permits within their metropolitan areas by more than double. This increase continued after the housing recession caused the number of permits to plummet in the outer suburbs. What is more, statistics showed, housing in cities and inner suburbs held their value during the recession far better than their exurban counterparts.

This seems to me a case in which common sense wins a battle of dueling statistics. Most of the major demographic trends right now in America work in favor of an urban preference, at least among a significant cohort of the emerging adult population: smaller households, later marriages, decisions not to marry at all, decisions not to have children, the emergence of a huge and active baby boom population in its sixties and seventies—all point to some form of reemergence of urban choice.

But suppose one grants many of the predictions made by those who attempt to debunk any significant back-to-the-city movement among the millennial generation. The generation is simply so large—by one conventional measure, sixty to seventy million people—that even a respectable minority of this cohort seeking an urban life is bound to change American metropolitan areas dramatically.

In a poll cited by *The New York Times* in 2009, 45 percent of Americans between the ages of twenty and thirty-five said they would like to live in New York City someday if they could. This is an absurdly large number of people—well over 20 million, in fact. It's a safe assumption that, other than the ones who already live in New York, not too many of them will ever get there. So the poll does not offer much insight into the future demographics of the nation's largest city. But it says a great deal about the values, tastes, and wishes of an enormous group of American young people.

There is a thirst for urban life among the millennial generation. It shows up in polls, in anecdotal conversation, in blogs and other casual writing. It is not based primarily on watching television shows such as *Friends* or *Seinfeld,* though those should not be discounted. It is based on an inchoate feeling that the cul-de-sac suburbia in which millions of them grew up is a cul-de-sac in more ways than one: It cuts off not only streets, but diversity and the casual outdoor experience they feel is crucial to meaningful human sociability.

Once again, it is necessary to say that exurbs are not going to empty out in the coming generation. They remain home to millions of current residents with families who like the space, are concerned about safety, and want to stay put; newcomers to this country who are determined to avoid the crowding they encountered in other parts of the world; and poorer people who are able to find acceptable housing on the periphery that is not available in the center.

One may object that the city-seeking young people are not a representative sample of their age group. They are more affluent, more often single, less affected by family life, more interested in spending an ample supply of disposable income on the entertainments available to them in urban precincts. But that seems to me only to provide evidence for the central arguments of this book. The inhabitants of the center cities of the twenty-first century will be largely those with money—those who have the greatest choice about where to live. Those who inhabit the periphery will be for the most part those for whom prices in the center are prohibitive. As the Urban Land Institute concludes, "Once the economy recovers and household formation resumes, the demand for urban housing will greatly outstrip the supply."

So to me, the bulk of the evidence points to the emergence of a city-seeking young population cohort—mostly singles, couples, and families with very young children. The question will be where to put them. This might not seem a very difficult question in light of the glut of empty or near-empty condominiums that line downtown Miami, Phoenix, and other Sun Belt cities that overbuilt in the center during the housing boom of the last decade.

But it is a crucial question nevertheless. Most cities are not Miami or Phoenix. They are more like Houston, with a tiny supply of downtown housing and little prospect of building or converting much more. Or they are more like Washington, where Dupont Circle, the traditionally hip point of entry for young people in the baby boom and Generation X, is now too expensive for their millennial successors.

There are several answers to the question of where we are going to put the emerging urban-seeking cohort. One, which might be called the D.C.-Chicago option, is simply to expand the range of desirable housing gradually outward from the center of the city, attracting young people to neighborhoods that were considered too dangerous to live in only a decade ago.

The other is more complicated, and more difficult. It is to urbanize the suburbs. There is currently a startling amount of abandoned and available land stretching across the diverse corners of suburban America. Much of this is "grayfields"—the land underneath enclosed shopping centers that were built in the 1960s and 1970s, flourished in the 1980s and 1990s, and were essentially dead by the first decade of the new century. Most enclosed shopping centers, if they are still holding on, are unlikely to do so much longer. The International Council of Shopping Centers estimates that there are one thousand enclosed malls left in the United States, but that most of them will not survive. The demographer Arthur C. Nelson calculated in 2009 that in the coming ten years, 2.8 million acres of grayfields will be open for redevelopment. Walmart alone has a real estate inventory of more than two hundred of its older stores that have become available for leasing.

The growing glut of grayfields is important for the urban future not because it represents the only block of developable suburban land—there is much more land that has never been built on at all—but because for hundreds of suburbs around the country, the shopping center was the one recognizable fulcrum of activity the community possessed. When the shopping center dies, there is no physical space to hold the community together at all. That is why, over the past ten years, suburbs around America have been struggling to convert dead or dying malls into something much different—town centers that emulate, as much as possible, the downtowns that exist within the city. Many—perhaps the majority—have been at best partially successful. They have failed to attract the residential, retail, and office combination that a successful downtown needs no matter where it is located.

But some have been trying very hard. If you are looking for evidence of that, you might want to go to Denver.

. . .

WHY DENVER should be emerging as the capital of the suburban town center phenomenon may seem a little perplexing at first. It is not, after all, a dense Eastern city. It is a sprawling, exceptionally auto-dependent Western metropolis. But there are good explanations. One is the glut of enclosed malls from the 1960s and 1970s that the Denver area somehow managed to produce. Strapped for cash by low income taxes and property taxes, Denver suburbs launched a competition with one another to bring in sales tax receipts by building shopping centers. In quite a few cases, this worked nicely for a while—until a newer, glitzier mall was built a few years later on land farther from the city. The ultimate result was that by the later years of the last decade, there were thirteen enclosed regional malls in the Denver area, and seven of them were failing and under serious consideration for some form of retrofit.

That is one reason Denver has produced so much original thinking and experimentation on the subject of suburban town centers. The other reason is Stapleton International Airport.

Stapleton was Denver's only major airport from the dawn of commercial aviation until the 1990s, when the much larger Denver International Airport was built some thirty miles from the city. Technically, Stapleton is not part of a suburb at all; it exists within the city limits. But when it was leveled in the 1990s, it launched a complex discussion of just what its 4,700 acres of suddenly empty and relatively convenient land might be used for. It was an immense piece of property less than ten minutes from the heart of Denver. And it was demolished and replaced by a huge new mixed-use development aimed at capturing as much as possible of the urban experience.

Stapleton does not seem, at first glance, to be an ideal spot for urban retrofitting. It is too big, for one thing. More than seven square miles in area, it is much larger than Manhattan's Central Park. There is no way to walk from one end to the other, even if one has the endurance; it is bisected by Interstate Highway 70. There is no public transportation inside it. Of the three major shopping centers within its borders, all built after the airport was torn down, one is little more

than conventional big-box retail. This least distinguished of the retail
centers was built first, to generate revenue that might make the other
two more financially feasible. But at the southern tip, as one walks
along the shaded sidewalks of Twenty-ninth Street, Stapleton offers a
hint of what suburban retrofitting might actually be like. It is, in some
of its development, an imitation of a city neighborhood. In fact, it is
the biggest neighborhood in Denver. The houses spread out over most
of its 4,700 acres, a blend of Victorian and Craftsman, Colonial, and
Mediterranean revival. All of them are on small lots, none larger than
a quarter acre. The fact that Stapleton was built this way, rather than
as one more cookie-cutter suburban subdivision, is a tribute of sorts to
the city of Denver, circa 1995; its master planner, Peter Calthorpe; and
its developers, Forest City Enterprises.

Moreover, it has generally been a success. Prior to the recession,
its 3,600 occupied units were increasing in value at a rate of roughly
10 percent a year. There are ten thousand residents of Stapleton now,

*Loft apartments and condominiums are standard housing at Stapleton,
a newly urbanized piece of Denver territory built to replace the city's
demolished airport.*

out of a projected population of thirty thousand people two decades from now, a fair proportion of them empty nesters but a startling number of families. There are so many young children during the day on Twenty-ninth Street that the developer had to put in "stroller corrals" for the double-wide contraptions that the more affluent residents in their twenties and thirties have become addicted to. Stapleton has an elementary school and a middle school, as well as the magnet Denver School for Science and Technology. There is a two-and-a-half-acre green where the Fourth of July is celebrated every year.

Stapleton is far from being the ideal retrofit, urban or suburban. Its efforts to attract multifamily housing largely have failed, and the office space has not filled out the way the developer wanted it to. It is, and will be, almost entirely car-dependent. But conceived as early as it was, at a time when suburban shopping-mall culture was still largely thriving, it was a bold and productive experiment. It got others thinking about what might be possible. "Stapleton was a significant proving ground," says Denver planning director Peter Park. "You could try anything if you were a developer, see if it might work elsewhere. It elevated developer confidence that urban projects could do well."

IT SEEMS ODD in a way to describe Stapleton as the progenitor of Belmar, the urbanist experiment on the other side of Denver, because their origins couldn't be more different. Stapleton was built on vacant land whose useful life as an airport had come to a planned conclusion. Belmar replaced a shopping mall that went from being highly profitable to being a financial disaster in the space of barely five years. And yet they are part of the same movement and fulfill some of the same desires: They are attempts to establish an urban environment on empty suburban space.

Belmar is in Lakewood, an inner suburb just five miles west of Denver, and it stands on the site of the demolished Villa Italia, a relatively nondescript enclosed shopping mall but the only real center Lakewood ever knew, the only real public place for more than one hundred thousand city residents to visit. And they did go there, for more than just shopping. As the current mayor, Bob Murphy, says, "People got married at Villa Italia, had their proms at Villa Italia. It was the cat's meow. But it wasn't a downtown. It was a mall."

As late as the mid-1990s, Villa Italia was still the engine whose tax revenues financed Lakewood's expanding public needs; but by 2000, it was dying. Villa Italia is a testament to just how fast an aging shopping mall can collapse. Its stores went from 90 percent leased to 50 percent leased in the space of five years, a victim of the glut of malls opening in suburban Denver and the retail industry consolidation that robbed it of its most important anchor department stores. Instead of a welcoming spot for weddings, it became a dangerous place with an increasing gang presence and the need for additional police supervision. In the words of Bob Murphy, "It was a boarded-up mall with a chain-link fence around it. We saw the future and it wasn't bright."

Something had to be done about Villa Italia, and done quickly, not only because its increasingly decrepit status was a civic embarrassment, but because Lakewood needed the money. There isn't much else to tax in Lakewood; in its heyday, the mall provided as much as 50 percent of the town's revenue base.

Compared to Stapleton, Belmar is a pygmy—104 acres compared to nearly 5,000. Its residential population, after more than five years of continuous development, is still less than three thousand. But in its own way, it represents a striking achievement. Stapleton was built on land that the city of Denver had already leveled. At Belmar, it cost $120 million to demolish Villa Italia and replace its acres of asphalt with twenty-three gridded streets. Much of this represents the vision of three men: then–city manager Mike Rock, then-mayor Steve Burkholder, and developer Mark Falcone, chief executive of a development firm called Continuum Partners. "The most important part of getting plans right is human scale," Falcone insists. "People are thirsting for something more intimate."

Sitting in a café at Wadsworth Boulevard and Alaska Drive on the busiest corner in Belmar, one finds it difficult to imagine that this was once the center of an indoor mall. Burkholder, Rock, and Falcone had to persuade the residents of a conservative and somewhat insular suburb of 140,000 people that it was ripe to become a major experiment in the retrofitting of suburban America. But they managed to do that.

And through a long sequence of advances and setbacks, Belmar has generally thrived. Its retail businesses have mostly hung on during the recession, although there are some vacant storefronts. Its restaurants are hard to get into on a pleasant summer night. It brings $1.3 million a year in revenues to Lakewood, although much of the sales tax money is scheduled to go back to the developer under a tax increment financing deal. It employs two thousand people, the largest employer being the Integer Group, a marketing company.

Most important, though, it is a residential success. Belmar opted for a different strategy than Stapleton; it never really went after families. There is no school located on the property. But it has been able to attract singles, young couples, and empty nesters, the demographic that a retrofitted suburbia is going to have to attract. Its dwelling places are two-thirds apartments; they are 95 percent rented, most of them at a premium of roughly 20 percent over market prices in nearby areas.

Actually, it is easier to combine work, play, and commerce in Belmar than it is in downtown Denver. From an apartment overlooking the town square, with its playground and wintertime ice rink, one can walk a quarter mile and find a Whole Foods grocery, a Target department store, a Nordstrom clothing store, and a wide variety of chain and local restaurants. The project's Italian Fest, a carryover from the Villa Italia days, draws one hundred thousand people in a week during the summer. There is a bocce court that was preserved intact from a spot inside the old mall. "It didn't take long for people to embrace it," the current mayor boasts. "It's now the core of our identity as a city."

Belmar may come as close to the model of retrofitted suburbia as anything that has been completed so far. There is only one component that it lacks: It has no transit system, and it is unlikely ever to get one.

OF THE NEARLY DOZEN SUBURBAN RETROFITS designed or planned in the metropolitan Denver area, only one really qualifies as a transit-oriented development, and that is CityCenter Englewood, on the east

The pedestrian-scale development at Belmar, built over the remains of a failed shopping mall in Lakewood, Colorado, is an experiment in creating an urban experience in a classic Denver suburb.

side of metropolitan Denver, not too far from Stapleton. One can ride a light-rail train right to the entrance of the town center, cross over a pedestrian bridge with impressive metal trusses, and stand in a civic courtyard in which the town hall has taken the place of an old department store in the middle of Cinderella City, an enclosed mall built in 1968 and dead by the last of the 1990s. CityCenter Englewood is the oldest completed retrofit in the Denver area; its opening in 2001 predated even the major elements of Stapleton. Promotional literature calls it "the first project in Colorado—and among a handful nationally—to replace a suburban shopping mall with a living, breathing, mixed-use downtown."

Some of the right elements for pedestrian scale are present: Surrounding the town hall is a small park dotted with sculptures and other modern art structures aimed at convincing the visitor that Englewood is an arts-minded community. There is a small, pedestrian-oriented street just beyond the park that suggests human scale.

But by most standards of suburban retrofit and pedestrian use, CityCenter Englewood is no triumph. The light-rail station is one of the busier ones within the metropolitan Denver system, but most of the people who come to shop or work there do not ride the train; they drive and park in one of two enormous open lots at either side of the project. The amount of pedestrian-oriented retail shopping is very small, about seven thousand square feet in all. A few hundred yards beyond the impressive civic building is a power center with Walmart and the usual giant big-box tenants. This center is an enormous help in paying the taxes of a community of about thirty-two thousand people, but it turns its back on the light-rail station and on transit-oriented development in general. Walking from the station to the Walmart is not only a difficult experience, it is barely a feasible one. CityCenter Englewood is essentially a small, pleasant enclave masking oceans of asphalt.

Perhaps the most remarkable thing about the project is that a few blocks beyond all of it, beyond the town green and the town hall, the power center with the big-box stores, there is an old, slightly seedy, but interesting prewar downtown, with locally owned businesses still open. Unless you are driving, you have to take a shuttle bus from the front entrance of the town hall even to discover that it is there. Instead of sprucing up the historic center that already existed, the town planners and developers razed the development of the 1960s and built on top of that.

In this respect, CityCenter Englewood is an entirely different creature from Belmar. In Belmar, there was no center, despite the fact that Lakewood was Colorado's fourth-largest city. There was no downtown to save. In Englewood there was one, but it was ignored. And this is a criticism that has been applied to the fledgling suburban retrofit craze and the New Urbanist design philosophy from which it has generally emerged. In spite of a commitment to infill projects and to saving what is most precious about the urban past, the most ambitious projects have been built on empty land.

And it is so hard to get all the elements working together. At least one of the major pieces of the puzzle—residential, retail, or office development—is nearly always missing. Belmar has never been able to attract the offices or multifamily housing that its planners envisioned at the start. Stapleton has the residential scale to be a meaningful part of the Denver housing scene, but like Belmar, it has no transit, and even when the commuter rail begins stopping at its northern end in a few years, the majority of residents will not be able to take advantage of it. CityCenter Englewood is a model of transportation efficiency, but the convenience of transit to the development seems almost irrelevant to most of those who use it. Each of the projects, even Stapleton, feels like a small oasis squeezed between multilane highways deemed necessary to attract the customers upon which retail success depends. Walk down the main shopping street of Belmar, and you can easily imagine yourself standing in the middle of a twenty-first-century urban experiment. But to venture outside the twenty-three gridded blocks of Belmar, even to cross the street at the edge of the project, is to be reminded that one is, for all the efforts at urban innovation, reentering the incomparably larger expanse of car-dependent suburbia.

And perhaps that is the most important point to make about Denver and its sincere interest in retrofitting the suburbs. The projects built so far, and even the ones in the planning stages, are drops in the bucket. Belmar, when it is fully built out, will have a population of about 3,000. Lakewood, the suburb that houses it, has a population of about 140,000. It would literally take a dozen Belmars to make an appreciable dent in the character of what has for virtually its entire existence been a suburb with precious little character at all.

The lesson is that if retrofitted suburbia is to meet the demands for classic urbanism that today's millennial generation tells so many poll-takers it wants, suburban retrofits will have to become much, much denser. They will need to move beyond sidewalk cafés and nighttime street life and build buildings with enough tenants and home owners to support the retail on the ground floor, without a six-lane highway whizzing by just a couple of blocks away. They will need to have transit stations integrated into the very fabric of the developments. Whether this is possible, I don't know. The suburban retrofits are, despite the number of examples that multiply every year, in only the earliest stages.

But if urbanized suburbia is going to be the answer for this generation, or even a large part of it, density—somewhere—is the only real choice.

DENSITY HAS BEEN, in many ways, the principal theme of New Urbanism, the movement that is now two decades old and has had a profound if not quite revolutionary impact on the shape of cities all over the Western world. In 1990, the New Urbanists were a small, close-knit coterie of architects and planners with a simple and heretical message: The automobile, and four decades of building homes, streets, and suburbs for the automobile's convenience, had drained American places of the community and intimacy that human beings naturally desire. Recapturing the attractiveness and livability of the traditional American city would require an effort to convince millions of suburbanites and a rising millennial generation that density was nothing to be afraid of. It was the way to live a life of sociability that placed walking at the center of the urban experience.

Many public officials and planning professionals were first introduced to the principles of New Urbanism through the vehicle of lectures and slide shows documenting the ugliness of suburban sprawl and the intelligence of urban design as practiced in many places in the preautomobile era. Andres Duany, Elizabeth Plater-Zyberk, Peter Calthorpe, and a handful of coconspirators carried these slides to countless audiences all over the country in the early and mid-1990s. As a model of their intentions, they offered Seaside, the residential community in north Florida that was designed by Duany and Plater-Zyberk in the 1980s, complete with sidewalks, front porches, a town square, and a whole array of other reminders of the old-fashioned, pedestrian-friendly American small town.

The first half of the 1990s brought the New Urbanism a reputation and a following far beyond what its founders could have predicted. Not that a whole collection of Seasides emerged on the American landscape—the number of communities built according to the original Duany principles remained tiny. But the march of the New Urbanists through the forest of American public opinion was all but unstoppable. By mid-1995, they had reached the cover of *Newsweek*. By 1996, *The New York Times* was calling them "the most important phenomenon to emerge in American architecture in the post–Cold War era."

Planners in cities and towns began drafting master plans laced with references to "mixed-use development," "pedestrian friendliness," "resource efficiency," and a whole battery of terms that might have come straight out of the New Urbanist charter. The annual summer meetings of the Congress for the New Urbanism quickly grew from single-room bull sessions into big-time extravaganzas, with hundreds of participants, dozens of speakers, and coverage by numerous reporters from America and overseas.

It was an extremely heady but also a dangerous position to be in. On the one hand, the New Urbanists couldn't be said to have altered the physical landscape of America in any significant way. On the other hand, they had done just well enough to spawn a growing army of imitators.

If there weren't many Seasides being built in the 1990s, there clearly were lots of little pieces of Seaside turning up in otherwise conventional suburban developments: sidewalks, porches, Victorian street lamps, and other snatches of neotraditional architectural detail. And there were lots of developers who felt that describing a subdivision as neotraditional—or New Urbanist—was a good way to get the houses sold.

The one convincing criticism of Seaside that continued for years was that there was nothing very urban about it. Seaside was (and is) a lovely little traditional town. It was the setting for the movie *The Truman Show,* much of whose purpose was to tell a story about a reality TV show set in an idyllic community. But it was largely a beachfront resort establishment, with few of its home owners living there year-round. There were no large or even midsize cities anywhere near it. It was a dazzling display of many of the refinements of the early twentieth-century small town. But it did not point the way to urbanizing suburbia, or urbanizing anything, for that matter.

Nor did Kentlands, the next major New Urbanist development, launched in the Maryland suburbs, more than twenty miles from Washington, D.C. Kentlands was no beachfront resort—it was a year-round residence for people who wanted sidewalks, porches, neigh-borly community, and all the other important accoutrements of New Urbanist thinking. Unlike Seaside, Kentlands was to include a success-ful retail component. When Kentlands was designed by Duany and Plater-Zyberk in the late 1980s, it had a clever plan for a shopping cen-ter that could be pedestrian-friendly and car-friendly at the same time. The stores, even the big-box retail units, would front on a tree-lined boulevard that the residents could use to walk to shopping and back home. The rear of the same stores would face a big parking lot and a busy highway, but nobody inside Kentlands would need to look at that. They could treat the village center as if it were a small-town Main Street in the 1940s.

There was no way to be sure how that plan would have worked, because the recession of the early 1990s came along and bankrupted the original developer, and the bank that took over the project didn't see it as practical. A shopping center was eventually built just across the road from Kentlands, and the residents could walk to it, but it was everything the New Urbanism abhors: cookie-cutter, strip mall–type retail units separated from the street by acres of parking lot.

Kentlands hasn't been a failure by any means. As the years went by, it regrouped in an increasingly urbanist direction and attracted a larger pedestrian-friendly retail component. But it is not a transit-oriented development: The way to get there is by car, and only by car. By 2005, the New Urbanists had demonstrated that they could build success-ful residential projects on greenfield suburban land. But they had not demonstrated that they could comfortably put together all the pieces that genuinely urbanizing suburbia would need: residential, retail, offices, and public transportation. In other words, density.

A more versatile effort turned up a few years later near Portland, Oregon, at Orenco Station, thirty minutes from the center of the city by light-rail train. It's a third-of-a-mile walk between Orenco's train station and its downtown, and the two are separated by a long stretch of land with condominiums on one side and an open grass field on the other. Downtown Orenco has what looks like a Victorian Main Street shopping block, with big bay windows in the storefronts and round turrets on top of the buildings. Surrounding this business district are modestly sized English cottages and Craftsman bungalows with the same period look as the shopping street. Behind the houses stands a village green.

Orenco was a developer's high-stakes gamble on two hundred acres of empty farmland, fifteen miles from downtown Portland. It was designed to be eighteen hundred residential units, twenty-seven thousand square feet of retail, and thirty thousand square feet of office space constructed around an old-fashioned main street, in the densest, most urbanized suburban project built anywhere in the country up to that point.

And it was the best test of the theory that traditional urban design, public transit, and suburban life could coexist in harmony. It is possible—perhaps not easy, but possible—to live in Orenco without a car. Hillsboro, a magnet for high-tech employment in what locals call "Silicon Forest," is on the same Westside rail line. Intel has a big facility not far from Orenco's borders.

The developers of Orenco were convinced they had created a path breaking new form of urbanity in the suburbs that would spread like wildfire in the next few years, appealing to empty nesters and a city-seeking younger generation as well. "It is so far beyond what anyone else has done," one of the developers exulted. "But it is going to be the future of the country."

When it came to merging the important elements of urbanized suburbia, Orenco jumped off to a flashy start. Within a year, Orenco's town center had a florist, a dry cleaner, a wine-and-cheese store, an Indian restaurant, a steakhouse, and an Italian café. A stockbroker, a dentist, and an insurance agent had set up shop in second-floor offices above the retail units. But there was very little shopping for everyday residential needs. For that sort of shopping, residents of Orenco had to drive a mile or so down Cornell Road, a four-lane arterial highway that ran in front of the town center and was carrying twenty-five thousand cars a day. After a decade, much of the main-street retail had disappeared. There was an upscale grocery store, but relatively few other shops in the center of town. And despite the presence of the light-rail station a third of a mile from the main street, most residents were still driving to work.

That highlighted what may have been the one flaw in this whole ambitious experiment. Bold as they were, Orenco's designers didn't dare build the traditional shopping street right next to the station, as would have been the case in an old-fashioned city or prewar suburb. If they had, Orenco might have had the compact charm of true urbanism. But then the local merchants would have had few customers other than the immediate residents. Placing the downtown one-third of a mile away, next to a multilane highway, created the opportunity to attract drive-by traffic as well. But it left the dream of a true urbanized suburb still unfulfilled.

The next decade saw the emergence of a series of New Urbanist communities, among them Celebration, the large-scale project created by the Disney corporation on empty land in central Florida just a few miles from the Disney amusement parks. In a way, Celebration was the most ambitious of the New Urbanist experiments. It was a brand-new town with a goal of ten thousand residents by 2010 (it actually reached about eleven thousand), and main-street shopping that the developer was in a position to subsidize. Celebration became a tourist attraction in its own right; many of the visitors to Disney World and Epcot Center drove a few extra miles to take a look at the built-from-scratch traditional community, its town square and main street, and its mixture of Victorian houses, Colonials, and Craftsman bungalows surrounded by generously sized parks. But like Orenco, Celebration didn't solve the density problem; it lacked transit connections and struggled to achieve the critical mass to make main-street commercial development viable on its own.

Nearly two decades after its founding, New Urbanism was still trying to create a community that embodied all the elements of its doctrine and seeking to retrofit or urbanize the suburbs in a way that assembled all the pieces of the puzzle. But there was an immense experiment aimed at doing just that. It was being built at Tysons Corner, in the Virginia suburbs ten miles west of Washington, D.C.

TYSONS CORNER has never been anything much to look at. That doesn't mean simply that it's unattractive—although it is—but that when you pass through it, along the main commercial strip of Route 7, in northern Virginia's Fairfax County, you don't even get the feeling that anything substantial is there. You see a long, loose string of office buildings built in the 1970s and 1980s, scattered over a stretch of two or three miles, few of them close together or in any way congruent with one another. You pass two huge regional shopping malls, both tucked behind vast parking lots and barely visible from the highway. You don't know for sure when you've reached the place, and there's no way to tell when you've left.

The utter placelessness of Tysons Corner is one important truth about it. But there's an even more important one: It is the twelfth-largest business district in the United States. More than one hundred thousand people work there. Every morning and every evening, forty thousand cars inch down Route 7 and Route 123, overwhelmed arterial roads that lack the capacity to handle the traffic at anything more than a glacial pace.

In the nearly five decades since the modern history of Tysons began, Fairfax County and its leaders have passed through several stages in trying to come to terms with what it is and what it means. First, there was sheer novelty—the presence of glass towers and upscale shopping on what had been farmland only a few years before. Then in the 1980s came an attitude of somewhat jaded acceptance: It's an eyesore, but it's a money machine, and besides, there's nothing we can do to change it now. Only with the start of the new century did planners and a few politicians dare to express a radical idea: A region that can produce the twelfth-biggest business center in the country ought to be able to civilize it and bring in some of the elements of urban living.

It was in the summer of 2001 that Andres Duany came to Fairfax with slides of San Francisco and Paris, and told an audience of suburbanites that he could build something equally appealing for them right there in the Virginia suburbs. Genuine urbanism was within their grasp—if they were willing to go for it. "This is a fantastic opportunity," he exulted, "to create a truly wonderful place." It was like Pinocchio being told that if he shaped up, he might eventually become a real live boy.

But when Duany presented his dream of urbanizing Tysons,

he wasn't simply talking about trees or parks or fashionable boulevards. He was talking about a dozen residential towers, tall enough
to accommodate twelve thousand people, big crowds on the streets,
and heavy-duty public transportation. He was talking about density.
He admitted it. "High density is not a punishment if it is built in true
urbanism," Duany insisted that day. "High density is a true delight."

The audience was not swept away. "What Duany wants to do is put
a city here," one resident complained. "We don't want a city here." One
of the elected county supervisors, Gerald Connolly, was even more
blunt. "I think he is being arrogant," Connolly said, "and, frankly, igno-
rant. Any proposal that intense is dead on arrival." And Connolly was
right: Duany's idea never went anywhere. Touchy as they might have
been about the reputation of Tysons Corner, the citizens of Fairfax
were not ready for density in 2001.

If you work in local government anywhere, the odds are you have
heard the joke that there are two things Americans can't stand: sprawl
and density. I refer to it as a joke, but in fact it comes close to being
a literal truth. Millions of Americans who live in places like Fairfax
County visit Boston and San Francisco and wish they could re-create
some of that urbanity and elegance for themselves. But faced with the
reality of what true urban sophistication requires—height, big crowds,
and strangers from the city flocking in on trains—they back off. That's
the deadlock of density.

It's quite plausible to argue that the deadlock will not be broken in
our lifetimes: that if the price of containing sprawl is to turn suburbs
into cities, it is a price American suburbanites simply will not pay. But
it is also plausible to argue that slowly and almost imperceptibly, the
deadlock of density is being replaced by a willingness to take a few
risks. It is even plausible to make that case in Fairfax County.

Fairfax didn't welcome Duany, but just five years later, the county
board gave its approval to a stunning amount of dense high-rise
development—as much as Duany ever proposed. In 2006, the board
voted for a plan designed to surround the original 1968 shopping mall
with eight towers, some as tall as thirty stories, containing 1,350 condos and apartments, four office buildings, and a three-hundred-room
hotel. And that was just on one side of the road. Across Route 123,

where the second big mall is located, there was a plan for eight more towers, most of them designed for offices.

The developer of this project, the Macerich Co. of California, pressed all the right New Urbanist buttons. Its computerized graphics envisioned spacious plazas, sculpture gardens, skating rinks, and performance space. Macerich talked about making the intersection of routes 7 and 123 into a new "Central Park," a "100 percent downtown corner."

Most intriguing of all, Macerich promised to take the blank acres of asphalt that have characterized Tysons for decades and superimpose a grid that would provide fifty-four additional pedestrian-friendly streets for traffic to move in, generate a huge increase in sidewalk capacity, provide up to fourteen thousand curbside parking spaces, and in the end create something that wouldn't just possess the density of a city but would actually look like a city.

All of this was to be timed to the extension of a Metro transit line, scheduled to reach Tysons Corner in 2013 or shortly thereafter. The Metro station will be right across from the redesigned mixed-use mall; all the residential towers are supposed to be within easy walking distance of the station—some literally in its shadow.

But there are some excellent reasons to be skeptical. The original transit plan, favored by Macerich as well as by local residents, was to place the subway line underground, leaving all the surface land around the station free for urban amenities. That didn't happen. The U.S. Department of Transportation and the Virginia congressional delegation said going underground would cost more money, and they didn't want to pay for it. So rail transit will come to Tysons in the form of a seventy-foot-high elevated track along Route 123, with disembarking passengers required to go down to the street and then climb back up a bridge to get to the plaza and the towers. It's not exactly the best way to signal the presence of an urban village.

However, the really important part—and the hardest part—is the grid. Developers know how to build thirty-story buildings; they know how to create plazas with skating rinks. But retrofitting seventeen hundred acres of suburban asphalt with a network of walkable streets will be an enormous challenge, one that will require huge investments of money and determination from both the developer and the government. The plain truth is that nobody has ever done this before—not on the scale that is being called for at Tysons Corner. And yet if the grid doesn't happen, Tysons may never be a vibrant city or any kind of city at all. It may just be a collection of tall buildings arranged a little more compactly than the ones that are there now.

In the summer of 2010, Tysons Corner was a jumble of construction activity, but it was all subway. The residential, retail, and office developers had all delayed their plans for the new walkable city, a casualty of the national bank lending crunch and a glut of suburban office space. But the county board had just reaffirmed its support for the entire project, residential towers, gridded streets, and all. The developers insisted they remained committed to it. All seemed convinced that when the transit line opens, New Urbanist development fervor will rise again. Macerich said officially that it would continue to take its time and "would be guided by market demand." A spokesman for another development company said that "it took forty years to get to this point, and significant changes are going to take another couple of decades." But Adam Ducker, of the real estate advisory firm RCLCO, remained exultant. "There are lots of places like Tysons Corner," he told a *Washington Post* columnist, "but nobody has demonstrated how you can really do this. Nobody has the mix of political, development community, and general population buy-in to make it happen."

None of this is made easier by the changes in transportation policy virtually guaranteed by the change in political leadership in a county such as Fairfax every several years. There will be many approaches to transportation based on electoral decisions in the long years before any elaborate plan for Tysons Corner is finally realized. But the crucial work has begun. It is hard to imagine any turning back from the overarching idea of an urbanized place in what would seem to be the unlikeliest of suburbs.

My guess is that when all of this development is completed, no matter how many years from now, Andres Duany's vision won't be close to realization. Nor do I expect that Tysons Corner will much resemble the green pedestrian oasis pictured in the computerized Mac-erich sketches. But I think it will meet the standards of retrofitted suburbia. I also think it will be a commercial success.

I'm convinced of that because I see all around me a generation of young, mainstream, middle-class adults who are looking for some form of midlevel urban experience: not bohemian inner-city adven-ture, but definitely not cul-de-sacs and long automobile commutes. There are more of them coming into the residential market every year. They like the idea of having some space, but they aren't fleeing in ter-ror at the mention of density. They aren't willing to sell their cars, but they appreciate the advantage of having another way to get around. If Tysons Corner is rebuilt on a reasonable human scale and with a modicum of physical appeal, they will go for it, imperfect as it may be.

And then we will begin to see experiments of this sort in suburbs all over the country, launched by developers and local governments that may still be a little nervous about density but will know one thing for sure: If Tysons Corner can be reborn, nothing in the suburbs is beyond hope. If the effort to rebuild Tysons Corner somehow succeeds, it will become a national model for retrofitting suburbia for the millennial generation.

CONCLUSION

WORLD WAR II was a long way from over at the beginning of 1944, but the outcome was taken for granted among the civilian population in the United States. The Allies would win, and a new kind of world would come into place. The debate among economists and public policy experts was about what that world would be like. Should the nation expect a return to the conditions of economic stagnation that had prevailed for more than a decade before the war brought three years of unexpected prosperity? Or would it be a different sort of world, operating under new rules that might make possible a sustained period of national economic health and stability?

A majority of economists took the pessimistic side. The war had brought the Great Depression to an end, they reasoned, but it was an artificial boom that had been caused by military production and could not be expected to last. Once the war was over, we would be returning to the same economic hard times that had prevailed prior to Pearl Harbor. A minority of specialists felt this was false: The coming elements of American civic life were unpredictable, they wrote, but there was no reason to assume that these would be the ones that had existed prior to the cataclysmic Second World War.

In a very different but interesting way, 2011 feels like 1944 might have felt to those who were living through it. The United States is gradually reaching the end of a cataclysm, economic rather than military, but a cataclysm nonetheless, and it is impossible not to wonder what ordinary American life will look like in the postrecession future. Some of the most intriguing questions this time are ones of culture, demographics, and the use of physical space. It is perfectly possible to argue, as critics such as Joel Kotkin and David Brooks do, that the rules are not about to change—that the auto-dependent existence, suburban expansion, and the urban decline of the late twentieth century will simply resume. It is also possible to argue, as do critics on the other side, such as Christopher Leinberger and Arthur C. Nelson, that the Great Recession will prove to be a cultural and demographic turning point. Cities and suburbs will cease to play the role that they played in the second half of the twentieth century. Indeed, it is plausible to contend—as this book largely does—that the roles of cities and suburbs will not only change but will very nearly reverse themselves. A demographic inversion will take place.

Much that is important remains unpredictable by anyone writing about the future of the urban and suburban experience. In the year 2020, will the price of gasoline be $3 a gallon? Five dollars? Ten dollars? We all saw what happened in the spring of 2008, when the price of a gallon of gas first rose beyond $4 in most parts of the country. The demand for expensive homes in the exurbs declined, and the interest in urban living among the affluent rose. I am not an expert on energy policy, but most of those who are predict that when the economies of the developed world regain their strength, the demand for oil will be great enough to drive gas prices in America beyond where they were in 2008, or where they are now.

On the other hand, what if cars powered by fuels other than gasoline become ubiquitous on American highways, and the cost of driving long distances each day remains what it is now, or even becomes cheaper? One has a right to be skeptical about this happening anytime in the near future. The arrival of these cars has been anticipated now for a generation, and still only a relative handful are in operation. But suppose something like this does occur. Suppose it becomes possible to buy a car at close to the current price that can travel eighty miles on one gallon of fuel. Will that allow the car-dominated outer suburb to continue flourishing? Perhaps. Or perhaps not. Fuel economy does not decrease traffic congestion or reduce the length of the daily commute. In many American cities, the question of where to live is already as much a question of time as it is of money. That will continue to be true in the postrecession world, no matter how much it costs in fuel to drive a mile down the road. People who live in the American cities of the next generation will be doing so as a matter of choice, and the question of whether to save two or three hours commuting back and forth to work each day rather than staying put in exurbia represents one of the crucial decisions that will determine what the cities and suburbs of the coming decades will look like.

I would go so far as to say that choice is what the urbanism of the next generation is all about. Traditional cities and the pockets of newly created urban design that are springing up around them, as in Denver, will give the millennial generation now entering adulthood a set of options that none of the emerging generations of the past sixty years has really had. Except in a very few places, metropolitan areas around the country did not offer the young adults of the 1960s or 1970s much of a menu when it came to deciding where they might choose to live and raise their families. Unless one was an extremely intrepid pioneer, it was not really practical to live in downtown Charlotte or Memphis or Milwaukee. The number of desirable housing units near the center of most cities was tiny, the supply of services and commerce available was meager, and high crime rates made urban living a dangerous experience that an overwhelming majority of the generation would not consider choosing.

Those problems have not disappeared, but they are disappearing. It is now possible to live in relative comfort in the middle of most of the big cities in America. This may mean doing without a few of the amenities that many middle-class adults like to have, such as a drugstore or grocery store within walking distance, but for others the convenience of walking or taking other quick transportation to restaurants, entertainment, and downtown jobs is a sufficient benefit.

In many cities, at the moment, there is a greater problem of oversupply than of unfulfilled demand. There are partially inhabited or partially complete condominium towers awaiting the return of an economy in which more people who find them attractive will be able to afford them. But this state of affairs will not last forever.

It is important to reiterate that demographic inversion and mass migration are not the same thing. Mass migration means, to me, at least, a reversal in which a much greater proportion of the residents

of a large metropolitan area will live near the center of the city than
have lived there for the past thirty or forty years. Robert Fishman,
one of America's most respected urban historians, believes that a "fifth
great migration" is taking place. This amplifies the contention of Lewis
Mumford in the 1920s that there had been three previous ones (west
across the frontier in the early nineteenth century; from farms to factory towns a few decades later; and to the great metropolitan centers around the beginning of the twentieth century), and Mumford's
accurate prediction that there would soon be a fourth, decentralizing
population away from city centers and into empty suburban land, as
the twentieth century unfolded.

Fishman's fifth great migration, back to city centers and away from
suburbs, is one he believes will dominate urban demographics in the
generation to come. In his view, this will be a full-scale city revival that
"will reurbanize precisely those inner-city districts that were previously
depopulated." These evolutionary changes will bring back to the city
(or retain there) middle-class blacks, newcomers from other countries,
and millions of members of the white middle class who have lived in
the suburbs for most of their lives, whether in childhood, youthful
family nurturing, or childless middle age. I am personally skeptical of
any significant revival of population in the center among blacks and
immigrants. Everything the census tells us suggests that a majority
among these groups, for a variety of reasons, wants to leave the center
and settle outside city borders. If there is a fifth migration, I would
hold that it will be very largely a migration of the white upper middle
class.

Fishman does not attach specific numbers to his urban migration,
so it is difficult to gauge just how large a cohort of migrants he is talking about. One thing that seems clear is that he is not talking about a
new American urbanism built on the massive construction of urban
skyscrapers located within classic downtown borders. It is possible to
talk about a twenty-first-century skyscraper urbanism in a few North
American cities, but in the much larger number of semisuccessful cities whose populations range from 250,000 to about a million, forests
of new downtown towers seem unlikely, whatever the larger appeal of

the fifth migration might be. There is limited land available for building these skyscrapers, difficulty (at least for a while) obtaining the rents or mortgages that make them profitable, and backlogs of empty units that need to be filled up before new ones can be constructed.

So it will turn out that much of the burden of the fifth migration will fall on the neighborhoods just beyond or reasonably close to downtown, regions that, as Mumford pointed out in the 1920s, long suffered from the annoyance of noise and congestion, the odors of industrialism, and the scourge of violent crime. We have already seen this in several places: in Sheffield in Chicago; in the rebuilding of the Fourth Ward in Houston; in the inner communities of Brooklyn in the first decade of the new century. We have also seen places where it will be very difficult to achieve, such as some of the neighborhoods just north of Center City in Philadelphia.

But when it comes to demographic inversion, the importance of the movement rests on the character of the new population group rather than on its size. There are those who predict that the distant exurbs that proved so attractive in the late twentieth century will turn into the slums of 2030. At the risk of repeating myself, I would argue something softer. I think the exurbs will be ports of entry for newcomers and minorities who will either not be attracted to, or not be able to afford, life in the center of a metropolitan area. This is what demographic inversion is about. It is why Chicago in 2030 will look more like the Paris of 1910 than like the Detroit of 1970.

Anyone who doubts that the adults of the coming generation will be making new sorts of choices need only look, as we did earlier, at raw demographics. For one thing, they guarantee a vast increase in the number of people over age sixty-five—the current baby boomers. The proportion of the U.S. population over sixty-five right now is about 13 percent. In 2030, it will be 19 percent. Tens of millions of these people will choose to stay where they are, to age in place. Others will move to a city center or its environs. But scarcely any will be buying large, detached single-family houses thirty miles from the city limits. No matter what young people may choose to do, the market for these houses is going to be limited. There will be a demand for them among some younger families and immigrants with children who are seeking more space. But the likelihood of an increased net demand for homes in exurban subdivisions is small.

Similarly, according to Professor Nelson, only about a quarter of American households in 2030 will be raising children. This compares to the roughly 50 percent that were doing so in the 1950s. Twenty years from now, there will be more single-member households than households with children. They will not all want to live in high-rise condominiums downtown. But to assume that they will maintain the demand for exurban single-family housing that existed before 2008 seems misguided.

Nelson believes that the percentage of Americans who are home owners of any sort will itself decline substantially. The American home ownership rate reached an all-time high of 69 percent in 2004 amid the ownership promotion programs of the Bush administration. Given demographic trends that are not subject to alteration, it is reasonable to expect a rate as low as 60 percent in the next decade or two.

One symbol of change, and to a certain extent of demographic inversion, is the remarkable reversal in the urban-suburban ratio of housing starts over the past two decades. In 1990, according to statistics compiled by John Thomas of the Environmental Protection Agency, the share of new residential housing permits in the New York metropolitan area that were awarded within New York City itself was 15 percent. In 2007, it was 55 percent. During that same period, the central-city permit share went from 7 percent to 40 percent in Chicago, and from 4 percent to 14 percent in Atlanta. In the depths of a housing recession, of course, there are relatively few permits being issued anywhere. But there is good reason to believe that the trends of the 1990s and 2000s will resume rather than reverse themselves.

OVER THE COURSE of this book I have avoided using the term "gentrification" except in a select number of places. This is for two reasons. One is that "gentrification" long ago became a word at the center of urban ideological debate, with those against it arguing that the return of affluent white residents to city centers was unfairly displacing impoverished minority renters, and those in favor of it insisting that it was gradually restoring the economic and social vitality of cities as a whole.

The other reason is that what is happening in American cities, most visibly in such places as Chicago, Atlanta, and Washington, is a much larger force than the coming of "gentry" to previously dilapidated neighborhoods. We are witnessing a rearrangement of population across entire metropolitan areas. "Gentrification" is too small a word for it. As I indicated at the beginning, "demographic inversion" comes closer to capturing the scope of what is going on.

Nevertheless, there are those in urban sociology who have argued for years that gentrification is the equivalent of mass displacement, and those in the same field who have denied that this is so. There is a song that goes back to the 1970s:

> *I woke up this morning*
> *I looked next door*
> *There was one family living where there once were four*
> *I got the gentrifi-gentrification blues.*

The word "gentrification" was actually invented in 1963 by the British sociologist Ruth Glass to describe the "invasion" of working-class urban neighborhoods by the wealthy. By the 1970s, there were two common theories of how gentrification actually worked. One was a demand-based theory that singles, couples, and disillusioned suburbanites provided an unmistakable critical-mass base for urban recolonization, and that developers were simply responding to it. The other, a supply-based concept, assumed that developers create a market for luxury living on unused inner-city land, and gradually convince those amenable to try living there.

I am not sure it is a debate that makes much sense. Developers respond to demand, and customers respond to supply. There is no need for these theories to be mutually exclusive, or even competitive. What matters is that the people have been coming since the 1970s, and the trend will continue. As Rowland Atkinson wrote in *Urban Studies* in 2008, "The bear pit of gentrification debates over the past four decades has not tended to be accompanied by significant attempts at creating reliable and useful estimates of its social harm."

What is new in the past decade is a collection of thorough studies, mostly by urban scholars Lance Freeman of Columbia and Jacob Vigdor of Duke University, concluding that the arrival of affluent newcomers to a neighborhood does only a small amount of damage to neighborhood life; it brings more benefits than it takes away. Vigdor argues that the rate of residential turnover in poorer black neighborhoods tends to be very high regardless of whether the affluent are arriving or not. He concludes there is little evidence that the rate spikes significantly higher when gentrification occurs. A 2002 study by the American Housing Survey reported that only about 4 to 5 percent of relocations in American neighborhoods in general are caused by displacement.

FOR STUDENTS of cities and community, perhaps the final intriguing question is what demographic inversion will do to the structure of urban life in general. Will the enhanced street vitality and personal contact that are already occurring in many of America's largest cities bring about a return to the casual social cohesiveness that Jane Jacobs wrote about in 1961? Or will the immense changes in human technological communication diminish the ultimate importance of the street life that seems to be a magnet for so many youthful newcomers in the first place?

When Jacobs wrote *The Death and Life of American Cities*, there were only two methods of real-time personal communication. One was the telephone. The other was face-to-face human interaction. The forms of communication that the microchip has wrought are so fast and so current as to make detailed explanation unnecessary. Our relationship with the person we run into on the street, possibly several times a day, the contact that Jacobs valued, has been compromised by iPods, cell phones, iPhones, e-mail, social media, and other devices Jacobs could not imagine in her wildest dreams.

To put the question simply, will technology be a substitute for the regular social contact of Jacobs's day, or will it provide a crucial supplement? As anyone who walks down an urban street knows, a significant proportion of the cell phone conversations that take place are simply logistical arrangements, as people seek to reveal to others where they are in space and how soon they can meet one another at an agreed-upon location. Social media are, among other things, ways for large numbers of people to settle on mutual congregating spaces instantly. And what of the long, personal conversations that take place on the street between lovers, coworkers, siblings, parents and children, and casual friends talking about that night's NFL football game? Are most of those simply replacing conversations that would have been held in the old days in person or over old-fashioned landlines? Or are they new forms of communication that would not have taken place in the old days?

Those are crucial issues, it seems to me, for the legacy of Jane Jacobs and for ourselves. There is no question that for people who have been displaced from their physical neighborhoods, or even have left them voluntarily, the products of the information technology industry are a startlingly effective way of maintaining relations that have been disrupted by the processes of physical dislocation. Young former residents of public housing projects in Cleveland who agree to meet on a corner in Cleveland Heights or East Cleveland are preserving social contact in ways that would have been utterly impossible before. The existing residents of Cleveland Heights may not be pleased with the gatherings that result, but social action has been preserved nevertheless.

But what of the coming generation of city dwellers—the millennials raised on suburban cul-de-sac streets who see no reason to live there as adults; the young people raised in cities who wish to live out their lives there? What are we to make of these people? One can argue that they are so plugged into the technological inventions of the past quarter century that it hardly matters where they live. They can tweet from anywhere. The closely connected world of physical contact that Jane Jacobs idealized may have no meaning for them. The point of living in the city, the argument could run, is to spend less time commuting and more time communicating via gadget to a circle of friends who hardly ever meet up in person.

That is possible. But to say it is to miss the whole point of demo-

graphic transformation. The more that people are enabled by technology to communicate with one another while remaining physically
solitary, the more they crave a physical form of social life to balance out
all the electronics. People do not move to the center of cities merely to
be able to get to and from work a quarter of an hour faster. They are
settling in cities—those who have a choice—in large part to experience the things that citizens of Paris and Vienna experienced a century
ago: round-the-clock street life; café sociability; casual acquaintances
they meet on the sidewalk every day. This is the direction I think we
are heading in.

The twenty-three-year-old student glued to a laptop computer in
a corner café in a Chicago neighborhood like Sheffield should not be
seen as too different from the Viennese reading his newspaper in a café
on Vienna's Ringstrasse in 1910. He remains a social animal. He merely
expresses the balance between his sociability and his individuality in a
different, twenty-first-century way.

ACKNOWLEDGMENTS

I am no Jane Jacobs, but over the past decade or so I have spent time in many cities and tried to remember the way she said cities were best understood: by walking around them with as few preconceptions as possible and trying to understand the way they worked and the ways in which they were changing. What I saw, to recapitulate briefly the argument of this book, was a radical rearrangement in which people who possessed money and choice were increasingly living in the center, while newcomers and the poor were settling in the suburbs, often in the outer reaches of suburban territory. In short, many American metropolitan areas were coming to look more like the European versions of a century ago than like the places we grew accustomed to in the latter decades of the twentieth century. The more places I visited, the more convinced I became that this was a development of crucial importance to American society, but it was one that had attracted comparatively little attention from the media or even from scholars whose business it was to write about the challenges of urban life.

By 2008, I found myself wishing to present what I had seen in a systematic way. I was fortunate to attract the interest of Frank Foer, then-editor of *The New Republic,* who encouraged me to write a long article, "Trading Places," which documented the altered urban arrangements of the previous few years to the extent that I understood them at that time. This article appeared as a cover story in *The New Republic* in August 2008.

There was much more for me to learn and to say, however, and I set about trying to expand my ideas into a broader argument that might be persuasive at book length. I was lucky enough to attract an outstanding literary agent in Chris Parris-Lamb of the Gernert Company, and eventually a talented editor in Andrew Miller at Alfred A. Knopf. Both have been patient listeners to my ideas, suggestions, and complaints over the past couple of years. Chris is the best agent I have ever worked with or hope to work with; he also returns e-mails faster than any agent I have ever heard of.

And so the article called "Trading Places" grew into a book, informed by extended visits I made to eight different American metropolitan areas during 2009 and 2010. The project benefited immensely from the generosity of many dozens of sources in the eight places I chose to focus on. There is no way for me to name them all, but I want to express my special gratitude to Frank Beal in Chicago, Marina Peed in Atlanta, Camille Barnett in Philadelphia, and Peter Brown in Houston, all of whom served as guides and facilitators as well as interview subjects. Frank and Marina were also kind enough to review chapter drafts that I sent them later, as were Alex Marshall in New York, Feather Houstoun in Philadelphia, David Crossley in Houston, Dennis Keating in Cleveland, Don Keuth in Phoenix, and Sam Mamet in Denver. I am particularly grateful to several of these people who spent considerable time reviewing my work even though they did not agree with everything I chose to say.

Meanwhile, I was discussing and developing my ideas through conversations with colleagues and friends at the two places where I have worked in the past few years: *Governing* magazine and the Pew Charitable Trusts. I particularly want to thank Chris Swope, John Buntin, Alan Greenblatt, Peter Harkness, Richard Greene, Katherine Barrett, and Elder Witt. David Kidd was a great help to me not only as a photographer but as a patient listener and sometime traveling companion. David Merrill produced just the maps I was looking for. Susan Urahn and Lori Grange of the Pew Center on the States provided a challenging and rewarding work environment upon my arrival there early in 2010.

As this process was unfolding, several urban scholars published work on the same subjects I was pursuing, and I have benefited from the opportunity to read the books and articles they have produced. In no particular order, I would like to single out Christopher Leinberger and William Frey of the Brookings Institution, Richard Florida of the University of Toronto, Witold Rybczynski of the University of Pennsylvania, and Edward Glaeser of Harvard University. While none of these authors would agree with everything I say in this book, each has been a source of new ideas and provocative arguments.

It is customary at the end of acknowledgment pages to thank the members of one's family, and I would be delinquent in not doing so now. My daughters, Lizzie and Jennie, have served as sounding boards and sources of ideas that added to the contributions of professionals in the field. And without veering off too far in the direction of sentimentality, I must try my best to express thanks to my wife, Suzanne, who has performed at various times the roles of critic, researcher, proofreader, counselor, and source of overall moral support. In this effort, as in so many phases of my life, I would be nowhere without her.

NOTES

PROLOGUE: TRADING PLACES

4 In some places, the phenomenon of demographic inversion: Data taken from American Fact Finder, U.S. Census Bureau, 2009.

4 At the time of the September 11 attacks: Survey by New York Downtown Alliance, 2007.

6 No American city looks like Vancouver: Alan Ehrenhalt, "Extreme Make-over," *Governing*, July 2006, p. 26.

7 Burgess was right about: Ernest W. Burgess, "The Growth of the City: An Introduction to a Research Project," 1925, www.tsjugephd.com/PCC.../file _Burgess_The_Growth_of_the_City.pdf.

8 "submerged regions of poverty": Ibid.

9 The urban historian Robert Bruegmann goes so far as to claim: Summarizes material in Robert Bruegmann, *Sprawl: A Compact History* (Chicago: University of Chicago Press, 2005).

12 In the peak baby boom period: Arthur C. Nelson, "The New Urbanity: The Rise of a New America," *Annals,* American Academy of Political and Social Science, November 2009.

15 If you were part of the servant class: Frederic Morton, *A Nervous Splendor: Vienna 1888/1889* (New York: Penguin, 1980), p. 58.

17 "an endless succession of factory-town main streets": A. J. Liebling, *Chicago: The Second City* (New York: Knopf, 1952), reprinted in *Liebling at Home* (New York: Wideview Books, 1982), p. 166.

19 Christopher Leinberger, the real estate developer and urban planning scholar: Christopher Leinberger, *The Option of Urbanism: Investing in a New American Dream* (Washington, D.C.: Island Press, 2008).

CHAPTER ONE: A BACKWARD GLANCE

22 "If we are to achieve an urban renaissance": Donald J. Olsen, *The City as a Work of Art: London, Paris, Vienna* (New Haven, Conn.: Yale University Press, 1986), p. x.

22 "the nineteenth century invented modernity": Jean-Christophe Bailly, Pref-

ace to François Loyer, *Paris Nineteenth Century: Architecture and Urbanism* (New York: Abbeville Press, 1988), p. 10.

23 "Apartment houses destroy private life": Sharon Marcus, *Apartment Stories: City and Home in Nineteenth-Century Paris and London* (Berkeley: University of California Press, 1999), p. 57.

23 "as soon as it awakes": Alfred Delvau, *Les Dessous de Paris,* 1860, quoted ibid., p. 149.

24 "we find it tiresome": Alfred Delvau, *Histoire anecdotique des cafés et cabarets de Paris,* 1862, quoted ibid., p. 148.

24 "the interior is going to die": Comments by Edmond and Jules de Goncourt, 1861, quoted ibid., p. 139.

25 "Gray does not have a good name": Bailly, Preface to Loyer, *Paris Nineteenth Century,* p. 9.

25 "It is not an illumination but a fire": Edmondo de Amicis, *Studies of Paris,* 1882, quoted in Norma Evenson, *Paris: A Century of Change, 1878–1978* (New Haven, Conn.: Yale University Press, 1981), p. 6.

26 "Everything is neat and fresh": Ibid., p. 2.

26 "The sidewalks provided": Evenson, *Paris,* p. 20.

28 "nothing can more thoroughly demoralize": Eugene Viollet-le-Duc, quoted in Marcus, *Apartment Stories,* p. 160.

28 "Montmartre was to become the dynamo": Nigel Gosling, quoted in Peter Hall, *Cities in Civilization* (New York: Pantheon, 1998), p. 230.

28 "The young artists": Hall, *Cities in Civilization,* p. 237.

28 "the smells from the kitchen": Fernande Olivier, *Picasso and His Friends* (New York: Appleton Century, 1965), quoted ibid., p. 227.

29 "the great ordering system": James Howard Kunstler, *The City in Mind: Meditations on the Urban Condition* (New York: Free Press, 2002), p. 3.

29 "Second Empire Paris became": Loyer, *Paris Nineteenth Century,* p. 232.

30 "For hours I could stand": Carl Schorske, *Fin-de-Siècle Vienna: Politics and Culture* (New York: Vintage, 1981), p. 46.

31 "the Minister-President or the richest magnate": Stefan Zweig, *The World of Yesterday* (Lincoln: University of Nebraska Press, 1964), p. 15.

31 "The first glance": Ibid., p. 14.

32 "It is a sort of democratic club": Ibid., p. 39.

32 "dismal tenement landscape": Frederic Morton, *A Nervous Splendor: Vienna 1888/1889* (New York: Penguin, 1980), p. 58.

33 "If the British empire was the most powerful": Jonathan Schneer, *London 1900: The Imperial Metropolis* (New Haven, Conn.: Yale University Press, 1999), p. 19.

34 "a true Londoner": Ford Madox Ford, quoted in Peter Ackroyd, *London: The Biography* (New York: Nan A. Talese, 2000), p. 569.

34 "The Strand of those days": H. B. Creswell, quoted in Jane Jacobs, *The Death and Life of Great American Cities* (New York: Vintage, 1992), p. 341.

35 "The leisure class in London": Olsen, *The City as a Work of Art,* p. 217.

35 "The East End became a terra incognita": Tristram Hunt, *Building Jerusalem* (New York: Henry Holt, 2005), p. 390.

35 "where filthy men and women live": Arthur Morrison, quoted in Asa Briggs, *Victorian Cities* (New York: Harper & Row, 1963), p. 326.

35 "a great mysterious movement": H. G. Wells. *Tono-Bungay,* quoted in Ackroyd, *London,* p. 581.

35 "some hoary massive underworld": D. H. Lawrence writing to Lady Ottoline Morrell, May, 14, 1915, in *The Letters of D. H. Lawrence,* vol. 2, ed. George J. Zytaruk and James T. Boulton (Cambridge, U.K.: Cambridge University Press, 1981), p. 339.

36 "the habit of living": Hunt, *Building Jerusalem,* p. 409.

36 "the little clump of shops": H. G. Wells, *Ann Veronica,* quoted in Briggs, *Victorian Cities,* p. 357.

36 "The center of population is shifting": Sidney J. Low, "The Rise of the Suburbs," *The Contemporary Review* 60 (October 1891): 550.

CHAPTER TWO: A NEIGHBORHOOD IN CHICAGO

43 "At first glance": Susan Chandler, "Flaunting It," *Chicago Tribune Magazine,* October 8, 2006, p. 12.

43 "The city is changing": Richard M. Daley quoted by Fassil Demissie, "Globalization and the Remaking of Chicago," in *The New Chicago: A Social and Cultural Analysis,* ed. John Koval et al. (Philadelphia: Temple University Press, 2006), p. 22.

43 The loss of factory jobs: Figures taken from John Koval, "An Overview and Point of View," Introduction to Koval et al., *The New Chicago,* p. 8.

44 "Manufacturing was still more important": David Moberg, "Economic Restructuring: Chicago's Precarious Balance," in Koval et al., *The New Chicago,* p. 36.

45 This did not change for a long time: Bill Testa, "What Are the Opportunities in Central Cities," in Midwest Economy, a blog from the Federal Reserve Bank of Chicago (www.midwest.chicagofedblogs.org), posted May 21, 2009.

46 "a watershed in Chicago planning history": Joseph P. Schwieterman and Dana M. Caspall, *The Politics of Place: The City in the Twenty-first Century* (New York: Pantheon, 2000), p. 70.

48 "Virtually every garage": Erich Teske, quoted in *Voices and Visions of Lincoln Park,* a film produced by the Lincoln Park Community Research Initiative, 2005.

48 "You ride the length of Chicago": Jack Mabley, *Chicago Daily News,* 1957.

50 "Living west of Halsted": Diane Levin, personal interview, June 2009.

51 The Ravenswood line was in financial trouble: Alan Ehrenhalt, "A City in Transit," *Preservation,* March/April 2001, pp. 43–49.

53 "They're turning what was a vibrant urban neighborhood": Blair Kamin, "Exercises in Isolationism," *Chicago Tribune Magazine,* October 8, 2006, p. 12.

55 "a tremendous diminution in participation": Martin Oberman, personal interview, June 2009.

55 "The young people here": Laura Wolfgang, *Midwest Magazine* of the *Chicago Sunday Sun-Times,* July 23, 1972, p. 12.

58 "In Chicago, . . . gentrification follows": Martin Oberman interview.

59 "High-rise villages and communities": Koval, "An Overview and Point of View," p. 12.

CHAPTER THREE: RE-CREATION IN NEW YORK

66 Following September 11, 2001, many predicted: Joseph J. Salvo, Arun Peter Lobo, and Joel A. Alvarez, "A Pre- and Post-9/11 Look (2000–2005) at Lower Manhattan," paper prepared for March 2007 annual meeting of the Population Association of America.

67 In 2009, the median family size: Alliance for Downtown New York, Survey of Lower Manhattan Residents, Summary of Findings, May 2010.

68 New residents of the Financial District were eligible: Lloyd Dixon and Rachel Kaganoff Stern, *Compensation for Losses from the 9/11 Attacks* (Santa Monica, Calif.: RAND Institute for Civil Justice, 2004), p. 78.

69 By the summer of 2009, official city estimates: Amanda Fung, "Shadow Units Cast Pall; Not-Yet-Marketed Condominiums Mean Apartment Glut Is Worse Than It Looks," *Crain's New York Business,* August 10, 2009, p. 2.

69 Some developers were making unsold units: Hilary Potkewitz, "Hotels Spring Up in Unsold Condos; Wall Street Area Contains New Crop of Illegal Rooms; Neighbors Annoyed," *Crain's New York Business,* December 15, 2008, p. 1.

70 One building on John Street: Vivian S. Toy, "The Diaper District," *New York Times,* February 22, 2009, p. RE1.

71 "Shaded by poplars and elms": Ron Chernow, *Alexander Hamilton* (New York: Penguin, 2004), p. 50.

73 "a residential population would stimulate": Jane Jacobs, *The Death and Life of Great American Cities* (New York: Vintage, 1992), p. 156.

74 "I live just about geographic dead center": Ro Sheffe, personal interview, August 2008.

76 "More than anywhere else in the city": Deborah Brown, personal interview, August 2009.

76 "We get a lot of calls from Europe": Kevin Lindamood, personal interview, August 2009.

76 In June 2009, the first Bushwick biennial: James Kalm, "Bushwick Biennial: Venice It Ain't," www.brooklynrail.org, July/August 2009, www.brooklynrail.org/2009/07/artseen/brooklyn-dispatches-new.

79 "I think it's bizarre": Jeremy Sapienza, comments section of "Vito Lopez to 'Yuppie Newcomers': Drop Dead," www.BushwickBK.com, September 11, 2008.

80 "in a five-year period": Martin Gottlieb, "F.H.A. Case Recalls Bushwick in 70's," *New York Times,* February 2, 1986, p. 35.

81 On July 13, 1977, Bushwick suffered through: Steven Malanga, "The Death and Life of Bushwick," *City Journal,* Spring 2008.

82 Bushwick began to change: Robert Sullivan, "Psst . . . Have You Heard About Bushwick?" *New York Times,* March 5, 2006.

82 "Fight, fight, fight": See Tom Robbins, "The Second Battle for Bushwick," *Village Voice,* June 19, 2007, p. 3.

83 "People move here because": Angel Vera, quoted by Sullivan, "Psst . . . Have You Heard."

84 "The train is the entire reason": Kevin Lindamood interview.

84 "I'm fine . . . with having no view": Deborah Brown interview.

84 "Gentrification can't be prevented": Vito Lopez, quoted in Yalissa Rodriguez, "Fires and Flames in Brooklyn," www.mixbook.com/photo-books/educa tion/the-bushwick-fires-and-aftermath-4415967, p. 16.

86 When Jacobs's own three-story redbrick townhouse: Michelle Young, posted on www.untappednewyork.com, September 28, 2010.

86 downed eighteen whiskeys: Biographer Andrew Lycett argues that Thomas was exaggerating: "The consensus was that he cannot have drunk more than six measures of Old Grand-Dad Whiskey" (*Dylan Thomas: A New Life* [Woodstock, N.Y., and New York: Overlook Press, 2003], p. 369).

87 "We must understand that self-destruction": Jacobs, *Death and Life,* p. 251.

CHAPTER FOUR: THE NEW SUBURBIA

91 It was later estimated: Jeffrey S. Passel, Randolph Capps, and Michael E. Fix, *Undocumented Immigrants: Facts and Figures* (Washington, D.C.: Urban Institute, 2004).

93 "had been driven to their madness by": "Georgia: Men in Despair," *TIME,* August 13, 1956.

93 "Gwinnett County, which has suffered": *Atlanta Constitution,* quoted in Elliott E. Brack, *Gwinnett: A Little Above Atlanta* (Norcross, Ga.: Gwinnett Forum, 2008), p. 170.

95 "Six lanes of black hardtop": Tom Wolfe, *A Man in Full* (New York: Farrar, Straus & Giroux, 1998), p. 520.

96 Meanwhile, just down the road, Gwinnett Place: Brack, *Gwinnett,* p. 12.

97 "It's almost like migrant workers": Bucky Johnson, personal interview, October 2009.

97 "Latinos are leaving": Letycia Pastrana, personal interview, October 2009.

98   "Illegal immigrants have already broken several laws": Paul Allen, letter to *Atlanta Journal-Constitution,* June 15, 2008.

99   "We are leading the region": Ellen Gerstein, personal interview, October 2009.

99   Lilburn limits occupancy: Diana Preston, personal interview, October 2009.

99   "If you don't enjoy and embrace diversity": Nick Masino, personal interview, October 2009.

100   "illegal immigration costs cities": Bob Griggs, quoted in Alan Ehrenhalt, "Suburban Influx," *Governing,* December 2009, p. 30.

101   Today, the numbers aren't even close: Audrey Singer, "Twenty-First-Century Gateways: An Introduction," in *Twenty-First-Century Gateways: Immigrant Incorporation in Suburban America,* ed. Audrey Singer, Susan W. Hardwick, and Caroline B. Brettell (Washington, D.C.: Brookings Institution Press, 2008), p. 15.

102   "Herndon is acquiring": Bob Rudine, quoted in Timothy Dwyer, "From Segregation to Immigration: For Longtime Residents, Day-Laborer Site Highlights Herndon's Transformation," *Washington Post,* January 15, 2006, p. C5.

103   "suburban immigrant nation": Susan Hardwick, "Toward a Suburban Immigrant Nation," in *Twenty-First-Century Gateways,* ed. Singer, Hardwick, and Brettell, pp. 31–50.

103   "You really have no choice": Lam Ngo, personal interview, October 2009.

104   At one point, Vietnamese in the Atlanta region: "Global Atlanta Snapshots: The Vietnamese," Atlanta Regional Commission, 2009, p. 1. This is one in a series of twenty-four informational brochures on ethnic communities in the Atlanta region.

104   By 2008, Indians formed the largest Asian immigrant group: "Global Atlanta Snapshots: Asian Indians," Atlanta Regional Commission, 2009, p. 3.

105   "They are buying houses": Charles Bannister, personal interview, October 2009.

106   "has regressed some in that respect": Ibid.

107   "That one shop brought people": Moses Choi, personal interview, October 2009.

108   "We're not as politically active": Herman Pennamon Jr., personal interview, November 2009.

110   "We don't have a lot of diversity": Diana Preston interview.

110   "It's about time for the Asian community": Lam Ngo interview.

110   "It will change the landscape": Moses Choi interview.

111   "Each minority kind of keeps to themselves": Bucky Johnson interview.

111   "Nobody moves out now": Ibid.

111   "the rubber band of suburban sprawl": Chuck Warbington, personal interview, October 2009.

112   "Gwinnett County . . . isn't really": Marina Peed, personal interview, October 2009.

CHAPTER FIVE: CAUGHT IN THE MIDDLE

119 "The cycle of decline": Kenneth T. Jackson, *Crabgrass Frontier: The Suburban-
izitation of the United States* (New York: Oxford University Press, 1987), p. 301.

119 "Half a century after Levittown": Herbert Muschamp, quoted in William
H. Hudnut, *Halfway to Everywhere: A Portrait of America's First-Tier Suburbs*
(Washington, D.C.: Urban Land Institute, 2003), p. 40.

120 "It's absurd": Thomas Bier, quoted ibid., p. 85.

120 Bernadette Hanlon provides a rich account: Bernadette Hanlon, *Once the
American Dream: Inner-Ring Suburbs of the Metropolitan United States* (Philadelphia: Temple University Press, 2010), p. 36.

120 persistence theory: Ibid., p. 40.

120 "life cycle" change: Ibid.

121 social stratification: Ibid.

123 Careful studies by William H. Lucy and David Phillips: University of Virginia, various studies, 1998–2006.

124 As the economist George Zeller reported from census data: Zeller figures
cited in Elizabeth Sullivan, "Despite Its Problems, Cleveland Has a Rosy
Future," Cleveland *Plain Dealer,* May 16, 2010, p. G1.

124 One perverse symbol: Thomas Bier, personal interview, May 27, 2010.

125 "This is the model community": Jennifer Kuzma, personal interview,
May 28, 2010.

126 When a riot takes place: W. Dennis Keating, personal interview, May 27,
2010.

127 "Everybody talks about regionalism": Ken Montlack, personal interview,
May 26, 2010.

CHAPTER SIX: UNEASY COEXISTENCE

137 Two notable events: Alan Ehrenhalt, "Guns and Caramel Sauce," *Governing,*
April 2009, p. 9.

138 A 2009 survey found: *State of Center City 2009,* published by Philadelphia
Center City District and Central Philadelphia Development Corporation.

139 In 2010, they frequented: *State of Center City 2011,* published by Philadelphia
Center City District and Central Philadelphia Development Corporation.

139 the apartment vacancy rate: *State of Center City 2009.*

139 Center City had a full-time residential population: Ibid.

139 In fact, a very dangerous place: Figures taken from Philadelphia Research Initiative, Pew Charitable Trusts, *Philadelphia 2011: The State of the City,* March
2011, p. 27.

140 "is as close to a European city": Feather Houstoun, personal interview, January 19, 2010.

141 Penn Center: John Kromer, *Fixing Broken Cities: The Implementation of*

Urban Development Strategies (New York: Routledge, Taylor & Francis Group, 2010), pp. 51–54.

141 Edmund Bacon was so widely admired: The *TIME* article is described on the Ed Bacon Foundation website, www.edbacon.org/bacon/site.htm.

141 the Gallery: Kromer, *Fixing Broken Cities,* p. 54.

142 "Center City is being despoiled": "For Future Seasons: Trash and Crime Have Reduced the Appeal of Center City, but Change Is Coming," *Philadelphia Inquirer* editorial, December 23, 1989, p. A8, quoted ibid., p. 56.

142 By the 1990s, Society Hill: Kromer, *Fixing Broken Cities,* p. 54.

142 Instead, it collects roughly 60 percent: Philadelphia Research Initiative, Pew Charitable Trusts, *Philadelphia 2009: The State of the City,* March 2009.

143 It enacted a ten-year tax abatement: Kromer, *Fixing Broken Cities,* pp. 17–47.

143 "Without tax abatements": John Kromer, personal interview, January 20, 2010.

144 "Center City has never looked better": John DiIulio, personal interview, January 19, 2010.

144 "These areas hem in the city": Anonymous source, personal interview, January 12, 2010.

144 "For miles on end": Metropolitan Philadelphia Policy Center, *Flight (or) Fight: Metropolitan Philadelphia and Its Future,* September 2001.

145 In 1950, 45 percent of the city's jobs: Philadelphia Research Initiative, *Philadelphia 2009.*

146 "it was a paradise in its way": John DiIulio interview.

147 "Lots of individual houses fail": Alan Greenberger, personal interview, January 20, 2010.

148 "When you pass under the elevated train tracks": Rob Gurwitt, "Betting on the Bulldozer," *Governing,* July 2002, p. 28.

149 In a study of eighty-three cities: Brookings survey, cited in Metropolitan Philadelphia Policy Center, *Flight (or) Fight,* p. 41.

150 "No one sitting in a sidewalk café": Anonymous source, personal interview, January 12, 2010.

150 "If you were to aggregate": Gurwitt, "Betting on the Bulldozer."

151 "What you generally see is tinkering": Bruce Katz, quoted ibid.

151 In the end, though, Street's initiative: Ehrenhalt, "Guns and Caramel Sauce."

152 The number of new arrivals: Audrey Singer et al., *Recent Immigration to Philadelphia: Regional Change in a Reemerging Gateway,* Brookings Metropolitan Policy Program, November 2008.

152 But when it comes to reviving: Harold Brubaker, "Philadelphia Is Lagging in Immigrant Population," *Philadelphia Inquirer,* December 6, 2009, p. D2.

152 Why did Philadelphia fail to attract: Camille Barnett, personal interview, January 12, 2010.

153 "Philadelphia has traditionally not been very tolerant": Feather Houstoun interview.

153 "We simply don't have enough economic vitality": Metropolitan Philadelphia Policy Center, *Flight (or) Fight.*

153 "The game is not keeping people": David Thornburgh, personal interview, January 13, 2010.

154 "New York considers itself the capital": Alan Greenberger interview.

154 "We don't have the economic juice": Ibid.

155 Any discussion of Philadelphia's economic development problems: "The Philadelphia City Wage Tax: A 'Special Case' Income Tax," *IssuesPA,* Pennsylvania Economy League, July 2003.

155 "Our employment trajectory": David Thornburgh interview.

155 It's the amount of tax: Philadelphia Research Initiative, *Philadelphia 2009.*

156 "It's a ridiculously weak executive form": John DiIulio interview.

157 "Being aggravated and contentious": Alan Greenberger interview.

157 "I've lived in the Midwest": Monica Yant Kinney, "Why Is Philly Still So Parochial?" *Philadelphia Inquirer,* December 22, 2010, p. B1.

CHAPTER SEVEN: THE URBAN SQUEEZE

159 Emancipation Park was the place: Museum of Fine Arts, Houston, "Historical Reflections on the Third Ward," paper written to accompany the museum's annual student photography exhibit, *Eye on the Third Ward* (date of paper unknown). This educational exchange with Houston's Jack Yates High School has been ongoing sine 1995.

161 Between the vacant lots: John Buntin, "Land Rush," *Governing,* March 1, 2006.

161 "We're supply-constrained": Bob Eury, personal interview, April 2010.

162 "The Third Ward is the epicenter": Bill White, unpublished interview with John Buntin, February 2006.

162 "I'm an egalitarian": Garnet Coleman, quoted in Steve Inskeep, "Fighting Gentrification with Money in Houston," *Morning Edition,* National Public Radio broadcast, September 17, 2009.

163 "If somebody's going to move into the Third Ward": Garnet Coleman, personal interview, April 2010.

163 "Quite frankly, this is personal": Ibid.

164 "Our goals are two-pronged": Ibid.

165 "is, 'Give us our blight' ": Tom Diehl, personal interview, April 2010.

165 "If we weren't banking land": Garnet Coleman interview.

165 The Fourth Ward was the home: Federal Reserve Bank of Dallas, "Houston's Fourth Ward: Old Neighborhood, New Life," *Perspectives* 2 (2002): 1–8.

166 Houston Renaissance: David Ellison, "A Neighborhood in Flux," *Houston Chronicle,* January 21, 2007, p. B1.

166 "When you look at what they were being displaced from": Larry Davis, quoted in Buntin, "Land Rush."

166 "If it's historic": Spencer Lightsy, quoted in Ellison, "A Neighborhood in Flux."

167 "Gentrification was never my goal": Bob Lanier, unpublished interview with John Buntin, 2006.

167 One is LARA: Carolyn Feibel and Bradley Olson, "Mayor Moves on the Great White Way," *Houston Chronicle*, January 1, 2010, p. 1.

167 More ambitious was Houston HOPE: Ibid.

168 "redevelopment that's the opposite": Buntin, "Land Rush."

168 One effort that Coleman has supported: Ibid.

168 "Every time one of these little old houses": Ibid.

169 In a survey conducted early in 2010: Stephen Klineberg, personal interview, April 2010.

171 "multicentered metropolitan region": Ibid.

171 "If the rich are going into downtown now": Ibid.

171 "one reason Houston is affordable": Mayor Bill White, unpublished interview with John Buntin, January 9, 2006.

171 "The unavoidable fact": Edward Glaeser, "Houston, New York Has a Problem," *City Journal*, Summer 2008.

172 "There are no tools": Peter Brown, personal interview, April 2010.

172 "As long as they can put forth the required cash": Tom Diehl interview.

174 "You've always loved trains": Frank Liu, personal interview, April 2010.

175 "You see people buying housing": Bob Eury interview.

175 "The higher the price": Frank Liu interview.

175 "They've already fallen in love": Ibid.

176 "pedestrian-friendly atmosphere": Woodlands promotional brochure, April 2010.

177 "Urban and Sugar Land were not always compatible words": Sugar Land promotional brochure, April 2010.

177 "Everybody wants that": David Crossley, personal interview, April 2010.

179 "There will be more transit-oriented real estate": Ibid.

179 "The people who want to live close in": Tom Diehl interview.

179 "If I had to take one thing": Peter Brown interview.

180 "is the most interesting city in America": Stephen Klineberg interview.

CHAPTER EIGHT: CREATING A DOWNTOWN

184 "to attract hip young professionals": Michael Smith, personal interview, April 2008.

184 "creative class": Richard Florida, *The Rise of the Creative Class* (New York: Basic Books, 2003).

184 "The common element of great cities": Phil Gordon, personal interview, November 2009.

185 As early as the end of the 1940s: Grady Gammage Jr., *Phoenix in Perspective: Reflections on Developing the Desert* (Tempe: Herberger Center for Design Excellence, Arizona State University, 2003), p. 36.

186 "Real estate is to us": Susan Clark-Johnson, personal interview, November 2009.

192 "We must solve the riddle": Michael Smith interview.

192 "Retailers are not pioneers": Ibid.

193 "to use entertainment in the service of downtown revival": William Fulton, "Planet Downtown," *Governing*, April 1997.

193 "For thirty years": Glendon Swarthout, quoted in Philip VanderMeer, *Phoenix Rising: The Making of a Desert Metropolis* (Carlsbad, Calif.: Heritage Media Corp., 2002), p. 102.

194 "If you want to create a real downtown": Don Keuth, personal interview, November 2009.

194 "looks like a truckful of buildings": Grady Gammage Jr., personal interview, November 2009.

195 "Our historic building stock": Jason Harris, personal interview, November 2009.

195 "Phoenix had Quonset huts": Don Keuth interview.

196 "There was a wildly optimistic view": Tom Franz, personal interview, November 2009.

196 "We've got all these edifices": Susan Clark-Johnson interview.

196 "this is not a Disneyland ride": Harry Mitchell, quoted in John Faherty et al., "Light Rail Packed for Grand Debut," *Arizona Republic*, December 28, 2008, p. 1.

198 "Now that it's up": Carol Johnson, personal interview, November 2009.

198 "Our presence will be catalytic": Michael Crow, quoted in Craig Harris, "Trio Frame Future for Downtown," *Arizona Republic*, January 4, 2006, p. 1B.

198 "ASU downtown is more than a few nuggets": Phil Gordon interview.

199 "People weren't buying to flip": Eric Brown, personal interview, December 2009.

200 "Life happens under five stories": Ibid.

201 "The less frequently you use your car": Grady Gammage interview.

201 "This isn't an urban city": Don Keuth interview.

202 "We have all these people": Carol Johnson interview.

202 "When I think about Chicago": Alicia Porter, quoted in *The Arizona We Want* (Phoenix: Center for the Future of Arizona, 2009), p. 32.

202 "There is something genuinely vital": Grady Gammage interview.

202 "We're not a global city": Don Keuth interview.

CHAPTER NINE: URBANIZING THE SUBURBS

205 77 percent of Generation Y: John McIlwain, *Housing in America: The Next Decade* (Washington, D.C.: Urban Land Institute, 2010), p. 15.

205 "Generation Y's attitudes toward home ownership": Ibid.

206 In a poll cited by *The New York Times* in 2009: David Brooks, "I Dream of Denver," *New York Times* op-ed column, February 17, 2009, p. 33.

207 "Once the economy recovers": McIlwain, *Housing in America*, p. 26.

208 The demographer Arthur C. Nelson calculated: Arthur C. Nelson, quoted in Ellen Dunham-Jones and June Williamson, *Retrofitting Suburbia: Urban Design Solutions for Redesigning Suburbs* (New York: Wiley, 2008), p. 10.

211 "Stapleton was a significant proving ground": Peter Park, personal interview, July 2010.

212 "People got married at Villa Italia": Bob Murphy, personal interview, July 2010.

212 "It was a boarded-up mall": Ibid.

212 "The most important part": Mark Falcone, personal interview, July 2010.

213 "It didn't take long": Bob Murphy interview.

214 "the first project in Colorado": City of Englewood, Colorado, website, http://englewoodgov.org/Index.aspx?page=468.

217 But the march of the New Urbanists: Alan Ehrenhalt, "The Dilemma of the New Urbanists," *Governing,* July 1997, p. 7.

218 "the most important phenomenon to emerge": Herbert Muschamp, "Can the New Urbanism Find Room for the Old?" *New York Times,* June 2, 1996, p. 27.

220 "It is so far beyond what anyone else has done": Quoted in Alan Ehrenhalt, "Suburbs with a Healthy Dose of Fantasy," *New York Times,* July 9, 2000, p. 15.

222 "This is a fantastic opportunity": Andres Duany, quoted in Michael D. Shear, "Density Debate's Large Stakes," *Washington Post,* July 19, 2001, p. T14.

223 "High density is not a punishment": Ibid.

223 "What Duany wants to do": Quoted in Shear, "Density Debate's Large Stakes."

223 "I think he is being arrogant": Gerald Connolly, quoted ibid.

224 "100 percent downtown corner": Quoted in Ehrenhalt, "Breaking the Density Deadlock," p. 11.

225 "would be guided by market demand": Quoted in Lisa Rein and Kafia A. Hosh, "Transformed Tysons Still Years Away in Fairfax," *Washington Post,* June 24, 2010, p. A1.

225 "it took forty years": Ibid.

225 "There are lots of places like Tysons Corner": Adam Ducker, quoted in Robert McCartney, "A Transit-Friendly Tysons Corner Would Support Growth, Cut Auto Traffic," *Washington Post,* June 27, 2010, p. C1.

CONCLUSION

227   It is perfectly possible to argue: See Joel Kotkin, *The Next Hundred Million: America in 2050* (New York: Penguin, 2010).

230   "fifth great migration": Robert Fishman, "The Fifth Migration," *Journal of the American Planning Association,* Autumn 2005, p. 11.

230   "will reurbanize precisely those inner-city districts": Ibid.

231   There are those who predict: See Christopher B. Leinberger, *The Option of Urbanism: Investing in a New American Dream* (Washington, D.C.: Island Press, 2008).

232   Similarly, according to Professor Nelson: Arthur C. Nelson, "The New Urbanity: The Rise of a New America," *Annals,* a journal of the American Academy of Political and Social Science, November 2009, p. 195.

232   In 1990, according to statistics compiled by John Thomas: John Thomas, "Residential Construction Trends in America's Metropolitan Regions," U.S. Environmental Protection Agency, February 2009.

233   "I woke up this morning": Lyrics from the song "Gentrification Blues," by Judith Levine and Laura Liben, 1982, quoted in Tom Slater, "A Literal Necessity to Be Replaced: A Rejoinder to the Gentrification Debate," *International Journal of Urban and Economic Research,* March 2008, p. 216.

233   "The bear pit of gentrification debates": Rowland Atkinson, "Gentrification, Segregation and the Vocabulary of Affluent Residential Choice," *Urban Studies,* November 2008, p. 2634.

234   What is new in the past decade: See, for example, Lance Freeman, *There Goes the 'Hood: Views of Gentrification from the Ground Up* (Philadelphia: Temple University Press, 2006), and Jacob L. Vigdor, "Is Urban Decay Bad? Is Urban Revitalization Bad Too?" National Bureau of Economic Research, working paper 12955, March 2007, www.nber.org/papers/w12955.

SELECT BIBLIOGRAPHY

Abbott, Carl. *Greater Portland: Urban Life and Landscape in the Pacific Northwest.* Philadelphia: University of Pennsylvania Press, 2001.

Ackroyd, Peter. *London: A Biography.* New York: Nan A. Talese, 2000.

Alexiou, Alice Sparberg. *Jane Jacobs: Urban Visionary.* New York: Harper Perennial, 2006.

Allman, T. D. *Miami: City of the Future.* New York: Atlantic Monthly Press, 1987.

Altshuler, Alan, and David Luberoff. *Mega-Projects: The Changing Politics of Urban Public Investment.* Washington, D.C.: Brookings Institution Press, 2003.

Ballon, Hilary, and Kenneth T. Jackson, eds. *Robert Moses and the Modern City: The Transformation of New York.* New York: Queens Museum of Art/W. W. Norton, 2007.

Bennett, Larry. *The Third City: Chicago and American Urbanism.* Chicago: University of Chicago Press, 2010.

Bishop, Bill. *The Big Sort: Why the Clustering of Like-Minded America Is Tearing Us Apart.* New York: Houghton Mifflin, 2008.

Blauvelt, Andrew, ed. *Worlds Away: New Suburban Landscapes.* Minneapolis: Walker Art Center, 2008.

Boorstin, Daniel J. *The Americans: The National Experience.* New York: Vintage, 1965.

Brack, Elliott E. *Gwinnett: A Little Above Atlanta.* Norcross, Ga.: Gwinnett Forum, 2008.

Briggs, Asa. *Victorian Cities.* New York: Harper & Row, 1963.

Briggs, Xavier de Souza, Susan J. Popkin, and John Goering. *Moving to Opportunity: The Story of an American Experiment to Fight Ghetto Poverty.* New York: Oxford University Press, 2010.

Bruegmann, Robert. *Sprawl: A Compact History.* Chicago: University of Chicago Press, 2005.

Calthorpe, Peter, and William Fulton. *The Regional City: Planning for the End of Sprawl.* Washington, D.C.: Island Press, 2001.

Carmona, Michel. *Haussmann: His Life and Times, and the Making of Modern Paris.* Chicago: Ivan R. Dee, 2000.

Chafets, Ze'ev. *Devil's Night: And Other True Tales of Detroit.* New York: Vintage, 1991.

Dallas, Gregor. *Metro Stop Paris: An Underground History of the City of Light.* New York: Walker & Company, 2008.

DeParle, Jason. *American Dream: Three Women, Ten Kids, and a Nation's Drive to End Welfare.* New York: Penguin, 2004.

Dillaway, Diana. *Power Failure: Politics, Patronage, and the Economic Future of Buffalo, New York.* Amherst, N.Y.: Prometheus Books, 2006.

Duany, Andres, Elizabeth Plater-Zyberk, and Jeff Speck. *Suburban Nation: The Rise of Sprawl and the Decline of the American Dream.* New York: North Point Press, 2000.

Dunham-Jones, Ellen, and June Williamson. *Retrofitting Suburbia: Urban Design Solutions for Redesigning Suburbia.* New York: Wiley, 2008.

Eberly, Don E., ed. *Building a Community of Citizens: Civil Society in the 21st Century.* Lanham, Md.: University Press of America and The Commonwealth Foundation, 1994.

Ehrenhalt, Alan. *Democracy in the Mirror: Politics, Reform, and Reality in Grassroots America.* Washington, D.C.: Congressional Quarterly, 1998.

———. *The Lost City: Discovering the Forgotten Virtues of Community in the Chicago of the 1950s.* New York: Basic Books, 1995.

Evenson, Norma. *Paris: A Century of Change, 1878–1978.* New Haven, Conn.: Yale University Press, 1979.

Feagin, Joe R. *Free Enterprise City: Houston in Political and Economic Perspective.* New Brunswick, N.J.: Rutgers University Press, 1988.

Flint, Anthony. *This Land: The Battle over Sprawl and the Future of America.* Baltimore: Johns Hopkins University Press, 2006.

Florida, Richard. *The Rise of the Creative Class.* New York: Basic Books, 2003.

Freeman, Lance. *There Goes the 'Hood: Views of Gentrification from the Ground Up.* Philadelphia: Temple University Press, 2006.

Gammage, Grady, Jr. *Phoenix in Perspective: Reflections on Developing the Desert.* 2nd ed. Tempe: Herberger Center for Design Excellence, Arizona State University, 2003.

Girouard, Mark. *Cities and People: A Social and Architectural History.* New Haven, Conn.: Yale University Press, 1985.

Glaeser, Edward. *Triumph of the City.* New York: Penguin, 2011.

Goldman, Mark. *City on the Edge: Buffalo, New York.* Amherst, N.Y.: Prometheus Books, 2007.

———. *City on the Lake: The Challenge of Change in Buffalo, New York.* Amherst, N.Y.: Prometheus Books, 1990.

Goodman, James. *Blackout.* New York: North Point Press, 2003.

Gottlieb, Robert, Mark Vallianatos, Regina M. Freer, and Peter Dreier. *The Next Los Angeles: The Struggle for a Livable City.* Berkeley: University of California Press, 2005.

Hall, Peter. *Cities in Civilization.* New York: Pantheon, 1998.

Hanlon, Bernadette. *Once the American Dream: Inner-Ring Suburbs of the Metropolitan United States.* Philadelphia: Temple University Press, 2010.

Hibbert, Christopher. *Cities and Civilizations.* New York: Weidenfeld & Nicolson, 1986.

Hiss, Tony. *The Experience of Place.* New York: Alfred A. Knopf, 1990.

Hudnut, William H., III. *Halfway to Everywhere: A Portrait of America's First-Tier Suburbs.* Washington, D.C.: Urban Land Institute, 2003.

Hunt, Tristram. *Building Jerusalem: The Rise and Fall of the Victorian City.* New York: Henry Holt and Company, 2005.

Jackson, John Brinckerhoff. *A Sense of Place, a Sense of Time.* New Haven, Conn.: Yale University Press, 1994.

Jackson, Kenneth T. *Crabgrass Frontier: The Suburbanization of the United States.* New York: Oxford University Press, 1985.

Jacobs, Allan B. *Great Streets.* Cambridge, Mass.: MIT Press, 1995.

Jacobs, Jane. *The Death and Life of Great American Cities.* New York: Vintage, 1992.

Johnson, G. Wesley, Jr., ed. *Phoenix in the Twentieth Century: Essays in Community History.* Norman: University of Oklahoma Press, 1993.

Katz, Bruce, and Robert E. Lang, eds. *Redefining Urban and Suburban America: Evidence from Census 2000.* Washington, D.C.: Brookings Institution Press, 2003.

Kennedy, Lawrence W. *Planning the City Upon a Hill: Boston Since 1630.* Amherst: University of Massachusetts Press, 1992.

Kingwell, Mark. *Concrete Reveries: Consciousness and the City.* New York: Viking, 2008.

Kostof, Spiro. *The City Assembled: The Elements of Urban Form Through History.* New York: Thames & Hudson, 1992.

———. *The City Shaped: Urban Patterns and Meanings Through History* Boston: Bulfinch, 1991.

Kotkin, Joel. *The City: A Global History.* New York: Modern Library, 2005.

———. *The Next Hundred Million: America in 2050.* New York: Penguin, 2010.

Kotlowitz, Alex. *Never a City So Real: A Walk in Chicago.* New York: Crown, 2004.

Koval, John P., Larry Bennett, Michael I. J. Bennett, Fassil Demissie, Roberta Garner, and Kiljoong Kim, eds. *The New Chicago: A Social and Cultural Analysis.* Philadelphia: Temple University Press, 2006.

Kromer, John. *Fixing Broken Cities: The Implementation of Urban Development Strategies.* New York: Routledge, Taylor & Francis Group, 2010.

Kunstler, James Howard. *The City in Mind: Meditations on the Urban Condition.* New York: Free Press, 2001.

Leinberger, Christopher B. *The Option of Urbanism: Investing in a New American Dream.* Washington, D.C.: Island Press, 2008.

Loyer, François. *Paris Nineteenth Century: Architecture and Urbanism.* New York: Abbeville Press, 1988.

Marcus, Sharon. *Apartment Stories: City and Home in Nineteenth-Century Paris and London.* Berkeley: University of California Press, 1999.

Marwell, Nicole P. *Bargaining for Brooklyn: Community Organizations in the Entrepreneurial City.* Chicago: University of Chicago Press, 2007.

Mennel, Timothy, Jo Steffens, and Christopher Klemek, eds. *Block by Block: Jane Jacobs and the Future of New York.* New York: Municipal Art Society of New York, 2007.

Miller, Ross. *Here's the Deal: The Buying and Selling of a Great American City.* New York: Alfred A. Knopf, 1996.

Morris, Charles R. *The Cost of Good Intentions: New York City and the Liberal Experiment, 1960–1975.* New York: W. W. Norton, 1980.

Morton, Frederic. *A Nervous Splendor: Vienna 1888/1889.* New York: Penguin, 1980.

Morton, Marian J. *Cleveland Heights: The Making of an Urban Suburb.* Charleston, S.C.: Arcadia Publishing, 2002.

Nicolson, Juliet. *The Perfect Summer: England 1911, Just Before the Storm.* New York: Grove Press, 2006.

Nivola, Pietro S. *Laws of the Landscape: How Policies Shape Cities in Europe and America.* Washington, D.C.: Brookings Institution Press, 1999.

O'Connor, Len. *Clout: Mayor Daley and His City.* New York: Avon Books, 1975.

Olsen, Donald J. *The City as a Work of Art: London, Paris, Vienna.* New Haven, Conn.: Yale University Press, 1986.

Owen, David. *Green Metropolis: Why Living Smaller, Living Closer and Driving Less Are the Keys to Sustainability.* New York: Riverhead Books, 2009.

Ozawa, Connie P., ed. *The Portland Edge: Challenges and Successes in Growing Communities.* Washington, D.C.: Island Press, 2004.

Pinkney, David H. *Napoleon III and the Rebuilding of Paris.* Princeton, N.J.: Princeton University Press, 1958.

Pomerantz, Gary M. *Where Peachtree Meets Sweet Auburn: The Saga of Two Families and the Making of Atlanta.* New York: Scribner, 1996.

Popkin, Nathaniel. *The Possible City: Exercises in Dreaming Philadelphia.* Philadelphia: Camino Books, 2008.

Rae, Douglas W. *City: Urbanism and Its End.* New Haven, Conn.: Yale University Press, 2003.

Rasmussen, Steen Eiler. *London: The Unique City I.* Cambridge, Mass.: MIT Press, 1974.

Royko, Mike. *Boss: Richard J. Daley of Chicago.* New York: New American Library, 1971.

Rybczynski, Witold. *City Life: Urban Expectations in a New World.* New York: Scribner, 1995.

———. *Last Harvest: How a Cornfield Became New Daleville.* New York: Scribner, 2007.

———. *Makeshift Metropolis: Ideas About Cities.* New York: Scribner, 2010.

Rykwert, Joseph. *The Seduction of Place: The City in the Twenty-first Century.* New York: Pantheon, 2000.

Schneer, Jonathan. *London 1900: The Imperial Metropolis.* New Haven, Conn.: Yale University Press, 2001.

Schorske, Carl E. *Fin-de-Siècle Vienna: Politics and Culture.* New York: Vintage, 1981.

Schwieterman, Joseph P., and Dana M. Caspall. *The Politics of Place: A History of Zoning in Chicago.* Chicago: Lake Claremont Press, 2006.

Sennett, Richard. *The Corrosion of Character: The Personal Consequences of Work in the New Capitalism.* New York: W. W. Norton, 1998.

Singer, Audrey, Susan W. Hardwick, and Caroline B. Brettell, eds. *Twenty-first-Century Gateways: Immigrant Incorporation in Suburban America.* Washington, D.C.: Brookings Institution Press, 2008.

Stone, Clarence N. *Regime Politics: Governing Atlanta, 1946–1988.* Lawrence: University Press of Kansas, 1989.

Suarez, Ray. *The Old Neighborhood: What We Lost in the Great Suburban Migration, 1966–1999.* New York: Free Press, 1999.

Teaford, Jon C. *The Metropolitan Revolution: The Rise of Post-urban America.* New York: Columbia University Press, 2006.

Vanderbilt, Tom. *Traffic: Why We Drive the Way We Do (and What It Says About Us).* New York: Alfred A. Knopf, 2008.

VanderMeer, Philip. *Phoenix Rising: The Making of a Desert Metropolis.* Carlsbad, Calif.: Heritage Media Corp., 2002.

Von Hoffman, Alexander. *House by House, Block by Block: The Rebirth of America's Urban Neighborhoods.* New York: Oxford University Press, 2003.

Weber, Eugen. *France, Fin de Siècle.* Cambridge, Mass.: Harvard University Press, 1986.

Wille, Lois. *At Home in the Loop: How Clout and Community Built Chicago's Dearborn Park.* Carbondale: Southern Illinois University Press, 1997.

Wolfe, Tom. *A Man in Full.* New York: Farrar, Straus & Giroux, 1998.

Zweig, Stefan. *The World of Yesterday.* Lincoln: University of Nebraska Press, 1964.

STUDIES AND REPORTS

Atlanta Regional Commission. *Global Atlanta Snapshots: A Look at Ethnic Communities in the Atlanta Region.* 2006.

Birch, Eugenie L. *Who Lives Downtown.* The Brookings Institution Living Cities Census Series. November 2005.

Center City District and Central Philadelphia Development Corporation. *State of Center City.* 2009, 2011.

Center for the Future of Arizona. *The Arizona We Want.* 2009.

Dixon, Lloyd, and Rachel Kaganoff Stern. *Compensation for Losses from the 9/11 Attacks.* RAND Institute for Civil Justice. 2004.

Frey, William H., Alan Berube, Audrey Singer, and Jill H. Wilson. *Getting Current: Recent Demographic Trends in Metropolitan America.* The Brookings Institution Metropolitan Policy Program. 2009.

McIlwain, John. *Housing in America: The Next Decade.* Urban Land Institute. 2010.

Metropolitan Philadelphia Policy Center. *Flight (or) Fight: Metropolitan Philadelphia and Its Future.* September 2001.

Metropolitan Policy Program at Brookings. *State of Metropolitan America: On the Front Lines of Demographic Transformation.* 2010.

New York City Department of City Planning. *Plan for Lower Manhattan.* October 1993.

Philadelphia Research Initiative, Pew Charitable Trusts. *Philadelphia 2009: The State of the City.* 2009.

———. *Philadelphia 2011: The State of the City.* 2011.

Puentes, Robert, and David Warren. *One-fifth of America: A Comprehensive Guide to America's First Suburbs.* The Brookings Institution Survey Series. February 2006.

Singer, Audrey. *The New Geography of United States Immigration.* Brookings Immigration Series. No. 3, July 2009.

Singer, Audrey, Domenic Vitiello, Michael Katz, and David Park. *Recent Immigration to Philadelphia: Regional Change in a Reemerging Gateway.* Survey Series for the Metropolitan Policy Program at Brookings. November 2008.

Singer, Audrey, and Jill H. Wilson. *From "There" to "Here": Refugee Resettlement in Metropolitan America.* The Brookings Institution Living Cities Census Series. September 2006.

Singer, Audrey, Jill H. Wilson, and Brooke DeRenzis. *Immigrants, Politics, and Local Response in Suburban Washington.* Survey Series for the Metropolitan Policy Program at Brookings. November 2008.

Taylor, Paul, and Scott Keeter, eds. *Millennials: Confident, Connected, Open to Change.* Pew Research Center. February 24, 2010.

Urban Land Institute. *The City in 2050: Creating Blueprints for Change.* 2008.

PAPERS AND ARTICLES

Aizenman, N. C. "Figures Show Migration to Outer D.C. Suburbs Nearly Halting." *Washington Post,* March 19, 2009, p. B3.

Allen, Paul. "Gwinnett Opinions." *Atlanta Journal-Constitution,* June 15, 2008.

Alliance for Downtown New York. "Survey of Lower Manhattan Residents, Summary of Findings," May 2010.

Atkinson, Rowland. "Commentary: Gentrification, Segregation and the Vocabulary of Affluent Residential Choice." *Urban Studies* 45, no. 12 (November 2008): 2626–36.

Bagli, Charles V. "Financial District Adapts as Banks Leave." *New York Times,* February 4, 2011.

Bernstein, David. "Daley vs. Daley." *Chicago,* September 2008.

Beyer, Gregory. "For Downtown Primary Schools, Ever Less Wiggle Room." *New York Times,* October 5, 2008.

Brooks, David. "I Dream of Denver." *New York Times,* February 17, 2009, p. A33.

Burgess, Ernest W. "The Growth of the City: An Introduction to a Research Project." Originally published in 1925 in "The Trend of Population," *Publications of the American Sociological Society,* vol. 18, 85–97; www.tsjugephd.com/PCC.../file_Burgess_The_Growth_of_the_City.pdf.

Chandler, Susan. "Flaunting It: Mammoth Mansions Rise in Lincoln Park as Chicago's Wealthiest Parade Their Bankrolls." *Chicago Tribune Magazine,* October 8, 2006.

Duany, Andres. "Three Cheers for 'Gentrification." *American Enterprise* 12, no. 3 (April 1, 2001).

Dwyer, Timothy. "From Segregation to Immigration." *Washington Post,* January 15, 2006, p. C5.

Ehrenhalt, Alan. "A City in Transit." *Preservation,* March/April 2001, pp. 43–49.

———. "Suburbs with a Healthy Dose of Fantasy." *New York Times,* July 9, 2000, p. 15.

Ellison, David. "A Neighborhood in Flux." *Houston Chronicle,* January 21, 2007, p. B1.

Faherty, John, Casey Newton, Glen Creno, and Kerry Fehr-Snyder. "Light Rail Packed for Grand Debut." *Arizona Republic,* December 28, 2008, p. 1.

Federal Reserve Bank of Dallas. "Houston's Fourth Ward." *Perspectives,* Issue 2, 2002, pp. 1–8.

Feibel, Carolyn, and Bradley Olson. "Mayor Moves on the Great White Way." *Houston Chronicle,* January 2, 2010, p. A1.

Fischer, Lauren, and Joseph P. Schwieterman. "A Kaleidoscope of Culture: Measuring the Diversity of Chicago's Neighborhoods." Chaddick Institute for Metropolitan Development, DePaul University, July 1, 2008.

Fishman, Robert. "The Fifth Migration." *Journal of the American Planning Association* 71, no. 4 (Autumn 2005): 357–66.

Florida, Richard. "How the Crash Will Reshape America." *The Atlantic,* March 2009, www.theatlantic.com/doc/200903/meltdown-geography.

Freeman, Lance. "Comment on 'The Eviction of Critical Perspectives from Gentrification Research.' " *International Journal of Urban and Regional Research* 32, no. 1 (March 2008): 186–91.

———. "Displacement or Succession?: Residential Mobility in Gentrifying Neighborhoods." *Urban Affairs Review* 40, no. 4 (March 2005): 463–91.

———. "Neighborhood Diversity, Metropolitan Segregation and Gentrification: What Are the Links in the U.S.?" *Urban Studies* 46, no. 10 (September 2009): 2079–101.

Fung, Amanda. "Shadow Units Cast Pall; Not-Yet-Marked Condominiums Mean

Apartment Glut Is Worse Than It Looks." *Crain's New York Business,* August 10, 2009.

"Georgia: Men in Despair." *TIME,* August 13, 1956.

Glaeser, Edward L. "Houston, New York Has a Problem." *City Journal* 18, no. 3 (Summer 2008).

———. "How Some Places Fare Better in Hard Times." Posted at www.econo mix.blogs.nytimes.com, March 24, 2009.

Gupta, Sapna. "Immigrants in the Chicago Suburbs: A Policy Paper." Prepared for Chicago Metropolis 2020, February 2004.

Gyourko, Joseph. "Looking Back to Look Forward: Learning from Philadelphia's 350 Years of Urban Development." *Brookings-Wharton Papers on Urban Affairs: 2005,* pp. 1–58.

Hampson, Rick. "Studies: Gentrification a Boost for Everyone." *USA Today,* April 20, 2005, pp. 13A–14A.

Hubbard, Burt. "Denver Gets Whiter; Suburbs More Diverse." *Denver Post,* March 29, 2009.

Immergluck, Dan. "Large Redevelopment Initiatives, Housing Values and Gentrification: The Case of the Atlanta Beltline." *Urban Studies* 46, no. 8 (July 2009): 1723–45.

Johnson, Kenneth M. "Demographic Trends in Metropolitan Chicago at Mid-Decade." *Working Papers on Recreation, Amenities, Forests and Demographic Change,* no. 6, 2007.

Kalm, James. "Bushwick Biennial: Venice It Ain't." *Brooklyn Rail,* July/August 2009, www.brooklynrail.org/2009/07/artseen/brooklyn-dispatches-new.

Kamin, Blair. "Exercises in Isolationism." *Chicago Tribune,* October 8, 2006.

Katz, Alyssa. "Gentrification Hangover," *American Prospect* 21, no. 1 (January/February 2010): 17–20.

Kinney, Monica Yant. "Why Is Philly Still So Parochial?" *Philadelphia Inquirer,* December 22, 2010.

Kotkin, Joel. "The American Suburb Is Bouncing Back." Posted on www .newgeography.com, April 6, 2009.

———. "The Luxury City vs. the Middle Class," *The American,* Journal of the American Enterprise Institute, May 13, 2009.

Lees, Loretta, and David Ley. "Introduction to Special Issue on Gentrification and Public Policy." *Urban Studies* 45, no. 12 (November 2008): 2379–84.

Lopez, Owen. "Downtown Albuquerque: The Next Step." *New Mexico Business Weekly,* September 26, 2008.

Malanga, Steven. "The Death and Life of Bushwick." *City Journal,* Spring 2008.

McCartney, Robert. "A Transit-friendly Tysons Corner Would Support Growth, Cut Auto Traffic." *Washington Post,* June 27, 2010, p. C1.

Metropolitan Institute at Virginia Tech. *Housing Policy Debate,* vol. 19, issue 3, 2008 (Special Opolis Issue).

Museum of Fine Arts, Houston. "Historical Reflections on the Third Ward." Paper written to accompany the museum's annual student photography exhibit, *Eye on the Third Ward.* N.d.

Nelson, Arthur C. "The New Urbanity: The Rise of a New America." *The Annals of the American Academy of Political and Social Science,* November 2009, pp. 192–208.

Newberg, Sam. "Light Rail in Charlotte." *Urban Land,* July 2009, pp. 53–55.

Newman, Kathe, and Elvin K. Wyly. "The Right to Stay Put, Revisited: Gentrification and Resistance to Displacement in New York City." *Urban Studies* 43, no. 1 (January 2006): 23–57.

O'Dell, Rob. "Lessons Can Be Learned from Albuquerque." *Arizona Daily Star,* November 5, 2007.

Ouroussoff, Nicolai. "The New, New City." *New York Times Magazine,* June 8, 2008.

———. "Reinventing America's Cities: The Time Is Now." *New York Times,* March 29, 2009.

Potkewitz, Hilary. "Hotels Spring Up in Unsold Condos; Wall Street Area Contains New Crop of Illegal Rooms; Neighbors Annoyed." *Crain's New York Business,* December 15, 2008, p. 1.

Rein, Lisa, and Kafia A. Hosh. "Transformed Tysons Corner Still Years Away in Fairfax." *Washington Post,* June 24, 2010, p. A1.

Robbins, Tom. "The Second Battle for Bushwick." *Village Voice,* June 26, 2007.

Salvo, Joseph J, Arun Peter Lobo, and Joel Alvarez. "A Pre- and Post-9/11 Look (2000–2005) at Lower Manhattan." New York City Department of City Planning, Population Division, paper prepared for annual meeting of the Population Association of America, 2007.

Sander, William, and William A. Testa. "Education and Household Location in Chicago." *Growth and Change: A Journal of Urban and Regional Policy* 40, no. 1 (March 2009): 116–39.

Senior, Jennifer. "Alone Together." *New York,* December 1, 2008.

Shaw, Kate. "A Response to 'The Eviction of Critical Perspectives from Gentrification Research.' " *International Journal of Urban and Regional Research* 32, no. 1 (March 2008): 192–94.

Shear, Michael D. "Density Debate's Large Stakes." *Washington Post,* July 19, 2001, p. T14.

Slater, Tom. " 'A Literal Necessity to Be Re-Placed': A Rejoinder to the Gentrification Debate." *International Journal of Urban and Regional Research* 32, no. 1 (March 2008): 212–23.

Steigerwald, Bill. "City Views" (interview with Jane Jacobs). *Reason,* June 2001, pp. 49–55.

Sullivan, Robert. "Psst . . . Have You Heard About Bushwick?" *New York Times,* March 5, 2006.

Testa, William A. "What Are the Opportunities in Central Cities?" Posted May 21, 2009, on the Federal Reserve Bank of Chicago blog Midwest Economy (www .midwest.chicagofedblogs.org).

Thomas, John V. "Residential Construction Trends in America's Metropolitan Regions." Working paper, U.S. Enviromental Protection Agency, January 2009.

Toy, Vivian S. "The Diaper District." *New York Times,* February 22, 2009, p. REI.

Troianovski, Anton. "Downtowns Get a Fresh Lease." *Wall Street Journal,* December 13, 2010.

U.S. Department of Housing and Urban Development. "Housing the Olympics: Atlanta 1996." *U.S. Housing Market Conditions, Summary,* Spring 1996.

Vigdor, Jacob L. "Does Gentrification Harm the Poor?" *Brookings-Wharton Papers on Urban Affairs,* 2002, pp. 133–82.

———. "Is Urban Decay Bad? Is Urban Revitalization Bad Too?" National Bureau of Economic Research, working paper 12955, March 2007.

Wolfgang, Laura. "The Sheffield Neighborhood: North Side's Mini Melting Pot." *Midwest Magazine, Chicago Sunday Sun-Times,* July 23, 1972.

Wyly, Elvin, and Daniel Hammel. "Commentary: Urban Policy Frontiers." *Urban Studies* 45, no. 12 (November 2008): 2643–48.

INDEX

Page numbers in *italics* refer to illustrations.

PHOTO CREDITS

A NOTE ABOUT THE AUTHOR

Alan Ehrenhalt was the executive editor of *Governing* magazine from 1990 to 2009. He is the author of *The United States of Ambition*, *The Lost City*, and *Democracy in the Mirror*. In 2000, he was the recipient of the American Political Science Association's Carey McWilliams Award for distinguished contributions to the field of political science by a journalist. He is currently executive editor of Stateline, a daily news service tracking developments in state government in all fifty states.

A NOTE ON THE TYPE

This book was set in Adobe Garamond. Designed for the Adobe Corporation by Robert Slimbach, the fonts are based on types first cut by Claude Garamond (c. 1480–1561). Garamond was a pupil of Geoffroy Tory and is believed to have followed the Venetian models, although he introduced a number of important differences, and it is to him that we owe the letter we now know as "old style."

Composed by North Market Street Graphics, Lancaster, Pennsylvania
Printed and bound by Berryville Graphics, Berryville, Virginia
Book design by Robert C. Olsson